WHAT WORKS AND WHY:

EFFECTIVE APPROACHES TO REENTRY

FOUNDED 1870

ICCA

AMERICAN CORRECTIONAL ASSOCIATION
LANHAM, MARYLAND

INTERNATIONAL COMMUNITY CORRECTIONS ASSOCIATION

Mission

The American Correctional Association provides a professional organization for all individuals and groups, both public and private, that share a common goal of improving the justice system.

Printed in the United States of America by Versa Press, East Peoria, Illinois

For information on publications and videos available from ACA, contact our worldwide web home page at: http://www.aca.org
Contact the ICCA at:http://www.ICCAWEB.org

This publication may be ordered from:
American Correctional Association
4380 Forbes Boulevard
Lanham, Maryland 20706-4322
1-800-222-5646

Library of Congress Cataloging-in-Publication Data

What works and why: effective approaches to reentry.
    p. cm.
  Includes bibliographical references.
  ISBN 1-56991-216-5 (pbk.)
1.   Community-based corrections. 2. Criminals-rehabilitation. 3. Police supervision. 4. Ex-convicts. I. American Correctional Association. II. International Community Corrections Association.

HV9279.W48 2004
365'.66-dc22   2004052984

TABLE OF CONTENTS

INTRODUCTION

After reading different theories and program evaluations from researchers, correctional practitioners still have to figure out what will work in their unique situation. No matter how good a certain idea sounds, the ultimate test is will it work in my environment with my constraints? Can I get my staff to buy into it? How will I measure success and over what period of time? These essays reflect some of the finest thinking in the field today. It's reading that demands your careful attention but rewards you with some long-sought answers.

What is useful about this book, published jointly by ACA and the International Community Corrections Association (ICCA), is that many of these practical questions are analyzed and realistic responses are proposed. ICCA asked researchers and practitioners to examine the theories of "what works," why some things work and under what conditions.

Warden Marc Carey, of the Minnesota Correctional Facility at Shakopee, has faced some of these daunting questions and offers some specific ways to blend social learning principles with philosophical theories to guide correctional programming. He discusses how risk reduction differs from restorative justice, community justice, and "broken windows" and how these approaches can be combined for different groups of offenders.

The authors of the second essay use a model they have developed at the London Family Court Clinic in Toronto to suggest an approach to supervision that holds offenders responsible for their actions and allows for staff growth and development. This is an essay that should be read and studied by counselors and social workers who have supervisory responsibilities.

The third essay, "Evidence-based Programming Today," presents a British point of view that rehabilitation of offenders in community corrections is practical, achievable, and cost effective. The author also points out that research panels have published sets of criteria for evaluating the design and delivery of prison-based interventions and these are used in almost half of the correctional institutions in England and Wales.

Peggy McGarry of the Center for Effective Public Policy suggests that the criminal justice system should be a partner in achieving and ensuring safety and freedom and she describes how this is occurring in drug courts, youth accountability boards, and other areas.

Joan Petersilia states in her essay that far too many offenders are returning to prison and detention facilities. We have to figure out how to stem the tide of recidivism not only because imprisonment is economically costly, but it also is socially costly. She presents several succinct suggestions that could become rallying points for politicians and others who want to truly reduce the cost of corrections.

Dr. Frank Porporino, who serves on ACA's research council, presents the idea that implementing only part of "what works" will not be successful and he outlines some of the steps that need to be taken in order to avoid potential pitfalls.

This collection of essays offers a roadmap for working more effectively with offenders and ex-offenders. By studying the ideas of these practitioners and researchers, we can learn how to do a better job rehabilitating offenders and keeping our communities safe.

James A. Gondles, Jr., CAE
Executive Director
American Correctional Association

SOCIAL LEARNING, SOCIAL CAPITAL, AND CORRECTIONAL THEORIES: SEEKING AN INTEGRATED MODEL*

1

Mark Carey
Warden
Minnesota Correctional Facility—Shakopee
Shakopee, Minnesota

Recent studies have called into question whether traditional methods of correctional interventions produce reductions in recidivism. The Bureau of Justice Statistics recently announced that two-thirds of inmates released from state prisons in 1994 were arrested for at least one serious new crime within three years of release (Langan and Levin, 2002). Yet, the knowledge about what works in reducing recidivism has never been so instructive or encouraging. At the same time, new models for framing how a correctional agency might approach crime, determine strategies, select its customers, and identify specific outcomes have emerged. Restorative justice, community justice, broken windows, and risk-reduction interventions based on social learning have found their way into mission statements of most correctional agencies.

---

* Funded by the National Institute of Corrections

In addition, information is increasing at an exponential rate. Futurist Ed Barlow noted that knowledge is doubling every two and a half years, and by the year 2012, it is projected to double every year. He estimated that 20 percent of what we need to know today to perform our jobs will be obsolete in one year. Incredibly, 60 percent of what we need to know to be successful in our field of work lies outside our industry (Barlow, 2002).

The popularization of these models and their guidance in helping agencies think through their response to crime has created a hodgepodge of differing targeted outcomes, primary customers, intervention strategies, and employee skill requirements, to name just a few. Senseless debate has broken out within the profession around which theory should be the dominant public policy, leading to occasional attempts to discredit one approach or another. This crazy-quilt work often has left those assigned the practical task of providing direct service scratching their heads and adopting a "wait and see" attitude related to how these theories, trainings, and tools will have an impact on their day-to-day jobs. Some of the main questions are the following:

- How does the modern correctional agency reconstruct itself to take advantage of this research knowledge and models, and how does it use this information to reverse the sobering statistics on repeat crime?

- How does the agency that has committed itself to being a learning organization integrate this growing body of information without becoming overwhelmed?

- How can the leadership in a progressive-minded organization help its human resources "stay the course" while still making improvements as new knowledge is gained?

One of the most promising approaches is the application of social learning principles to philosophical theories and research findings that guide correctional supervision and programming. Social learning principles also provide direction for how an agency manages its own internal affairs. These principles are largely in alignment with the tenets of restorative and community justice. Integrating these models and new knowledge in the highly politicized and bureaucratized world of justice professionals has become one of the more recent and stubborn challenges. Perhaps even more daunting is the next step: translating this information into activities and expectations that are clear to those who are called upon to carry out the new model of correctional reform.

When it comes to the tedious task of implementation, some agencies have had greater success with clarity of vision and integration of concepts than others. Correctional agencies have long histories and strong cultures that make the application of social learning to internal affairs difficult. The agencies that have made the greatest inroads toward the outcomes of reducing the risk of future crime, restoring crime victims, and engaging communities are those that have been comprehensive and intentional in their approach.

This essay is written for practitioners who are committed to applying research knowledge to correctional practice in a way that reflects the most effective models and outcomes. Confusion often arises during a time of knowledge expansion. Agencies struggle with the hard task of integrating that knowledge in a way that informs each contributing member of a correctional agency as well as their stakeholders. The field is fortunate to benefit from recent investments in research and experimental practices.

However, this bombardment of ideas and knowledge, while providing an invigorating learning environment, also can create chaos. On which of these conceptual frameworks and their corresponding outcomes does an agency focus? And, on which activities does an individual staff member focus? Should one address all of them at the same time? Does it depend on the circumstances or nature of the case? How does one know how to prioritize among the various theories and intended outcomes? How can there be some continuity so members of an organization can show initiative around a common vision and understand the purpose and techniques used by an agency? The modern day challenge, then, is not that of struggling to find the most promising ways to address crime and the restoration of the public's sense of peacefulness and safety. Rather, it is how to apply what is known in such a way that there are clarity and movement toward solid outcomes. This paper covers two essential components of this issue:

- the need for integration of theory and research into one (or at least a partially blended) articulated model

- how to apply that model in an effective manner so an organization can reach its intended goals

Integration of Theory and Research into One Model

Both frameworks for thinking about crime theory and effectiveness research that guides the development of an agency's intervention strategies recently have been forwarded and popularized through literature and trainings. In fact, although theories about crime and effective interventions have never been scant with causation theories (ranging from body type to biomedical factors to media influence and so on), more recent concepts are being introduced at exponential speed. At first blush, these concepts appear disparate in that they might emphasize one customer or one outcome or be driven by one overarching principle. Upon closer examination, however, there are some common threads that pull portions of these concepts together and give rise to a potential integrated framework. Below are some definitions, principles, and practical examples of four recent major theories that have gained a foothold in correctional agencies. Each has a different set of emphases and outcomes related to public safety and public satisfaction. Each has varying levels of research support, ranging from well validated to promising but not yet meeting rigorous standards. Each has a group of proponents that use the theories' corresponding set of principles, outcomes, and research findings to justify its rightful place as a core philosophical model from which to build a comprehensive correctional response.

There are major differences in how jurisdictions seeking to apply these theories define them and carry out their principles. Developing a common understanding is challenging, and even more daunting is finding common practices under multiple theories or philosophical approaches. Furthermore, there is significant overlap within each of these theories that often causes practitioner debate about whether a practice lines up with a particular theory label. As agency missions have evolved and as new theories are popularized, these mission statements contain such a unique blend of differing philosophies that finding a dominant theory or approach is difficult. The following are four major correctional theories recently popularized.

Risk Reduction is also often referred to as "what works." This theory asserts that people develop a "cognitive structure" of attitudes, feelings, and behaviors largely through the observation of other people and events followed by individual practice of thoughts and behaviors. Approval and disapproval, rewards and punishments are key factors in the learning

4

process. Behavior is driven by attitudes, beliefs, and environment. The greatest risk factors for criminal behavior are antisocial attitudes and beliefs, association with antisocial peers, and temperament/personality factors. The most promising interventions for medium- to high-risk offenders include a cognitive/behavioral approach that addresses the offender's thinking processes, beliefs, values, and life skills.

Restorative Justice is a philosophical approach to correctional intervention, in which crime is seen as a conflict between individuals and their community whereby the party that causes the injury incurs an obligation to make things right—whenever and however possible. There are three primary players involved: the victim, the offender, and the community. All three are harmed by a criminal act and all should be given the opportunity to be involved in addressing the conflict. The objective is to balance the goals of public safety, accountability to the victim, and offender-competency development. Programs under restorative justice promote face-to-face dialog between the offender and the victim, community participation in advisory groups, and opportunities for the offender to repair the harm through redemptive means such as meaningful community work service and direct service to victims.

Community Justice is similar to restorative justice but with a stronger emphasis on prevention. Community justice involves a partnership between the justice system and community organizations to control crime and social disorder. Its ultimate customer is the public, and therefore community justice seeks to accomplish community-level outcomes. It looks at systemic patterns of criminal behavior rather than individual incidents. The community provides guidance for the justice system in terms of its priorities and activities; therefore, justice activities are community driven.

Broken Window, in the context of this article, is highly associated with an emphasis on pubic safety, since serving the community and ensuring its safety is the bottom line. It is often associated with surveillance techniques to ensure that those who have been placed under supervision are being held accountable and are not recommitting crime while under correctional authority. "Broken windows" gets its name from the idea that all social disorder such as unrepaired buildings and broken windows contribute to the breakdown in community standards and greater levels of disorder and crime (Wilson and Kelling, 1982). Its emphasis, therefore, is on partnering with the community to address factors that lead to crime, with a special emphasis on offender accountability and surveillance.

Figure 1

Model	Principles	Practice Examples
Risk Reduction/ "What Works"	— We learn best through observation. — Modeling works best when we identify with the person doing the modeling. — Rewards and consequences help us learn. — Reinforcement/approval/disapproval are effective forms of teaching strategies. — Not all learn exactly alike (responsivity).	— Cognitive/behavioral programming — Motivational interviewing — Multi-systemic therapy — Aftercare — Booster sessions — Strength/asset-based interventions
Restorative Justice	— Crime is an injury against another. — Restoration is the primary goal of justice. — Crime creates an obligation by the offender first and foremost to make things right. — All affected parties should be part of the response to the crime: the victim, the offender, and the community. — The victim's perspective is central to deciding how to repair harm. — The community is responsible for the well-being of all its members, including victims and offenders. — Crime control cannot be achieved without active involvement of the community.	— Family group conferencing — Victim/offender dialog — Crime repair crews — Community work service that provides earned redemption — Circle sentencing — Restitution programs — Reparative boards — Neighborhood accountability boards
Community Justice	— The community is the ultimate customer of the justice system. — The justice system must work closely with the community in true partnership. — Justice system assists in addressing causes of crime such as social disorder and social justice.	— Community policing — Community prosecution — Community courts — Beat probation (neighborhood based)
Broken Windows/ Surveillance	— Public safety is the first priority. — Deal with all behavior, even petty acts. — Quick response and accountability for violators. — Strong partnership with law enforcement. — Supervision should occur in the community and during nontraditional times. — Work with community, not alone.	— Creation of absconder units — Intensive supervision — Law enforcement ride-alongs, Operation Nitelite, and so forth — Administrative revocation hearings — Participate with police in block clubs — Use of urinalysis, electronic monitoring, and other surveillance tools — Storefront offices or work out of car

If the goal is to have a clearly articulated single, integrated model of crime response for correctional agencies that takes advantage of the contributions of each of the major theories, then some kind of framework might help bring these conceptual elements together. There are two contributory concepts that can serve as a type of glue that binds portions of these theories together and enhances the outcomes the theories purport to advance. The two concepts are social learning and social capital. They can help keep the correctional agency from veering too far off course from their primary vision. Indeed, they are like "street curbs" or bumpers used for bumper bowling, keeping the ball moving in the right direction and preventing gutter balls and poor results.

Social Learning

There is no empirical evidence that probation and control models reduce recidivism (Taxman, 2002). Moreover, recidivism is not reduced with increased probation officer contacts with offenders or smaller caseloads. In fact, increased time available due to smaller caseloads is often used for more of the same activities conducted during original probationary appointments, or for increased administrative duties. So, Taxman raises the question of how to restructure correctional supervision to produce more meaningful outcomes. It should be pointed out that probation and parole objectives are more encompassing than just reducing recidivism, especially under the other models of restorative justice and broken windows. For example, some noteworthy objectives outside of lowering recidivism include making the victim whole to the degree possible, restoring and involving the community, providing information to the courts and other legal authorities, partnering with the community to prevent crime, and so on.

There are as many contributing factors for the commission of crime as there are interventions to reduce the risk of future crime. Some of these factors listed by theorists and researchers are genetic predispositions, family dysfunction, chemical abuse or dependency, poor moral character, criminogenic neighborhoods, biological factors, and so on. Despite the veracity of these contributing factors, the social learning approach appears to have the greatest potency for long-lasting behavior change and therefore holds utilitarian value to the corrections professional. From an outcome perspective, effectively applied social learning models deliver the greatest known outcomes toward risk reduction and for other objectives such as victim restoration. The interventions with the largest reductions in recidivism rely on social learning principles in whole or in part. Some of these include cognitive/behavioral programming, multisystemic therapy, and functional foster care. These programs rely on role modeling, mentoring, connecting a disenfranchised community member to the larger, prosocial environment, using positive reinforcement and consequences, employing cognitive skills and restructuring, using a network of social supports, and experiential learning.

Under social learning theory, people develop a "cognitive structure" made up of attitudes, feelings, and behaviors. This structure is created largely through the observation of other people and events followed by actual practice of thoughts and behaviors. Behavior is driven by attitudes, beliefs, and the environment. Learning through social interaction, by its very nature, means that it does not occur in a vacuum. It thrives in the context of families, neighborhoods, and communities. Since our cognitive structures are created within an environment, the interactions that occur within families and communities are critical contributors to how people learn.

Some of the key principles of social learning are the following:

- People learn best through observation.

- Modeling of that behavior most likely occurs when the individual identifies with the person modeling.

- Rewards and consequences play a significant role in how one chooses to act.

- The use of reinforcement and approval/disapproval are key shapers of how we think and behave.

As a result, professionals working in a social learning environment must have the skills to instruct, model, give feedback, express empathy and encouragement, use nonauthoritarian methods, and provide effective reinforcement and approval/disapproval.

Social learning promotes self-efficacy so offering choice is another key component. Recent trends toward training correctional staff on motivational interviewing techniques are a good example of applying a social learning principle to a correctional practice that reaps better outcomes such as acquiring more comprehensive information and increased ownership and commitment by the offender to take steps to make changes.

Social Capital

Each individual lives in a community in which social and economic exchanges are made every day. These exchanges occur as a result of social interaction whether they are informal (for example, talking with a neighbor while doing yard work) or more formal (for example, when one joins a political party, organized recreational activity, or civic organization). We use our human and social capital to get what we need to be successful and gain happiness (Coleman, 1994). The use of this capital is crucial to getting ahead. It might mean the difference between gaining something deemed necessary and not getting it at all.

Robert Putnam, in his book, *Bowling Alone* (2000), points out that social capital involves social networks, and those networks have value. He refers to networking as a "bounteous Rolodex file" which benefits 1) the individual who gains access to critical and timely information, contacts, and access as well as 2) the community at large through the benefits derived from the rules of conduct they sustain, mutual obligation, and the actions that follow. This connection among individuals produces "capital" that requires reciprocity and trustworthiness "akin to a favor bank." There is mutual obligation and responsibility that reduces the incentives for opportunism and malfeasance.

When multiple members of a community act for each other's benefit, an overarching sense of good will and community spirit develops (Coleman, 1994). When there are patterns of such reciprocity, a sense of community capital emerges, and this capital can reap strong returns in reducing crime and establishing standards of conduct among its members. It can also be instrumental in overcoming highly contentious issues such as NIMBY (not in my back yard) and other isolationist responses (Carey, 2000). Even in impoverished, inner-city neighborhoods, social capital can suppress criminal activity (Sampson, 1997). Threats against strong social capital exist in all communities. Figure 2 illustrates how the traditional community vehicles of prosocial capital (businesses, faith communities, social agencies, and so forth) can see their efforts diminished through a variety of "isms" and social disorders that erode one's motivations and motives when engaging with others in that community.

Social capital can be used for increased personal and community benefit through a prosocial value system, or it can be used to further antisocial activities. Gangs, crime networks, and illicit partnerships maintain their antisocial beliefs and activities by exercising social learning and social capital. The question is how values play a part in the application of social capital techniques.

Figure 2: The Forces Which Support or Threaten Pro-Social Capital

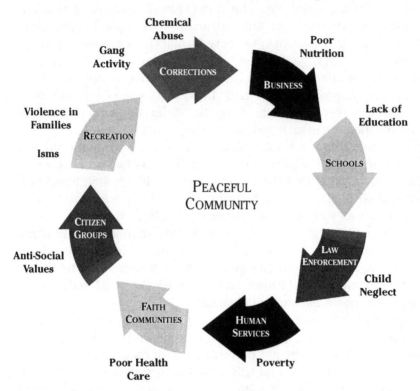

Combining Models into Practice

With at least four major correctional theories popularized today and the increasing onslaught of information supporting those theories, and with vendors and advocates promoting their wares and causes, how does an agency integrate the best components of these ideas and practices and still maintain program integrity and clarity of roles? How does this agency avoid the vertigo that sets in when too many ideas, seemingly disconnected from each other, are touted as preferred methods of structuring agency's resources and priorities? How does the leadership keep its staff well informed and trained without expecting them to perform such a diverse array of services for a diverse set of consumers so that the messages do not get lost in the confusion?

As the public scrutiny of correctional agencies increases along with the demand for outcomes and accountability, the need for clarity around the agency goals also increases. Agencies which seek to be on top of the information chain and who sponsor the most recent and progressive trainings often find themselves unintentionally giving mixed messages to the very staff who are asked to carry out the agency mission. In addition to the age-old correctional questions such as "Am I a social worker or an enforcer?", "Should I hold them accountable or rehabilitate them?", "Am I a deliverer of service or a broker of service?", we are now facing new questions such as "Am I supposed to be prioritizing victims or offenders?", "What is my role with the community and with prevention?", and "If you don't want me to facilitate cognitive/behavioral groups what role am I supposed to play?"

Too often, correctional administrators express frustration that agency staff is not doing what is expected of them. This disillusionment can be misdiagnosed as resistance to change, fear, lack of training, or laziness. In the meantime, in the break room and in the hallways, staff are scratching their heads in frustration wondering what is expected of them at this point in time. The failure to conceptualize a clear and embraced mission, unclear staff roles, and outcomes inevitably will result in the agency falling short of meeting its goals. It also can lead to subsequent blaming and disenchantment between staff, administration, and stakeholders. As indicated earlier, the major, recent correctional themes all have merit, but the failure to integrate them into a single conceptual model and well-articulated staff roles will inevitably render them ineffective.

The overarching principles of social capital and social learning have value under any utilitarian philosophy adopted by a correctional agency. If its purpose is to improve offender behavior or improve the benefits to the larger community through an agency's intervention strategy, then social capital and social learning can provide guidance to the framework. It should be noted that not all correctional theories are utilitarian. For example, many of the "just deserts" philosophical applications are primarily, if not solely, built around fairness and proportionality. Subsequent offender behavioral change or the provision of services for victims is either not found in the goals attached to the just deserts model or is added as a separate goal outside of its framework. As such, these models are not utilitarian in nature, and the fit with social learning and social capital principles is poor. On the other hand, restorative justice and "what works" can be highly complementary as research-validated practices

Figure 3

RISK REDUCTION:		
Maintenance (low risk)	Reduction (moderate/high risk)	Control (high risk)

RESTORATIVE JUSTICE:		
Accountability (victim)	Competency (offender)	Safety (community)

JUST DESERTS:		
Proportioned by	Deterrence	Fairness

around risk reduction can be integrated with the competency development practices promoted under the restorative justice approach.

Figure 3 shows three examples of correctional models, each having differing applicability to the principles and benefits of social learning and social capital.

Combining Theories into an Integrated Model

Most agencies are likely to select one or two theories that will guide their agency and activities. The important decision is the decision to pick. By selecting one or two theories that can be combined and by being clear on how they will be applied, an agency can achieve coherent integration. For purposes of illustrating how a partially integrated model could work by combining social learning and social capital with a dominant correctional theory, we will explore two of the major models. Any of the four models (risk reduction/what works, restorative justice, community justice, and broken windows/surveillance) could be combined with social learning and social capital principles for an integrated framework.

However, the degree to which integration of social learning and social capital interfaces with a correctional theory is dependent on whether that theory purports to produce a benefit to an individual or a community. If, for example, the theory is based on a general concept of fairness or proportionality (such as just deserts) or that of retribution, the relationship with social learning and social capital is much less compatible.

The first example to be considered is the "what works" model. An agency that embraces a "what works/risk reduction" orientation that is based on understanding and responding to an offender's risk and need areas naturally would be interested in the integration of social learning and social capital components as they are highly compatible and will strengthen the veracity of the programs designed to reduce risk and recidivism. To examine how these theories can be combined, it is important to break down the risk-reduction framework into categories. Figure 4 shows how managing risk can be viewed within three groupings of offenders along a continuum.

Figure 4

RISK/NEED RESPONSE CONTINUUM

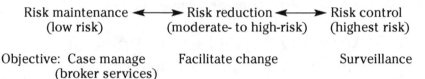

Risk maintenance ◄────► Risk reduction ◄────► Risk control
(low risk) (moderate- to high-risk) (highest risk)

Objective: Case manage Facilitate change Surveillance
(broker services)

Under this continuum, risk maintenance is the objective for the category of offenders who are deemed to be low risk and who are not likely to return to criminal behavior no matter what correctional intervention is applied. The justice process usually requires some form of punishment for any crime committed but court conditions, for this low-risk population, usually are geared more toward a quick sanction instead of treatment or other intrusive requirements.

For the second group of offenders who fall in the moderate-to-high-risk category, interventions are applied to those who possess one or more criminogenic needs that are dynamic in nature and can be changed. These individuals can benefit from a variety of risk-reduction programs such as cognitive restructuring, life skills, mentoring, education, and treatment. Effective application of these strategies has reduced reoffense rates by an average of 40 percent (Andrews et al., 1989).

The last objective is that of risk control. It is generally viewed as a set of strategies employed for the highest-risk offenders who are not projected to be responsive to interventions that would reduce their risk to reoffend. For this group of extremely high-risk offenders, no intervention is known to exist short of incapacitation that has a statistical probability of altering the course of their future criminal behavior over the long term. The strategies that are best employed include models whereby offenders are monitored very closely and are given little freedom to minimize the time and opportunity to reoffend at least while they are under the control of the justice system. Effective intensive supervision models have been successful in the short term as measured by the percentage of offenders who commit a crime while under supervision. These programs have not been successful at reducing reoffense rates once the supervision is lifted, nor were they designed to do so. They are structured in such a way to repress criminal behavior, not change the offender's attitudes, beliefs, and skills.

Under this model, offenders in all three risk/need categories would receive similar risk/need intake assessments, a range of graduated responses, procedural justice processes, and motivational interviewing techniques. However, other practices would differ due to the offenders' unique risk levels and corresponding criminogenic needs.

Figure 5: Applying Social Learning/Social Capital to Risk/Need Response

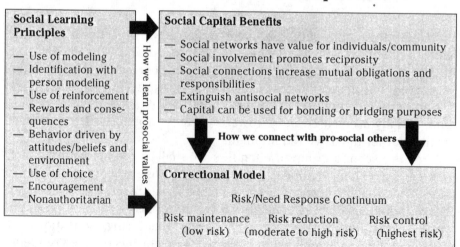

Figure 5 shows how the social learning and social capital principles could be applied to the risk reduction/what works philosophical model. Since the "what works" approach is based on social learning theory, effective risk-reduction techniques are riddled with social learning processes such as modeling; using guided interaction and behavioral techniques; employing cognitive instruction; using rewards and consequences; employing responsivity, and so on. The "value added" to the programs in the risk-reduction area with this integrated model would fall mostly in the social capital area because most social learning programs rely almost exclusively on individual programming and do not necessarily enhance the social capital and prosocial networking that is available in the community. Figure 6 describes possible enhancements to existing "what works" interventions when combined with social learning and social capital.

The second example of an integrated model, shown in Figure 7, is the combination of restorative justice with social learning and social capital. There are three goal components to the restorative justice approach: accountability, competency development, and public safety. All three are considered to be equally important and the justice system and treatment intervention response should be balanced in giving equal attention and priority. The primary receiver of services under accountability is the victim since the offender is obligated to restore the victim whenever possible. Within the restorative justice framework approach, the public is the primary benefactor under public safety. As the public is involved by partnering with the justice system to address both a specific criminal act as well as conditions that breed crime, the public improves its own safety. And, offenders benefit when programming to improve their competencies and skills is successfully applied by their successfully integrating back into the community.

Figure 8 shows how restorative justice interventions can be enhanced when combined with social learning and social capital principles. Here again, restorative justice appears to be highly compatible with these principles, especially in the competency development area. It is more difficult to apply the principles to the role of victims but easy to do with the community since social capital is a "community" affair by definition, whether this social networking is motivated by geography, special interests, or a common goal by those attending the events.

Figure 6

Potential enhancements using principles of:		
Common "what works" applications	Social learning	Social capital
Risk Maintenance: emphasis on • monitoring court conditions • limited justice system involvement, • efficient case monitoring and closure — fines — community work service — unsupervised probation — suspended sentence	Due to low risk/need level of this offender population, no social learning techniques are required; however, the community can provide the means of reinforcing offender learning.	Due to low risk/low need level of this offender population, no social capital techniques are required; however, the community can provide the means of reinforcing bonding in the prosocial community.
Risk Reduction: emphasis on • criminogenic need areas • cognitive/behavioral programming — use of cognitive-behavioral groups — residential treatment — life skills teaching — chemical and mental health services	— Catch offender doing things right and provide rewards and recognition. — Use ex-offenders, professional athletes, or other individuals that the offender respects for purposes of programming. — Use sole gender groups and culturally specific curriculum. — Combine/integrate mental and chemical health services with cognitive/behavioral programming. — Provide intensive aftercare including use of booster sessions.	— Harness community energy (fear, anger, anxiety) into offender monitoring and offender support functions. — Use court or community-based public recognition for improved behavior. — Use community work service projects that are good for the community and for which the court makes public statements of appreciation of the offender. — Get the offender involved in clubs or associations that match offender's assets and interests.

continued on page 17

Figure 6 (continued)

Risk Control: emphasis on • surveillance • limit opportunity to commit crime • increase motivation to want to make prosocial changes (limited) — community notification of sex offenders — intensive supervision — use of random urinanalysis — motivational readiness techniques — mapping — GPS electronic monitoring	Due to risk level and nonresponse to behavioral change techniques, interventions are limited. Examples could include: — Show quick consequences to antisocial behavior and lack of compliant behavior such as reduced residential placement time or supervision intensity. — Identify offender goals and create cognitive dissonance by pointing out how behavior is inconsistent with goal attainment. — Locate concentration of justice personnel in neighborhoods with crime and be highly visible.	Due to risk level and nonresponse to behavioral change techniques, interventions are limited. Examples could include: — Establish clear message by communicating that crime is not acceptable. — Elevate standards for conduct by, for example, a neighborhood march, protest, newspaper articles, development of neighborhood crime reduction plan. — Justice system partner with law enforcement and community by attending neighborhood block meetings and ride-alongs. — Use gang disruption techniques. — Use crime reduction strategies in housing complexes with an active offender population.

Figure 7: Applying Social Learning/Social Capital to Restorative Justice

Social Learning Principles

— Use of modeling
— Identification with person modeling
— Use of reinforcement
— Rewards and consequences
— Behavior driven by attitudes/beliefs and environment
— Use of choice
— Encouragement
— Nonauthoritarian

How we learn prosocial values

Social Capital Benefits

— Social networks have value for individuals/community
— Social involvement promotes reciprocity
— Social connections increase mutual obligations and responsibilities
— Extinguishing antisocial networks
— Capital can be used for bonding or bridging purposes

How we connect with prosocial others

Correctional Model

Restorative Justice:

Accountability	Competency	Safety
(victim)	(offender)	(community)

Figure 8

Potential enhancements using principles of:		
Common restorative justice applications	Social learning	Social capital
Accountability: emphasis on • monitoring court conditions • holding offender accountable to victim and community • obligation to repair harm — family group conferencing — victim/offender dialog — crime repair crew — community work service — restitution — reparative boards — victim-impact panels	— Combine cognitive program with accountability-based intervention to elevate learning. — Conduct offender orientation sessions to explain purpose of intervention. — Require letter by offender when restitution payment is late even if offender does not send letter (due to victim request). — Give victim and offender a choice on how to hold offender accountable.	— Ensure victims have a network of support that crosses one-dimensional areas. — Make sure the community rewards offender for good behavior (reciprocity). — Do not hold offender accountable in such a way that the offender feels unsupported and more disconnected from the community. — Find ways the offender can restore the victim and community and regain acceptance.
Competency Development: emphasis on increasing offender skills that the community values, offender obligation to reduce risk to reoffend, prepare for earned redemption and reintegration — victim empathy curriculum — cognitive behavior program — redemptive community work service that also teaches a life skill	— Combine cognitive programming with community work experience to elevate learning. — Hold celebration events when offender completes programming successfully. — Use non-justice system personnel to provide programming, especially involve those in recovery.	— Ensure community work project is meaningful to the public. — Provide visible means of appreciation by the public for completed work service project. — Provide community-based incentives for good behavior (for example, jobs, access to recreational club memberships, and so forth).
Public Safety: emphasis on community involvement; tight offender control (until risk to reoffend is reduced) — circle sentencing — citizen advisory boards — mentorship — circles of support — reparative boards	— Ensure diverse group of community members participate on boards or in circle sentencing to reflect community and offender population. — Balance accountability with lots of positive reinforcement and benefits for participation. — Ensure behavioral accountability if offender violates social contract.	— Provide for long-term relationships between the community and the offender even after criminal sanctions are removed. — Ensure mentors provide offender access to diverse activities and opportunities to join. — Make sure there is a mixture of offender taking and receiving so mutual responsibility and obligation is taught. — Provide opportunities for offender to give to less fortunate (e.g., a soup kitchen or Habitat for Humanity).

The Difficult Task of Integration

We have examined the integration of two separate correctional models with social learning and social capital principles. A more difficult task exists for those agencies that seek to combine more than one major correctional theory and still be able to articulate clearly the mission, practices, customers, staff responsibilities, and outcomes expected. Some models are more naturally combined than others (such as restorative and community justice). Many agencies are finding themselves in a "mission funk" as they try to embrace too many philosophies and strategies to be progressive and responsive to perceived needs as expressed by their stakeholders. Most often, the results are not improved outcomes but a crazy-quilt work of unrelated practices, philosophies, and models. Rather than achieving a coherent, integrated model where services relate to and flow into the other, there exists disjointed incrementalism. In most cases, it would be best if those agencies not try to be all things for all people, but rather decide where their emphasis should be based on discussions with policymakers, elected officials, and the communities they serve. Picking one clear, overarching model and doing it well will reap better returns than trying to apply a diverse and disconnected set of principles and goals.

Integration of research knowledge and philosophical models are difficult under most conditions. There is a tendency for employees or managers to gravitate toward an application of an integrated model based on their own beliefs, experiences, or biases even when the agency is clear on the integrated model and subsequent expectations. For example, many agencies have combined restorative justice and "what works" concepts into one model. On the surface, this appears to be a reasonable combination. There are few philosophical inconsistencies. The programs are complementary, and the set of outcomes (such as reduced recidivism, increased input and satisfaction of victims, improved restitution collection, and community participation in direct services) can be articulated with some degree of clarity.

However, agencies that have sought to combine these models have found that the risk-reduction strategies tend to dominate the training and emphasis. Victim restoration becomes an afterthought. Worse, some use restorative measures designed to improve victim input and participation as a means to reduce offender risk of reoffense. For example, victim-offender mediation and victim-impact panels are applied to teach the offender empathy or to hold the offender accountable. When this happens, often the procedures and safeguards against revictimizing victims are minimized. Even the outcomes for such programs identify offender-related outcomes. The victim's involvement becomes a means for an offender-outcome instead of a victim-outcome valid in its own right.

There are two management tools that are extremely useful in gathering together an agency's expectations under an integrated model in a way that reduces confusion about staff roles or agency mission. These tools are case plans and outcome measures. The offender case plan articulates what is expected of the offender and of the service provider as identified in the intervention plan. It is a central point where agency philosophy is translated into expected practices and customer outcomes (Carey et al., 2000):

> [P]roperly developed and administered case plans target specific strategies for maximum and measurable effectiveness. They are structured so key objectives are not forgotten or unduly minimized, and so less essential activities are given a lower priority. . . . Agencies seeking to implement best practices can be overwhelmed with mission statements, vision statements, action plans, strategic plans, challenges, outcomes, objectives, goals, performance plans, and so on. For those agencies that have not exerted much effort toward planning, visions, and outcomes, case plans provoke questions about what agency staff truly believe about the work they perform. Case plans are perhaps the most effective single vehicle for pulling together the diverse agency activities into a case-by-case, laser-like purpose. Properly developed, these plans are clear, specific, and measurable, and they ultimately tie directly back to the agency mission and outcomes.

There should be no ambiguity. If the offender is expected to participate in programming that reduces the risk of reoffending, then the agency philosophy is clear. If the case plan spells out actions intended to restore the crime victim, then the restorative elements of the agency mission are clear. The objective is to develop and use case plans that take advantage of assessment tools, apply motivational interviewing techniques, build on offender assets, seek to reduce the risk of reoffending, emphasize restorative ends, and hold the offender and caseworker accountable to case plan goals.

The other management tool that articulates an agency's philosophical model is that of a clearly defined set of outcome measures. The identification and ongoing reporting on agency outcomes simultaneously help the agency know if its interventions are producing intended results, and promotes clarity about what is ultimately expected of employees. (It exposes the bottom lines.) By visually and continuously reporting on agency outcomes, little room is left to wonder what the agency mission is. One might argue that the set of outcomes reaches too far by encompassing more than it should or is too limited in scope within the areas for which the agency is willing to be accountable. Either way, both the philosophy and the staff expectations can be articulated from such an exercise.

Full integration of a philosophy among all staff levels in an organization requires the provision of time and space. Staff should have time to dialog with colleagues about the model framework as it relates to actual crime conflict and correctional intervention. Exchanges of ideas can enhance the learning and excitement that come from applying models to challenging cases. But, staff needs the time to do this and it should not be so rushed as to limit the free flow of ideas. And staff needs comfortable physical and psychological space so that thoughts may be expressed without fear of ridicule or disrespect. It is through these kinds of processes (case plans, outcome measures, and respectful case consultation) that models can take on a life that is meaningful to all involved.

Adopting a Single Hybrid Model

As noted above, attempts by agencies to combine too many correctional theories into one mission could produce an overly diverse set of expectations leading to confusion. Some combination of theories is inconsistent with each other as they emphasize different outcomes or target different customers. For example, restorative justice elevates the victim's role and influence while broken windows/surveillance does not necessarily prioritize this "customer." The "what works/risk reduction" model has emphasized services to the offender and provides limited comment on the role of the victim or community.

While an agency's attempt to combine the best of the major theories into one framework is laudable, it is a challenging task that requires clarity of thought and constant training, communication, and leadership. Corrections is a complex task and adopting a blended model may make the system response too brittle when a more fluid, adaptable approach is called for. It may be possible, however, for an agency to adopt a "single hybrid model" under a case-specific integration plan. For example, an agency might adopt a broken windows/surveillance model for the highest-risk offenders who will not likely benefit from programming, a "what works model" for the moderate- to high-risk offenders, and overlay it all with a restorative justice philosophy that provides victim input and restoration and community participation. This blended model is adaptable based on the type of offender but embraces the restorative features in all cases. Or a different combination of major theories might be applied.

What will separate the successful agencies from the ones that fail with their implementation of this blended model is how they manage the complexity. Clear communication and outcomes for which individuals in an agency will be held accountable are necessary. In a residential care facility, for example, the agency might have a group of offenders with a mixture of risk levels. While most could benefit from social learning and social capital techniques, they should be treated quite differently. The extreme high-risk offender should not have privileges that require freedom and trust while the low-risk offender might not need any programming but just needs to be monitored for individual and program accountability purposes. For both groups of individuals, however, the victims and communities affected by the crime have needs that should be addressed. The offenders can play a role in helping attend to those needs by participating in victim-offender dialog sessions, completing work service that is redemptive in nature, meeting with community members to discuss how they can protect themselves from crime, and so on. Key to this is a clear message about expectations and goals for all involved for each of the risk/need level offenders.

Figure 9 shows how the four correctional models might be applied to the different offender groups based on their risk/need level. While the philosophies do not fit neatly in each box, they tend to fit a particular objective or group of offenders better than others. It is not perfect. For example, broken windows also addresses the nuisance crimes and low-level offenders in an attempt to raise the community standards. In most correctional applications, however, the emphasis by agencies under a broken window model has been largely on the high-risk offender, and the activities geared more toward surveillance and public safety. With this kind of integrated model based on category of offender type, the staff could distinguish the differing goals and intervention strategies based on whom they were dealing with at the time.

Figure 9

	Low risk/need offender	Social Learning and Social Capital Techniques Applied ↓	↓
		Medium to high risk/need offender	Extreme high risk/need offender
Risk reduction		X	
Restorative justice	X	X	X
Community justice	X	X	X
Broken windows			X
Correctional staff activities involved	— family group conferencing — diversion — community work service — group supervision	— treatment programming — residential care — victim/offender dialog and circles — cognitive-behavioral facilitation — supervised work crews — probation supervision	— police-corrections partnerships — residential care — victim/offender dialog and circles — specialized surveillance — intensive supervision
Expected outcomes	Correctional staff and agencies who work with differing risk/need level offenders would inherit different expectations as identified by outcomes. For example, while all risk/need level offenders would be obligated to contribute toward victim and community restoration whenever possible and each agency would provide for victim input and participation, expectations around programming for offenders would differ significantly. Some measures would be intense and designed around behavioral-control surveillance and monitoring, others around risk reduction, and others solely around sole sanctioning. Community participation would involve all risk/need levels; however, the nature of that participation would vary from monitoring of the extremely high-risk offenders to programming interventions for medium- and high-risk offenders to diversion techniques for low-risk offenders.		

The following is an example of an agency belief statement that attempts to integrate a number of theories and social learning/capital into a blended philosophy:

> We believe in the social learning theory of behavior that people develop as individuals largely through meaningful and timely social interaction. Values are transferred through role modeling and systems of rewards. Healthy families tend to produce healthy individuals. Healthy communities provide opportunities for their members to serve meaningful roles and such contribution to other community members help shape their ownership and loyalty to prosocial values. We believe that crime is largely caused by a breakdown of these value-producing environments. But, an antisocial orientation can be unlearned or retaught through the same social learning methods of modeling, rewards, and cognitive restructuring.
>
> Restorative justice is a concept that dovetails with social learning in that it uses similar techniques to help communities, victims, and offenders invest in each other's well being. A community harmed by crime is less healthy and has less social capital to invest. The criminal and juvenile justice system should seek ways to repair that harm and increase community capacity. The victim needs to be rallied around by caring individuals and be made whole to the degree possible. And, the offender must understand his/her role as a contributing and vested member to keep his/her behavior within acceptable bounds of the community. To do so, opportunities for repair, redemption, and reunification must occur.
>
> As a corrections agency, we recognize that we play an integral role in facilitating a social learning process for victims, offenders, and communities. Each staff member from the probation officer, to the secretary, to the case aide, to the manager is a role model (a restoration officer, and a community organizer in whichever community within or outside the agency he/she is involved with). As such, we are committed to practicing social learning in every aspect of our organization, from the services offered, to how incoming phone calls are answered, to how management makes decisions, to how

mistakes are rectified. Every encounter is a teaching and learning opportunity.

We recognize that we have a variety of roles to play, the most significant being that of pubic safety. We perform duties that line up with risk control, risk reduction, and/or risk maintenance. In each of these areas we apply social learning and social capital techniques to keep the community safe, to restore victims, to improve the skills and reintegration of offenders into society, and to create a staff-friendly work environment.

Bringing It Home to Direct Service Staff: The Effect on Day-to-Day Operations

The difficulty with discussing correctional models, frameworks for thinking about crime, integration of concepts, and theories in general is that it has a tendency to lose its punch when it gets to the individuals giving direct service. It becomes an academic discussion for those who enjoy the banter of philosophy and theories. By the time it is translated into practice, its strength is diluted. And, too often, service providers do not see its utility or practical application. It is incumbent on the administration and staff of these correctional agencies to avoid these problems. A clear mission under an integrated model with measurable goals must be communicated to the direct service staff or it is just verbiage that looks good in a mission statement tacked on a lobby wall without providing any direct service benefit.

One of the most useful ways to implement a theory or model is to translate the theory principles into a set of questions that reframe the approach in a given situation. For example, restorative justice proponents helped reshape how the justice system and treatment providers approached their jobs by redefining the questions. The difference between a retributive justice set of assumptions (or questions) and those of restorative justice can be delineated as follows:

Retributive justice
1. Who did it?
2. Which laws were broken?
3. What should the punishment be?

Restorative justice
1. What is the harm?
2. What needs to be done to repair the harm?
3. Who is responsible for this repair?

Regardless of the philosophical framework an agency picks, the following examples of questions could be asked to determine whether social learning and social capital benefits are being accrued in the correctional intervention:

Social learning: Do offenders receive behavior they can model and are the models people they look up to or with whom they can identify?

Does staff reinforce and effectively use approval/disapproval?

Is the most effective social learning environment present (use of empathy, nonauthority, choice, and so forth)?

Are the social learning steps to teaching used (in other words, instructing, modeling, practicing, and so forth)?

Does the community engage in any positive reinforcement activities when the offender makes marked improvement?

Social capital: Are offenders in risk-reduction programs actually given opportunities and encouragement to engage in prosocial networks, clubs, associations, and social activities?

Are these networks strategic in terms of the offender's strengths, assets, and criminogenic needs?

Will access to these networks allow the offender to learn trustworthiness and reciprocity?

How can the offender and community move toward extinguishing antisocial connections?

How can the offender increase a bridging form of social capital so he or she can gain access to more diverse activities and personal contacts that will increase his or her chance for economic and social success?

How can the offender give his or her time and talent to others, particularly the less fortunate to better understand that he or she has assets that the community values?

Applying a Planned Approach to an Integrated Model

There are six key areas that require close attention to transform an agency from its existing set of beliefs and values to a new, integrated mission. It is an unfortunate truism that most well-intentioned reforms and restructures fail not because the new model or practices were flawed or untimely, but because the implementation was not strategically applied. Poor communication; demands for quick turnarounds; insufficient attention to human resource needs such as training, tools, and understanding; lack of, or too much, patience; and not bringing other stakeholders on board with the change results in doom for a reform effort.

In addition, reform efforts fail when the attitudes and beliefs of the people who have to apply them do not change. Hiring staff with the right skills and attitudes, involving the existing agency staff in the implementation of the changes so they become part of the solution, and paying attention to agency culture are all necessary steps. No matter the agency and no matter the nature of the change, administrators should anticipate obstacles, unforeseen challenges, longer timelines than originally expected, and the need for personal involvement by all levels of staff and administration. The following six stages require attention and strategic planning:

1. Clearly Articulated and Communicated Information and Vision/Theory Are Needed

As discussed throughout this chapter, the absence of a clear and appropriate correctional intervention theory is a primary cause of reengineering failures. Too often, agency missions and values are ignored, too comprehensive, overly narrow, or just not well communicated. Agencies that use training, intra-staff communication, and all-staff events to predominantly focus on policy issues or peripheral topics (instead of the act of clarifying what the agency's contributing role is and how to best get there) are in trouble. It is easy for "mission creep" to occur (as opposed to strategic and conscious evolution) without constant attention to identifying and extinguishing noncore beliefs and activities that worm their way into an agency's cultural milieu. Of equal concern is when an agency does not take advantage of the latest research and theories by applying that learning. These organizations grow stagnant. Some staff naturally will gravitate toward such promising changes without the support of the organization creating fragmented application of theory and practice. Managing an organizational culture and mission is a dynamic process that requires the constant hard work of clarifying and challenging existing values and models of correctional intervention.

2. Staff Must Develop Ownership and Skills

Staff participation in the development of the agency mission increases their ownership and contribution toward the organization. Once the mission and vision is clear and well communicated, it is incumbent on the agency to examine its existing staff complement and ask whether the staff is properly trained in the areas needed. For example, under community and restorative justice, there is an increased role for organizing members of a community toward collaboration and partnerships. Many staff may become trained in mediation. Or, under the risk reduction model, staff takes on a group-facilitation role with offender cognitive/behavioral groups. New roles and expectations for direct service staff can be a threatening proposition as anxiety and concern for future roles in the agency arise.

Changing staff expectations and skills may be as difficult as changing offender behavior. Agencies should use the same social learning techniques to help change staff skills as is used with offenders such as modeling, practicing, reinforcing, and so forth. And, recruiting new staff takes on a new emphasis. The preferred staff profile may be different than the existing complement. Under social learning, correctional agencies need staff, managers, and administrators who are flexible, good communicators, interpersonal, capable of de-escalation and mediation, verbal, critical thinkers, and enthusiastic.

In addition, it is crucial that interested staff be involved in the agency change. Staff participation in crafting an agency mission, implementing the change, and communicating expectations will inevitably increase staff ownership and the sense that they have influence.

3. Leadership/Management Commitment, Passion, and Persistence Are Necessary

Rarely does significant agency change occur without a passionate leadership team. Not only does the leadership need to be clear and enthusiastic about the change, but it should be personally involved. This leadership needs to pay attention to details and areas where the change is breaking down. Involved leadership means that key leaders participate in discussions with all levels of the organization and that data is collected and analyzed to determine the degree to which the agency is making the mission shift. For example, it is one thing for an agency to say it emphasizes a "what works" philosophy. It is another to see the agency examine research, hold learning discussion groups, analyze what percentage of the agency training is balanced toward risk control versus risk reduction, or apply quality assurance and improvement techniques. Furthermore, does the leadership role model the practices expected of direct service staff? It is not enough for the leadership to know and articulate the vision, it also must know how to move an organization and be willing to have the rules and expectations apply to them as well.

4. Stakeholder Cooperation Is Necessary

No agency in the justice arena works alone. Rather, each agency's actions have a ripple effect on the others. No one agency can experience success without the cooperation of its sister agencies. If a residential facility changes its program without gaining the support of the courts or referral sources, it can suffer from lack of credibility and ongoing referrals. If a probation agency changes its revocation procedures without gaining input from the prosecutor's office, then it can find itself fighting against a system player. Most often, the system does not operate like a system. Each entity acts independently. Each agency might emphasize a different objective of justice and find itself in disagreement. If, for example, a corrections agency is working toward risk reduction, the prosecutor is emphasizing surveillance and risk control, the courts are seeking restorative measures, and the primary treatment provider works under a community justice model, there is a good chance that there will be poor communication and poor outcomes, if not outright chaos. A system that identifies common goals and agreed-upon strategies to reach those goals is much more likely to succeed in attaining the corresponding objectives than a system that either does not communicate or holds differing values and expectations. Ideally, there should be clear alignment within an agency and across stakeholder groups to fulfill commonly agreed upon goals as measured by specific outcomes. Contracts with vendors should articulate these expectations and consideration should be given to holding joint training sessions.

5. Infrastructure Alignment Is Vital

Organizations tend to be complex in the manner in which deliverables are obtained. Many activities must be coordinated to gain success. Staff recruitment, orientation, training, performance appraisals, reward systems, communication vehicles, position descriptions, management, auditing and quality control, information systems, and so on make up the administrative infrastructure. Any one activity that falls outside the philosophical framework can jeopardize the successful application of a model or program. For example, assume a probation agency is seeking to apply social learning to its population and uses early discharge from probation as a reward for the offender who is cooperative and successful. If the agency collects probation fees and relies on those fees to fund staff, there is a disincentive to discharge offenders early. Or, if management wants the staff to apply social learning to the work with offenders but fails to walk the talk by not being good listeners or empathetic to staff, there is no alignment. Principles of a particular model need to be adhered to throughout the entire agency for proper alignment and outcomes to be reached.

6. A Feedback Loop (Evaluation and Quality Improvement) Is Needed

Once the philosophical model is clear, staff are recruited and trained, stakeholders are involved and cooperative with the values and interventions, programs are in place, and the various agency activities are aligned with the principles of the selected model, there is still a need for some assurance that the work is achieving its intended purpose. Omitting or neglecting feedback to indicate whether the agency is meeting the expected outcomes is like golfing in the fog. Programs need to be evaluated, process measures set up, auditing conducted, and outcomes measured. From this, information areas in need of improvement will be identified and revisions to interventions can be made.

Figure 10 shows a graphic illustration of how one might think about implementing steps within an integrated theoretical framework. While

Figure 10

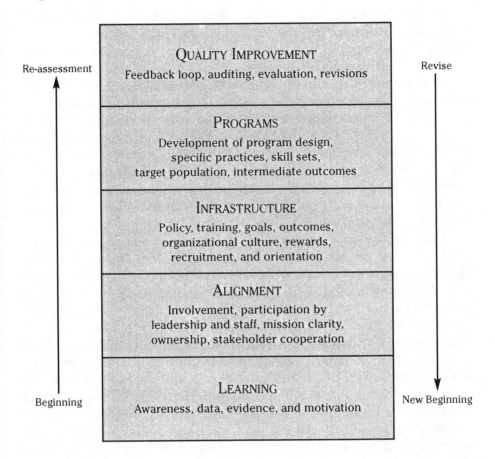

change is rarely linear, following a step-by-step process, it is helpful to think about the various actions that will need to be taken at some point.

In summary, once enough data and information is collected about what works for what purpose, a mission can be selected. Staff participation and stakeholder input is key during this time. Upon agreement on a theoretical framework, management needs to examine the agency infrastructure to determine whether there is alignment with the mission and framework. It then can develop and implement the programs and set up a process for feedback and examination of outcomes. Reassessment and refinement would follow the feedback and the process would begin anew.

Staying the Course

In an interesting article shortly after September 11, 2001, Frank Domurad (2002) described the state of affairs in the New York City probation department after the World Trade Towers collapsed. He poignantly and alertly observed the state of confusion and period of turmoil and how the department staff and management struggled to find its role during the aftermath of the tragedy. The department did not know how to respond, he argued, in part, because it was no longer clear to department staff what their mission was. The insurance companies knew how to respond. Certainly, the New York Police Department and the New York Fire Department kicked into immediate action. Why was the probation department filled with such ambiguity and confusion? He suggests that each correctional agency should be different today as a result of the September 11 crisis.

Major events should shape how we respond. While this is an appropriate call for periodic self-examination of its mission, each agency should protect itself from being whipsawed back and forth based on a new philosophy or new event. For example, restorative justice emphasis on victims is not a passing fad, and engaging communities is not a silly idea that will someday go away. These are real changes that require a proactive and thoughtful response. The danger is that agencies will either 1) vacate a tried and true approach to addressing crime and its aftermath to pursue the newest trend or 2) fail to change and integrate the new reality into the existing philosophy and mission. The failure to integrate these realities reaps confusion and frustration leading to individual interpretation of where the agency is going. And, when the vision is no longer commonly shared and team members no longer are pulling in the same direction, disparate results and inefficient operations occur.

While the correctional field is fortunate to be the recipient of new research findings and models of intervention for differing outcomes, it must be careful how to expose its agency to such ideas and learn how to integrate those concepts that make the most sense. In light of the rapid increase in information, the careful application of new knowledge is a modern-day challenge. A well-articulated and integrated model that is understood by all members of that agency with clear outcomes should be the goal.

References

Andrews, D. A., I. Zinger, R. Hoge, J. Bonta, P. Gendreau, and F. Cullen, 1989. Does *Correctional Treatment Work? A Clinically Relevant and Psychologically Informed Meta-Analysis.* Paper presented at the Research Seminar of National Associations Active in Criminal Justice, Ottawa, Canada.

Barlow, Ed. 2002. Speech to the American Probation and Parole Association annual training institute, Denver, Colorado. September 25.

Carey, Mark. 2000. Overcoming Fear, Misunderstanding, and NIMBY through Restorative Covenants. *Corrections Management Quarterly.* 43: 12-20.

Carey, Mark, Dave Goff, Gary Hinzman, Al Neff, Brian Owens, and Albert, Larry. 2000. Field Service Case Plans: Bane or Gain? *Perspectives.* Spring. 24(2).

Coleman, J. S. 1994. Social Capital in the Creation of Human Capital. *American Journal of Sociology,* Supplement, S121-S153.

Domurad, Frank. 2002. Managing the Unimaginable, Community Corrections and World Trade Disaster. *Perspectives.* Spring. 26(2).

Langan, Patrick A., and David J. Levin. 2002. *Recidivism of Prisoners Released in 1994.* Bureau of Justice Statistics, Special Report. June, NCJ 193427. Washington, D.C.: U.S. Department of Justice.

Putnam, Robert D. 2000. *Bowling Alone.* New York: Touchstone, Simon and Schuster, Inc.

Sampson, R. 1997. Neighborly Concern Lowers Crime. *Science.* 27(7): 918-923.

Taxman, Faye. 2002. Supervision: Exploring the Dimensions of Effectiveness. *Federal Probation.* 66(2): 14-27.

Thackray, John. 1993. Fads, Fixes and Fiction. *Management Today.* June.

Wilson, J. Q. and G. Kelling. 1982. Broken Windows: The Police and Neighborhood Safety. *Atlantic Monthly.* March: 29-38.

Zehr, Howard. 1990. *Changing Lenses.* Scottsdale, Pennsylvania: Herald Press.

Models of Supervision Relevant to the Delivery of Effective Correctional Service[*]

2

Alan W. Leschied Ph.D., C. Psych.
Professor
University of Western Ontario
London, Ontario, Canada

Anne L. Cummings Ph.D., C. Psych.
Professor
University of Western Ontario
London, Ontario, Canada

Linda L. Baker Ph.D., C. Psych.
Executive Director
London Family Court Clinic
London, Ontario, Canada

[*]In Harry Allen, ed. 2000. *Monograph Series on Community Corrections.* La Crosse, Wisconsin: International Community Corrections Association.

Introduction

Mental health and correctional workers often find themselves in challenging roles not only within the facilities in which they work, but also in the public attitudes they confront. Frequently, the commitment to support and rehabilitate offenders is contrary to the wishes of the public, which views the primary role of corrections as punitive. Hence, among the numerous juxtapositions in which correctional workers find themselves is their role of holding the public's trust in extending accountability for antisocial behavior of offenders along with the role of extending current effective practices to rehabilitate these same offenders. This obligation on the part of correctional workers is extremely challenging. This chapter focuses on the importance of supervision in supporting correctional and mental health practitioners who work with offenders. The current status of empirically derived interventions is summarized in the context of the accountability "burden" on correctional workers. We review models of supervision for effective service delivery and provide a detailed overview of the supervision model developed at the London Family Court Clinic.

Overview of Effective Practice in Corrections

During the past two decades, shifts in criminal justice policy have significantly influenced the role of correctional workers in both the adult and youth justice systems. Beginning in the late 1970s, the lingering effects of the "nothing works" pronouncements gave rise to "get tough" policies such as "three strikes," boot camps, and strict discipline programs. The impact from the negative reviews of the correctional literature by Martinson (1974) in the United States and Shamsie (1979) in Canada cannot be overstated. For mental health and correctional workers, the influence from these reviews was reflected in the perception that their role with clients was to be punitive in nature (Gendreau, 1998). Palmer (1996) reported that as a result of these pessimistic literature reviews, program funding was rolled back, staff-to-client ratios were increased, and rehabilitative programming was minimized in importance. In its place, was a rise in the importance of "static" security and strict behavioral programming, which was not intended to *change* the behavior of correctional clients as much as it was to contain it until the completion of an offender's sentence (Gendreau, 1998; Puritz and Scali, 1998).

A second major shift in correctional policy that influenced the role of correctional workers began in the late 1980s and early 1990s, reflecting the results of the meta-analyses by Mark Lipsey (1992; Lipsey and Wilson, 1997) and was furthered in the work by Don Andrews (Andrews, Zinger, Hoge, Bonta, Gendreau, and Cullen, 1990). In stark contrast to the conclusion of "nothing works," findings by Lipsey and Andrews suggested that correctional approaches based on punishment or accountability alone were related to actual *increases* in reoffending on completion of a sentence. Even more importantly, however, were the results from the Andrews' et al. meta-analyses reflecting that the addition of *human service* within the accountability measures for the offender accounted for decreases in client risk and reductions in reoffending.

With the encouragement from these reviews of the literature, practitioners in corrections are currently in the throes of redefining themselves in their role of *rehabilitating* offender attitudes and behavior to *reduce risk* and *increase community safety*. Since the conclusions from the reviews by Lipsey and Andrews have significantly influenced current correctional practice, and hence the role of supervision, the following section will detail their major findings.

Components of Effective Service from the Meta-analyses

Meta-analyses have helped in organizing the literature on effective intervention, not only in the field of corrections, but in many areas of human service. For readers unfamiliar with the concept of meta-analysis, this analysis reviews existing knowledge in an area from a *quantitative* perspective, giving numerical value to client type and the nature of intervention while specifying the desired outcome.[1] For corrections, the results generated from such reviews have assisted in understanding the prediction for risk (Andrews, Leschied, and Hoge, 1992), promising interventions (Lipsey and Wilson, 1997), and policies that can support effective practice (Gendreau, Goggin, and Cullen, 1999). To be effective, correctional practitioners need to be aware of the current knowledge in their area to maximize their effectiveness. This knowledge, in turn, will determine the kind of supervision that is reflected in effective correctional programs. The following section summarizes the major findings from the meta-analyses in providing the groundwork for understanding the role of supervision with correctional workers.

Risk Prediction and Assessment

Summary of Risk Factors. Andrews et al. (1992) provided a summary of the cross-sectional and longitudinal literature related to antisocial outcomes in youth. In their review, the principal factors that accounted for prediction included: early behavioral history, peer associates, early and current family conditions, interpersonal relationships, personal attitudes/values/beliefs, and school-based risk factors. These factors, considered *dynamic* in nature, were as predictive *in toto* as the static predictors of gender and age (for example, being young and male). The group of factors summarized in that review contributed to the body of work that Andrews and Bonta (1998) refer to as the *Psychology of Criminal Conduct*: a generalized term for criminogenic risk factors that reflect a psychosocial understanding of the nature of criminal conduct in general as well as pertaining to youth in particular. The complete list of factors and descriptors is found in Table 1.

Table 1: Summary of Major Risk Factors for Adolescents

(excerpted from Andrews et al., 1992)

Factor	Descriptors
1. Personal temperament, aptitude, and early behavioral history	Early generalized misconduct, aggression, a taste for risk, lack of problem-solving ability, egocentric.
2. Peer associates	Association with antisocial others, isolation from prosocial others.
3. Interpersonal relationships	Indifference to the opinions of others, weak affective ties.
4. Early and current family conditions	Low levels of family affection/cohesiveness, low levels of supervision, inconsistent discipline.
5. School-based risk factors	Below average effort, lack of interest, truancy.
6. Attitudes, values, and beliefs	High tolerance for deviance, rejection of the validity of the law, applies rationalizations for law violations, thinking style and content are antisocial.

Effective Intervention

Major Findings from the Meta-analysis. Mark Lipsey's reporting of two separate analyses (Lipsey, 1992; Lipsey and Wilson, 1997) suggested that the overall effect size linking treatment with reductions in reoffending lie between 20 to 40 percent as contrasted with no-treatment comparison groups, and only slightly less when compared to groups receiving some type of usual service. As stated in the Andrews et al. (1992) review, "Thanks to the meta-analyses, the evidence favoring treatment services is now undeniable" (p.148). Stronger effect sizes were found in the Lipsey studies in the following variables: higher-risk cases, longer duration of treatment, and behavioral-oriented multimodal treatment with a stronger emphasis on sociological than psychological orientation of service delivery.

Institutional Versus Noninstitutional Placement for Treatment. Lipsey and Wilson's (1997) subsequent review distinguished placement of treatment—residential versus community—in differentiating characteristics of effective programs. This is a critical differentiation because much of the debate regarding effective youth justice policies centers on the importance of incarceration as a relevant factor in community safety. Lipsey and Wilson (1997) noted in their analysis that effective outcomes were more likely to be found in community as opposed to residential settings. Table 2 summarizes factors relevant for effective programs in institutional and noninstitutional placements.

Table 2: Program Factors Contributing to Effectiveness for Institutionalized and Noninstitutionalized Young Offenders

Institutional-based Components
Interpersonal Skills
Teaching Family Model
Multiple Services
Behavioral Programs
Individual/Group Programs

Noninstitutional-based Components
Interpersonal Skills
Individual/Group Programs
Multiple Services
Restitution/Probation
Employment/Academic Programs

Effect sizes—accounting for total program outcome across both institutional and noninstitutional programs—suggested that the three factors comprising the highest ranking were interpersonal skills training, individual counseling, and behavioral programs. The second grouping of lesser, yet significant contributions were the two program factors of multimodal services and restitution for youths on probation.

The work of Don Andrews and his colleagues (Andrews et al., 1990; Andrews et al., 1992) are consistent with the findings of Lipsey. However, Andrews' work provides more specificity about appropriate targets for intervention, known as the risk principle, and increasing sophistication regarding style and type of intervention, namely the importance of cognitive-behavioral interventions. On a broader level, Andrews' work outlined characteristics of promising programs as including:

- systematic assessment that emphasizes factors relevant to criminality
- therapeutic integrity
- relapse prevention
- appropriate targets
- appropriate styles of service

Policies that Promote Effective Service

Perspectives from the Criminal Justice Policy Literature. There is further evidence from the criminal justice literature that some criminal justice policies further the efforts of effective criminal justice practitioners over others. These findings reflect the importance of the context in which the interventions take place. For example, Henggeler, Schoenwald, Borduin, Rowland, and Cunningham (1998) suggest that effective intervention for high-risk youths is more appropriately delivered in a community rather than in a residential context due to the opportunities of delivering systemically based family preservation services with environmental integrity. Hence, Henggeler and his colleagues suggest that justice policies, if they are to support successful intervention effectively, should emphasize community-based interventions over accountability provisions, which are typically reflected in a youth placed in custody. In a recent review of the larger literature on incapacitation and incarceration, Gendreau et al. (1999) concluded with the following:

- Custody should not be used with the expectation of reducing criminal activity.
- Excessive use of custody has enormous cost implications.
- Custody can have an aversive effect on some youths.
- The primary justification for the use of custody is to incapacitate offenders for reasonable periods of time to exact retribution.

Evidence for the Importance of Supervision in Effective Correctional Treatment

There is increasing recognition of the importance of supervision in supporting therapists in the corrections field. Though still limited, there is a developing empirical literature that identifies the roles that supervisors can play in helping deliver effective correctional treatment.

Correctional Program Assessment Inventory. Gendreau and Andrews (1996) have developed a measure of the components for effective service known as the Correctional Program Assessment Inventory (CPAI). The CPAI measures the extent to which services draw on components that are consistent with the meta-analyses on effective correctional treatment. The CPAI scales include: program implementation, preservice assessment, program characteristics, therapeutic integrity, relapse prevention, staff characteristics, and evaluation. The importance of staff supervision is reflected in items under both program characteristics and therapeutic integrity and focuses primarily on "quality assurance" assessments of staff performance (for example, behaviors of supervisors that monitor staff behavior through group and individual means, taped sessions, and reviewing progress notes). In the largest study to date using the CPAI, Hoge, Leschied, and Andrews (1993) found in a review of 131 young offender programs that items relating to staff supervision were correlated with higher scores on program integrity and staff characteristics as well as with the total score on program effectiveness.

Treatment Fidelity. As a refinement on the more global CPAI, Henggeler, Melton, Brondino, Scherer, and Hanley (1997) reported the specific importance of staff supervision and *treatment fidelity.* Treatment fidelity reflects the degree of adherence to the components of a theoretically derived treatment. Henggeler et al.'s (1997) research focuses on treating high-risk youths with an intervention known as multisystemic therapy (MST). MST is an intervention that places importance on clinical and peer supervision in the delivery of service. These researchers found that the variance accounting for positive outcomes from this home-based family preservation intervention was highest with therapists who adhered to the principles of MST.

Henggeler and Schoenwald (1998) have suggested that treatment adherence is closely linked to the quality of staff supervision. These authors have identified the primary objectives of effective supervision in MST as helping therapists stay on task as well as conveying knowledge to maximize therapist adherence to achieve specified youth outcomes. These therapist-supervisor goals are best achieved with supervisors who are adaptive to the differing structural needs of therapists (for example, being appropriately directive—when necessary) along with a well-developed knowledge base of offender characteristics and interventions consistent with a systemic view of child-family dynamics.

Supporting the Therapist-client Relationship. There is also empirical support for the importance of supervision in assisting therapists who work with conduct disordered antisocial youths in developing a therapeutic relationship with clients. Kann and Hanna (2000) suggest that developing a *therapeutic relationship* based on mutual respect with conduct disordered youths is a vital part of counseling. However, what makes the role of counselors who work at developing such therapeutic alliances with offenders challenging are the feelings of "irritation, disgust, anger, resentment, sympathy, and feeling defeated" that can be engendered from working with offenders (Church, 1994). Supervision, in this context, is essential in helping counselors manage feelings of countertransference that, if not managed, could damage whatever therapeutic alliance has been developed (Van Wagoner, Gelso, Hayes, and Deimer, 1991).

One aspect of countertransference that is increasingly coming to the attention of service agencies is the need to support their staff in dealing with their experiences of "vicarious traumatization." Several clinicians (Herman, 1992; McCann and Pearlman, 1990) have described vicarious traumatization as the ongoing exposure to the traumatic experiences of clients which then results in counselors exhibiting some of the symptoms of posttraumatic stress: intrusive imagery of clients' traumatic stories, nightmares, challenges to the counselor's basic faith in the goodness of people and the world as a safe place, a heightened sense of vulnerability, and feeling hopeless. With the high incidence of a history of abuse in offenders, correctional workers are prime candidates for experiencing vicarious traumatization. Herman (1992) believes that counselors who work with traumatized people *require* ongoing support to cope with these types of symptoms. This belief was confirmed by a study of 148 psychologist and sexual assault workers (Schauben and Frazier, 1995) who reported that two of their top four ways of coping with their work-related stress were seeking emotional support from friends and seeking instrumental support, such as advice.

Responding to Ethical Issues. In addition to dealing with issues of countertransference and vicarious trauma, one of the most important reasons for ongoing supervision is to provide correctional workers with a forum to discuss and resolve the many ethical dilemmas that any frontline worker confronts on a daily basis (Leschied and Wormith, 1997). Although most service providers expect to receive supervision on such issues while they are students in training programs, very few correctional workers receive continuing supervision on ethical conflicts that arise in their professional positions. There seems to be an expectation that once employed, helpers are autonomously functioning practitioners with little need for supervision. Yet, there are often instances where correctional workers may feel that the needs of a particular client are in conflict with ethical guidelines concerning such issues as dual relationships or confidentiality. In these cases, it can be extremely beneficial for helpers to have a regular forum to discuss and problem solve the situation. Finally, in these litigious times, it is imperative that correctional workers have close supervision on their cases to ensure that ethical and legal standards for service delivery are maintained at a high level.

Summary. This section has broadly summarized major themes from the correctional literature that direct the role therapists and correctional workers fulfill with offenders. For supervisors working in the corrections field, the following suggestions are found in the literature:

- There is a knowledge base that can provide direction for the nature of service within corrections that can influence the client's probability of reoffending. *The role of correctional supervisors is to monitor and convey that knowledge to frontline workers.*
- Treatment adherence has been shown to be a critical component of effective service. *The role of correctional supervisors is to monitor the ability of therapists to deliver treatment that is consistent with the principles of effective service.*
- The therapist-client relationship is a critical part of effective service delivery. The role of correctional supervisors is to be

aware of the development of respectful therapeutic alliances with particular attention to countertransference issues that correctional workers may be prone to developing.

The following section will outline models of supervision that complement the delivery of effective service.

Models of Supervision

Supervision has been defined by Holloway (1992) as, "literally, to 'oversee,' to view another's work with the eyes of the experienced clinician, the sensitive teacher, the discriminating professional" (p. 177). Numerous models of supervision have been proposed by educators. We have chosen to describe two of these models, solution-focused (Juhnke, 1996) and empowerment (McWhirter, 1998), as being most applicable to correctional workers.

Solution-focused Supervision Model. Based on the solution-focused therapy model of de Shazer (1991), solution-focused supervision has been adapted for family therapy trainees (Marek, Sandifer, Beach, Coward, and Protinsky, 1994; Wetchler, 1990) and for counseling trainees (Juhnke, 1996). As the name implies, the emphasis in this approach is on reaching solutions rather than highlighting problems. In this regard, supervisors are to emphasize the strengths and competencies of staff rather than their weaknesses or deficits. The supervision process begins by having supervisees identify their current clinical skills and personal characteristics that contribute both to effective work with clients and to their own feelings of self-confidence in working with clients (Juhnke, 1996). Then supervisees need to discuss how they will use their strengths with their clients and set some achievable, time-specific goals for self-growth (for example, "By the end of eight weeks, I will set clear boundaries with my clients"). The focus for supervision sessions is on the improvement that the supervisee has made since the last session.

Empowerment Supervision Model. McWhirter's (1998) empowerment model of supervision fits well with the solution-focused approach because it also emphasizes strengths and competencies of supervisees and clients in its goals of empowering both groups. However, McWhirter adds important aspects about the power dynamic between supervisor and supervisee. Traditional models of supervision mirror traditional models of counseling with the supervisor and counselor having more power than the supervisee and client. McWhirter seeks to decrease this power differential by conceptualizing the relationship between supervisor and supervisee as a collaboration between active members of a team with both members being co-learners and co-teachers in a continuing learning process. Even the client "is viewed as an active member of a team rather than a passive recipient of services" (p. 15). Porter and Vasquez (1997) expand the collaboration theme further by using the term "covision" instead of supervision to encompass a process of mutuality, collaboration, safety, and regard for each person's ideas.

In addition, McWhirter (1998) emphasizes the importance of addressing the context that shapes the power dynamics in providing supervision to staff and service to clients. This context includes the broader social forces of sexism, racism, classism, homosexual prejudice, and empowerment of the client. For example, when the supervisor is male, middle class, heterosexual, able-bodied, or from the dominant culture and the supervisee is female, working class, lesbian, has a disability, or is from a minority culture, the supervisor inherently will have more power in the relationship. In this situation, it is particularly necessary for supervisors to be aware of the possibility that their own biases could have a negative impact on the supervision process.

Bernard and Goodyear (1992) recommend the following interventions to reduce gender and cultural bias in the supervision process: (a) having a pluralistic philosophy that values diversity and multiple perspectives; (b) gaining cultural knowledge so that both supervisors and supervisees are reading and acquiring knowledge about relevant multicultural, gender, and sexual issues; and (c) using consciousness-raising activities to help supervisors gain awareness of their biases and stereotypes. Several authors (Daniels, D'Andrea, and Kim, 1999; Leong and Wagner, 1994) believe that it is important for supervisors and supervisees to discuss openly each other's cultural backgrounds and related values that may be influencing the supervision process and counseling with clients.

Supervisor Characteristics. In Holloway's (1992) review of the literature on counseling supervision, she reports that the ideal supervisor is described as empathic, understanding, flexible, open, concerned, attentive, curious, and conveying unconditional positive regard, all qualities that are helpful in any working relationship. Although Porter and Vasquez (1997) also include unconditional positive regard as necessary in a good supervisor, they believe that intellectual and personal challenge is equally important: "Unconditional positive regard without challenge seems patronizing, and challenge without relationship seems unsafe or disrespectful" (p. 157). They additionally describe positive supervisors as respecting the knowledge and experience of supervisees, promoting reciprocal dialog in supervision, and aiding supervisees in articulating their own ideas. They also assert that supervisors need to do continuous self-examination and reflective thinking about the relationship with the supervisee during the supervision process.

The Supervision Process. The challenge for supervisors is how to provide a safe forum for supervisees to discuss their cases while at the same time encouraging growth in case management. When supervision occurs individually, the supervisor must be particularly sensitive to the potential power differential in the relationship, as previously discussed. Instead, some agencies use group supervision with an all clinical staff meeting once a week to process cases in either peer-led groups or with a supervisor. There are several advantages for using group supervision: (a) multiple viewpoints can be brought to the issues and dilemmas of cases; (b) it may be easier to implement a collaborative model with more equal sharing of power among group members and a supervisor; (c) it is a more efficient use of agency personnel and time; (d) other group members can role play a particular client issue and allow the counselor to experiment with different approaches.

Whether supervision occurs individually or in a group, clear guidelines are needed for how correctional workers communicate with each other so that the principles of a solution-focused/empowerment approach are implemented. Even though many counselors will have had previous training in communication skills, it is useful to provide them with a refresher workshop to practice giving respectful, helpful feedback to their colleagues. Corey and Corey (1997) list a number of guidelines for giving and receiving feedback in groups that could form a basis for this workshop:

- *Specific rather than global*—feedback needs to describe specific behavior rather than making global generalizations (for example, "I notice that when you used silence with your client that she revealed something new to you.")
- *Nonjudgmental rather than evaluative*—simply describe behavior without adding a good or bad evaluation to that behavior.
- *Concise rather than an overload*—provide one piece of feedback at a time so that the receiver does not become overwhelmed with too much information.
- *Readiness of the receiver*—feedback needs to be well timed when there are clear indications that the receiver is ready to be aware of it and use it.
- *Focus on strengths.*

Johnson and Johnson (2000) suggest the following guidelines for receiving feedback in groups:

- *State what you want feedback about*—let givers know specific things about which you would like their reactions.
- *Paraphrase what you heard*—check that you understand what the giver is trying to say.
- *Share your reactions to the feedback*—givers need to know what was helpful or not helpful to improve their ability to give you useful feedback in the future.

Once all members of the supervisory relationship are clear on the theoretical approach, goals, and ground rules for supervision, it is then possible to begin the collaboration process that will be a valuable learning experience for all members. We will now provide a specific example of supervision in an agency that serves youthful offenders and their families.

Case Study of an Effective Supervision Model

The preceding sections have explained why supervision is important and what it involves. The next step is to examine how supervision actually happens, the translation of theory into practice. To achieve this goal, we will describe a specific program and the supervisory approach developed to complement the service, and the staff team that delivers it. The supervisory process will be brought to life through case studies.

Description of the Clinical Supports Program

The Clinical Supports Program provides clinical services for adolescents in secure and open detention and custody programs in six correctional facilities located in a Canadian urban center (approximate population 300,000) and a nearby rural setting. Client-centered services include the following: (a) solution-focused and cognitive behavioral interventions with youths and, in some cases, their families; (b) consultation with custody staff teams about client programming and plans of care; (c) assessment of the need for emergency psychiatric services; and (d) facilitation of linkages to community resources (for example, schools, adolescent mental health services, recreational programs).

A pilot expansion to the program enables clinicians to continue working for up to three months with selected clients after their release from correctional institutions to support successful reintegration into their communities. The focus is on reducing recidivism by assisting clients to continue to build and use their strengths to meet prosocial goals, and to develop or enhance their linkages to supports within their primary social settings.

Arms-length Service Delivery Model. The Clinical Supports Program is external to the correctional agencies within which clinical services are provided. It is operated and staffed by a community-based mental health center that specializes in working with children, adolescents, and families involved in the justice system (for example, the London Family Court Clinic). The following advantages are derived from this "arms-length" model:

> *Client-centered.* Clinician activities are client driven (for example, counseling sessions and home visits). With the exception of clinical documentation, which is kept to a minimum, the Clinical Supports Program team is largely freed from administrative and other agency responsibilities.
>
> *Continuity of Service.* Clinicians follow and continue to work with their clients through frequent transfers between correctional programs or facilities that occur for administrative reasons and because clients are moving through different stages of their sentences (for example, from detention to custody, from closed to open custody, and/or from custody to community parole or probation). When clinicians follow the youths, an increased "dosage" of the intervention is possible, when needed. This approach is consistent with research, which indicates that a dosage consistent with the level of a youth's need is a critical component to an effective program (Lispey and Wilson, 1997).
>
> *Therapeutic Role.* Clinicians are positioned to work hand in hand with correctional staff teams, while not being associated with roles and responsibilities that by their very nature may compromise client advocacy and the therapist-client relationship (for example, physical restraints, strip searches, "lock downs").

Team Qualifications. Clinical services are provided by three, graduate-trained (master's level) clinicians educated in social work or counseling psychology and with experience working with clients within the justice system. A clinical psychologist assumes supervision and administrative responsibilities. In addition to clinical skills, team members hired have experience with client advocacy; demonstrate respectful, collaborative, and solution-focused approaches to working with clients and coworkers; and, are willing to engage in team supervision.

Collaboration between Clinical Supports Program and Correctional Staff Teams. The Clinical Supports Program team works collaboratively with correctional managers and other correctional front line teams. While all clinicians work in all six facilities at various times, each setting is assigned a primary clinician who attends team meetings, provides program consultation, and accepts new referrals. Relationships are further strengthened during bimonthly, joint meetings between the Clinical Supports Program team and the correctional managers. Meeting agendas emphasize successes, challenges, and ethical issues related to clients, stakeholder organizations, the Clinical Supports Program, and the broader justice system.

Summary. The Clinical Supports Program is an "arms-length," client-centered model for providing interventions for youthful offenders. It embraces holistic, collaborative, and solution-focused approaches and maximizes the amount of intervention by enabling service to flow with the client throughout the youth justice system. External evaluations of the program (Avison and Whitehead, 1998; 2000) have identified the effectiveness of the supervision as a critical component of the Clinical Supports Program. The features of the supervision model are described next.

Supervision for the Clinical Supports Program

There are many models (for example, collaborative, solution-focused) and different structures (for example, individual, dyads, group, and team) for supervision (*see* Storm and Haug, 1997). The success of supervision is compromised if the supervisory process and format are not matched with the people and program for which they are designed. In the case of the Clinical Supports Program, the following factors were considered in choosing the supervision goals, structure, and model that would be most effective:

> *Clinician/supervisee Characteristics*—Clinicians possess substantial experience working in the justice system; possess well developed clinical skills; demonstrate excellent interpersonal communication skills and values that complement

the program philosophy and objectives (for example, respect, egalitarianism, and empowerment).

Clinical Supports Program Characteristic—Challenges and supervision issues are associated with cross-agency clinical service provision by an external organization (for example, differing or competing value systems and objectives, increased challenges for monitoring adherence to the principles of effective service).

Correctional Program Characteristic—Power differentials and other characteristics (for example, mandatory placement; impending court matters; peer dynamics of group residential setting) may compound the complexity and challenge of providing clinical services to youthful offenders (for example, confidentiality, vicarious trauma, countertransference).

Resource Allocation—Fiscal restraints and government policies necessitate a cost-efficient supervision model.

Supervision Goals

Four goals were established for supervision in the Clinical Supports Program. They emphasize the following:

1. Ensure ethical practice
2. Ensure fidelity to the goals of the Clinical Supports Program and to the principles of effective intervention
3. Foster continued development of skills and knowledge within all team members
4. Promote standardization within this area of practice

Supervision Structure. A team supervision structure was viewed to be the best match with the Clinical Supports Program, its staff members, and the supervisory goals. All clinicians attend the weekly session on supervision for the Clinical Supports Program team each Monday morning for two-to-three hours. Writing on supervisory structures, York (1997) indicated that team supervision affords an opportunity for greater complexity of relationships and distinct opportunities for colearning through team sharing, peer mentoring, and role modeling. This approach is most effective when supervisees, like those in the Clinical Supports Program, possess similar skill and experience levels. Group dynamics are experienced during team supervision that may parallel clinical situations.

Clinicians have the opportunity to practice advanced skills such as challenging coworkers within a supportive context, identifying and expressing biases or conflicts that may impact on their work with particular clients, and giving or receiving feedback related to clinical performance. This supervision structure also can strengthen team functioning and enhance support among clinicians. The latter benefits are particularly important with initiatives such as the Clinical Supports Program where supervisees may feel removed from the staff community in their own agency because they are constantly off-site and spread their time across multiple facilities. Finally, team supervision requires fewer resources in terms of time and cost, which complements the fiscal realities for the Clinical Supports Program.

Supervision Model. The Clinical Supports Program developed a supervision model that is best described as a combination of McWhirter's (1998) empowerment and Juhnke's (1996) solution-focused models that were described in an earlier section of this chapter. The combination of these models results in an emphasis on collaboration and competencies. This approach, combined with the team structure for supervision, enables the supervisor and supervisees to be both teachers and learners who work with each other to achieve the goals of supervision. Each team member brings competencies and valued experiences that both assist themselves and others. Ongoing learning is emphasized for all team members within this process. While supervision by definition has been described as "inherently hierarchical" (Storm and Haug, 1997, p. 2), the model used in the Clinical Supports Program serves to significantly decrease the power differential typically characterizing supervisor-supervisee relationships. Individual and team goals are established and reviewed every three months.

Empowerment and solution-focused supervision fosters investment in, and responsibility for, the treatment program by individual team members. In addition, this hybrid model parallels the approaches adopted by the Clinical Supports Program team for working with correctional clients and staff teams. The consistency between supervision and clinical approaches increases opportunities for further skill development. The following section details the supervision model within the Clinical Supports Program team drawing on case examples to describe specific processes of supervision.

Supervision Issues in Correctional Settings. Supervision provides a safe and regular opportunity to discuss dilemmas in a way that takes into consideration the context within which supervisory issues emerge. This approach concurrently emphasizes the best interests of the client, the organizations providing services, the public, and the profession. By thoughtfully exploring the context of the dilemma and these multiple perspectives, clinicians are supported in making effective clinical as well as ethical decisions. The supervisory role facilitates the supervisee to:

- consider all relevant perspectives
- generate ethical options
- identify the relative benefits and detractions of each option
- support the clinician's decision to choose one alternative over another

The supervisor's role should assist and benefit both clinicians/supervisees and their clients in supporting their rights in making autonomous decisions. Situations where supervisors are unable to support a supervisee's direction should be rare when the supervisory process described above has been followed. However, if such an exception occurs, the relationship established with the supervisee provides the context within which to discuss the intentional or unintentional consequences that may occur if the planned direction is followed. The clinician/supervisee should then be supported to consider other options and select the most appropriate one.

The issues highlighted in this section were chosen because of their pertinence to supervising clinicians that provide service in correctional programs. We start with the ethical issue of *confidentiality*, followed by a discussion on *countertransference*. Issues presented in supervision with the Clinical Supports Program team have provided the material for two composite case studies.

Confidentiality. By its very nature, therapeutic content and process are inherently personal. Clients need to be able to trust that their private communications will not be disclosed without their permission in order to engage in the therapeutic relationship. There is agreement among mental health disciplines that counselors have an obligation to maintain client confidentiality within the limits of the law and a specific profession's ethical guidelines. Client welfare is the practitioner's primary guiding principle.

However, unique in corrections is the obligation to balance both the client's welfare and the community's safety (Monahan, 1980). The need to balance the clinician's responsibilities to clients and others means that confidentiality is not absolute. For example, practitioners are required to disclose client information when it is necessary to prevent harm to clients or to others (for example, suicidal risk and serious threats of violence against another). Ethical practice dictates that clinicians identify and clearly inform clients of the limits of confidentiality at the onset of treatment. Counselors frequently encounter situations that fall into gray areas that make it difficult to determine whether the scales are tipped in favor of confidentiality or disclosure. *These dilemmas occur even when the limits of confidentiality have been clearly defined and communicated.* Accordingly, counselors need to have a well-developed sense of professional ethics on which to draw in order to make decisions. Ethical decision making is supported by effective supervision. Consider the following case:

> *Case A: Disclosure of a Crime*
>
> *Holly, a fifteen-year-old youth on probation for charges related to theft and trespassing, began working with Jane, a clinician, during the three-month open custody portion of her sentence. Trusting others is difficult for Holly who is estranged from her mother and is the survivor of multiple placement breakdowns. She currently lives with her father and his common-law partner whose relationship is volatile, and at times violent. Correctional staff members have told Jane that this is the first time Holly has engaged in counseling. During a weekly session, Holly reveals to Jane that she can't stand the fighting at home and that she has made plans to run. In response to Jane's concern about Holly's welfare, Holly indicates that she has stolen money from her father to help support herself until she gets work. Jane helps Holly to consider the consequences of her theft and running, including the violation of her probation order, and discusses alternate options for coping with her home situation. However, Holly states that her mind is made up and that she only told Jane because she "is different from the rest and isn't just doing her job." Jane is worried that if she informs the probation officer about Holly's theft and/or intentions, that she will damage the trust that Holly placed in her. Jane wonders if Holly may change her mind about running.*
>
> *During supervision, the team learns that Jane believes the psychological harm that Holly may experience if her trust in Jane is threatened is as great or greater than the risks Holly may experience on the run. Jane indicated that she wants to*

> *maintain confidentiality regarding the information Holly disclosed. At the same time, however, Jane expressed that "something just doesn't feel okay." She wonders if she has lost perspective, questions what is the right thing to do, and is seeking assistance through supervision.*

The question Jane brings to supervision is whether she is right in maintaining confidentiality about Holly's theft and intention to run. Within the empowerment and competency model of supervision, Jane would be asked to transform this question from a "yes or no" format into a range of possible options that include preserving confidentiality. Jane also would be strongly encouraged to attend to her own "unease" and to explore what the source of this feeling is about and how it can facilitate her movement through the current process. The team recognizes that Jane possesses the most knowledge about the case. The goal of supervision is to foster a process that enables the supervisee to synthesize and assign significance to various pieces of information, and when necessary, to provide additional input.

Client welfare is paramount in dilemmas pertaining to confidentiality. The team supervisory process will fully assess how various possible actions may impact Holly. Careful consideration will have to be given to determining whether a child protection issue exists due to either Holly's exposure to violence or the risks associated with running. Jane is assuming that Holly will benefit from the preservation of trust that she will experience if Jane maintains confidentiality. Effective supervision will assist Jane in considering what unintended consequences may result and what their respective impacts would be on Holly's present and future adjustment.

The supervisory process promotes professional development. For Jane, this may involve understanding what contributed to her sense that her regular judgment is compromised (for example, home and work variables, experience through previous cases), and how this may or may not have implications for her work with other clients. It will be important for Jane to draw on her strengths in this situation. A case overview would suggest that she might be underestimating her ability to engage and establish relationships with youths that have relationship difficulties. Supervision also should explore the impact of Jane's professional judgment on other members of the Clinical Supports Program team, as well as on the team's working relationship with probation services.

54

Countertransference. This term refers to the feelings aroused in the counselor in relation to clients and the projection of a counselor's biases, prejudices, and attitudes onto the client. These feelings have more to do with unrecognized or unresolved issues in the counselor's past relationships than with the therapeutic relationship where they are played out (Corey and Corey, 1997; Pearlman and Saakvitne, 1995). Such transfers are problematic because they can serve to distort clinical perceptions and lead to flawed decision making. While this phenomenon can occur in any therapeutic relationship, the subject matter of much of the counseling with youthful offenders may be more likely to evoke such transfers (for example, abandonment, victimization, perpetration). The harmful offenses that some correctional clients have committed may increase the likelihood of negative countertransference in some counselors. It is important to remember, however, that not all, negative feelings towards clients involve countertransference. Supervision helps to accurately identify countertransference early in the therapeutic relationship, thereby minimizing harmful effects on clients. Common expressions of countertransference are manifested in the need for either constant approval, or in an inability to separate personal feelings from those of the client (Corey, Corey, and Callanan, 1993). Consider the following case:

Case B: Counter-transference

Bob, a clinical intern with the Clinical Supports Program, had been working with Wendy for three months. He recommended that Wendy be suggested for the pilot program that would enable him to continue working with her in the community. Team members queried whether Wendy met the criteria for the program given that she had a number of formal and informal supports in the community. Bob described how Wendy indicated that she preferred meeting with him over other helpers and that this was a youth who really needed him. When asked why, Bob replied that, "I'm really getting through to her and I feel like I can help her." He asked if he could meet with her on his own time if she did not meet the requirements for the program until she was settled in the community.

In this scenario, Bob is not seeking assistance in supervision, but rather, the need for supervisory input becomes apparent when his reasons for referring a client to a specific program are discussed. The team format and the collaborative approach of the empowerment model of supervision are viewed to be particularly effective in engaging staff and students in the supervisory process in a way that promotes active "buy in" and participation. Sensitivity to the fact that Bob is an intern in the program and consideration of how that might be impacting his clinical decisions also is needed.

The focus of the supervision will be on the possible countertransference that Bob is experiencing. Bob's comments about the case center on himself and his needs. There is nothing in the information provided that tells us about the client's needs. When a client becomes "invisible" in the supervisory process, it is often an indication that the *boundaries* between counselor and client have become blurred. At these times, there is a risk that clinical decisions may not be in the best interests of the client. Accordingly, supervisory goals will focus on assisting Bob to use his strengths to shift his emphasis to the client, to determine the client's needs, and to work on role and boundary clarification and enforcement. Supervision can facilitate Bob's professional development by encouraging him to examine what personal needs are being met by this therapeutic relationship and to ensure that he understands the role that countertransference may be playing at this point in the therapeutic relationship.

Conclusion

Considerable research now exists to support the selection of specific services over other services that are consistent with the expanding research on effective treatment in corrections (Leschied and Cunningham, 1999). Further, supervision models in counselor training exist to provide direction on the selection of appropriate models that will enhance the delivery of services that focus on client need, as well as on the larger responsibilities of community safety and professional ethical practice. This chapter has highlighted two of these models based on the important components of empowerment and solution-focused supervision. Cases were presented that highlight the nature and process of supervision in the context of two recurring themes in supervision, namely the importance of therapist confidentiality and countertransference.

Finally, the role of supervision in the delivery of effective correctional programs cannot be understated. In a forthcoming review of program implementation factors in effective correctional practice, ten of thirteen chapters reviewing effective treatment implementation comment on the importance of therapist/worker supervision in monitoring the delivery of effective service (Bernfeld, Farrington, and Leschied, 2001).

As indicated in this chapter, two of the most well-established correctional treatment adherence measures, the Correctional Program Assessment Inventory (CPAI) and the Therapist Adherence Measure (TAM), strongly emphasize the role of supervision in program fidelity. Practitioners, correctional managers, and policymakers are well advised to acknowledge the critical role that supervision plays in delivering services that not only meet client need, but also contribute to promoting community safety.

References

Andrews, D. A. and J. Bonta. 1998. *The Psychology of Criminal Conduct.* 2nd ed. Cincinnati, Ohio: Anderson Publishing Co.

Andrews, D. A., A. W. Leschied, and R. D. Hoge. 1992. *Review of the Profile, Classification and Treatment Literature with Young Offenders: A Social Psychological Approach.* Toronto, Ontario: Ministry of Community and Social Services.

Andrews, D. A., I. Zinger, R. D.Hoge, J. Bonta, P. Gendreau, and F. Cullen. 1990. Does Correctional Treatment Work? A Clinically Relevant and Psychologically Informed Meta-analysis. *Criminology.* 28: 369-404.

Avison, W. R. and P. C. Whitehead. 1998. *Clinical Supports Program for Family and Children Interventions: An Implementation Evaluation.* London, Ontario: Ministry of Community and Social Services.

————. 2000. *Evaluation of the London Family Court Clinic's Clinical Supports Program.* London, Ontario: Ministry of Community and Social Services.

Bernard, J. M. and R. K. Goodyear. 1992. *Fundamentals of Clinical Supervision.* Boston: Allyn and Bacon.

Bernfeld, G. A., D. P. Farrington, and A. W. Leschied, eds. 2001. *Offender Rehabilitation in Practice: Implementing and Evaluating Effective Programs.* London: United Kingdom: John Wiley Press.

Church, E. 1994. The Role of Autonomy in Adolescent Psychotherapy. *Psychotherapy.* 31: 101-108.

Corey, M. S., and G. Corey. 1997. *Groups: Process and Practice.* 5th ed. Pacific Grove, California: Brooks/Cole.

Corey, G., M. Corey, and P. Callanan. 1993. *Issues and Ethics in the Helping Professions.* 4th ed. Pacific Grove, California: Brooks/Cole.

Daniels, J., M. D'Andrea, and B. S. K. Kim. 1999. Assessing the Barriers and Changes of Cross-Cultural Supervision: A Case Study. *Counselor Education and Supervision.* 38: 191-204.

de Shazer, S. 1991. *Putting Difference to Work.* New York: Norton.

Gendreau, P. 1998. Rational Policies for Reforming Offenders. Presentation to the International Community Corrections Association, Arlington, Virginia.

Gendreau, P., and D. A. Andrews. 1996. *Correctional Program Assessment Inventory.* St. John, New Brunswick: University of New Brunswick.

Gendreau, P., C. Goggin, and F. T. Cullen. 1999. *The Effects of Prison Sentences on Recidivism* (Cat. #J42-87/1999E). Ottawa, Ontario: Public Works and Government Services Canada.

Gendreau, P., C. Goggin, and P. Smith. 2000. Cumulating Knowledge: Some Ways in Which Meta-analysis Can Serve the Needs of Correctional Clinicians and Policy Makers. In L. Motiuk, ed. *Compendium on Effective Correctional Programs.* Ottawa, Ontario: Correctional Services Canada.

Henggeler, S. W., G. B. Melton, M. J. Brondino, D. G. Scherer, and J. H. Hanley. 1997. Multisystemic Therapy with Violent and Chronic Juvenile Offenders and Their Families: The Role of Treatment Fidelity in Successful Dissemination. *Journal of Consulting and Clinical Psychology.* 65: 821-833.

Henggeler, S. W. and S. K. Schoenwald. 1998. *Multisystemic Therapy Manual: Promoting Quality Assurance at the Clinical Level.* Charleston, South Carolina: Family Services Research Center, Medical University of South Carolina.

Henggeler, S. W., S. K. Schoenwald, C. M. Borduin, M. Rowland, and P. B. Cunningham. 1998. *Multisystemic Treatment of Antisocial Behavior in Children and Adolescents.* New York: The Guilford Press.

Herman, J. L. 1992. *Trauma and Recovery.* New York: Basic Books.

Hoge, R. D., A. W Leschied, and D. A. Andrews. 1993. *An Investigation of Young Offender Services in the Province of Ontario: A Report of the Repeat Offender Project.* Toronto, Ontario: Ministry of Community and Social Services.

Holloway, E. L. 1992. Supervision: A Way of Teaching and Learning. In S. D. Brown and R. W. Lent, eds. *Handbook of Counseling Psychology.* 2nd ed. New York: John Wiley and Sons.

Johnson, D. W. and F. P. Johnson. 2000. *Joining Together: Group Theory and Group Skills.* 7th ed. Englewood Cliffs, New Jersey: Prentice Hall.

Juhnke, G. A. 1996. Solution-focused Supervision: Promoting Supervisee Skills and Confidence through Successful Solutions. *Counselor Education and Supervision.* 36: 48-57.

Kann, R. T. and F. J. Hanna. 2000. Disruptive Behavior Disorders in Children and Adolescents: How Do Girls Differ From Boys? *Journal of Counseling and Development.* 78: 267-274.

Leong, F. T. and N. S. Wagner. 1994. Cross-Cultural Counseling Supervision: What Do We Know? What Do We Need To Know? *Counselor Education and Supervision.* 34: 117-131.

Leschied, A. W. and A. Cunningham. 1999. A Community-based Alternative for High-Risk Young Offenders. *Forum in Corrections Research.* 11(2): 25-29.

Leschied, A. W. and J. S. Wormith. 1997. Assessment of Young Offenders and Treatment of Correctional Clients. In D. R. Evans, ed. *The Law, Standards of Practice, and Ethics in the Practice of Psychology.* Toronto, Ontario: Emond Montgomery Publications Ltd.

Lipsey, M. W. 1992. Juvenile Delinquency Treatment: A Meta-analytic Inquiry into the Variability of Effects. In T. D. Cook, H. Cooper, D. S. Corday, H. Hartman, L. V. Hedges, R. J. Light, T. A. Louis, and F. Mosteller, eds. *Meta-analysis: A Casebook.* New York: Russell Sage Foundation.

Lipsey, M. W. and D. B. Wilson. 1997. *Effective Intervention for Serious Juvenile Offenders: A Synthesis of Research.* New York: Russell Sage Foundation.

Marek, L. I., D. M. Sandifer, A. Beach, R. L., Coward, and H. O. Protinsky. 1994. Supervision without the Problem: A Model of Solution-Focused Supervision. *Journal of Family Psychotherapy.* 5: 57-64.

Martinson, R. 1974. What Works: Questions and Answers About Prison Reform. *The Public Interest.* 35: 22-54.

McCann, I. L. and L. A. Pearlman. 1990. Vicarious Traumatization: A Framework for Understanding the Psychological Effects of Working with Victims. *Journal of Traumatic Stress.* 3: 131-149.

McWhirter, E. H. 1998. An Empowerment Model of Counselor Education. Canadian *Journal of Counselling.* 32: 12-22.

Monahan, J. 1980. *Who Is the Client? The Ethics of Psychological Intervention in the Criminal Justice System.* Washington D.C.: American Psychological Association.

Palmer, T. 1996. Programmatic and Nonprogrammatic Aspects of Successful Implementation. In A. T. Harland, ed. *Choosing Correctional Options That Work:*

Defining the Demand and Evaluating the Supply. Thousand Oaks, California: Sage Publications.

Pearlman, L. A. and K. W. Saakvitne. 1995. *Trauma and the Therapist: Countertransference and Vicarious Traumatization in Psychotherapy with Incest Survivors.* New York: W. W. Norton and Company.

Porter, N. and M. Vasquez. 1997. Covision: Feminist Supervision, Process, and Collaboration. In J. Worell and N. G. Johnson, eds. *Shaping the Future of Feminist Psychology: Education, Research, and Practice.* Washington, D.C.: American Psychological Association.

Puritz, P. and M. A. Scali. 1998. *Beyond the Walls: Improving Conditions of Confinement for Youths in Custody.* Washington, D.C.: Office of Juvenile Justice and Delinquency Prevention.

Schauben, L. J. and P. A. Frazier. 1995. Vicarious Trauma: The Effects on Female Counselors of Working with Sexual Violence Survivors. *Psychology of Women Quarterly.* 19: 49-64.

Shamsie, J. 1979. Our Treatments Do Not Work, Where Do We Go From Here? *Canadian Journal of Psychiatry.* 26: 357-364.

Storm, C. L., and I. E. Haug. 1997. Ethical Issues: Where Do You Draw the Line? In T. C. Todd and C. L. Storm, eds. *The Complete Systemic Supervisor: Context, Philosophy, and Pragmatics.* Needham Heights, Massachusetts: Allyn and Bacon.

Van Wagoner, S. L., C. L. Gelso, J. A. Hayes, and R. A. Deimer. 1991. Countertransference and Reputedly Excellent Therapists. *Psychotherapy.* 28: 411-421.

Wetchler, J. L. 1990. Solution-focused Supervision. *Family Therapy.* 17: 129-138.

York, C. D. 1997. Selecting and Constructing Supervision Structures: Individuals, Dyads, Co-Therapists, Groups, and Teams. In T. C. Todd and C. L. Storm, eds. *The Complete Systemic Supervisor: Context, Philosophy, and Pragmatics.* Needham Heights, Massachusetts: Allyn and Bacon.

Endnote

[1] For a detailed description of the meta-analytic approach in reviewing the literature in corrections, *see* the chapter by P. Gendreau, C. Goggin, and P. Smith in Harry Allen, ed. 2000. *Monograph Series on Community Corrections.* La Crosse, Wisconsin: International Community Corrections Association.

EVIDENCE-BASED PROGRAMMING TODAY

3

James McGuire, Ph.D.
Professor of Forensic Clinical Psychology
University of Liverpool
Liverpool, United Kingdom

The field of community corrections recently has begun to be significantly influenced by accumulating evidence that the rehabilitation of offenders, hitherto regarded as an elusive and probably unrealistic goal, is practical, achievable, and cost effective. A primary means of accomplishing this much sought-after objective is through the use of structured programs of psychosocial intervention. Evidence relating to this has emerged with a sizable degree of consistency from several large-scale reviews of relevant research literature.

The overall objective in this chapter is to summarize the findings from that literature. To accomplish this, the author will describe some of the methods used to conduct this work and arrive at conclusions. He will delineate the principal patterns and trends observed from the obtained findings. That will lead to an overview and discussion of their potential implications for correctional and other criminal justice services, and he will give some illustrations of this from a number of sources. Finally, he would like to consider several gaps in knowledge and identify areas requiring further investigation and make proposals on how to make further advances in this field.

Context and Background

The entire field of crime and justice is one in which it is frequently difficult to separate scientifically valid findings from individual opinion and belief. As crime touches the lives of many citizens, and is commonly in the media spotlight, it is the focus of much moral and political debate. It is not always clear whether more dispassionate presentation of research findings can have a meaningful influence on the direction of disputes.

One much-debated issue within this sphere is the question of whether recidivist offenders—individuals who frequently have broken the law, and have been prosecuted, convicted, and penalized—can be induced to change, and their rates of reoffending reduced as a result. Society's traditional approach to this, which remains the centrepiece of practice and policy in most jurisdictions, is the use of punishment or deterrent sanctions. As part of what follows, the author will briefly consider the net value of that approach and ask to what degree it achieves its desired impact. This will be set alongside evidence concerning the value of other types of interventions, generally grouped under the collective heading "treatment," with the general objective of "rehabilitation" of the offender.

Reviews of the latter area in the 1970s drew predominantly negative conclusions, the pronouncements of which are widely known. Following the increased use of methods of systematic, statistically based research review from the 1980s onwards, a different pattern of findings could be discerned. This suggested that interventions that effectively reduce offender recidivism are not as rare as had been supposed; on the contrary, that rehabilitative efforts of a variety of forms can be shown to yield significant benefits. To create a context for the rest of the paper, we will survey that historical background briefly, as it still constitutes a useful framework within which to present more recent surveys of the field.

Initial Research on the Effectiveness of Correctional Treatment

Interventions designed to reduce crime are sometimes represented as occupying one of three levels: primary, secondary, and tertiary (Guerra, Tolan, and Hammond, 1994). The first, sometimes called *developmental prevention*, entails provision of services to families and children in environments, such as socio-economically deprived neighborhoods, with the aim of reducing long-term difficulties including delinquency but also mental health problems and substance abuse (Yoshikawa, 1994).

Secondary prevention is focused on known "at-risk" groups, for example, individuals who have conduct disorders, in attempts to avert subsequent involvement in juvenile offending (Kaufman, 1985), or to help avoid low-level aggression escalating to a more serious level (Goldstein, 2002). Tertiary prevention is addressed to adjudicated offenders, those already convicted of crimes, with the objective of reducing their rates of recidivism (Gendreau and Andrews, 1990). This third level of preventive efforts is the main focus of this chapter.

In the field of corrections, the issue of effective interventions at the tertiary level began to be intensely debated from approximately the mid-1970s onwards when, almost simultaneously, research reviews were conducted in both North America and Europe. The primary objective of most evaluative research in this field has been to discover methods of reducing offender recidivism. In the United Kingdom, Brody (1976) reviewed 100 studies of the impact of different types of court sentences and other interventions, which attempted to evaluate this outcome. His attempt to arrive at clear conclusions was hampered by the poor quality of much of the research that had been undertaken, but the available findings appeared to point towards very little if any notable impact in terms of reduced rates of reoffending.

Perhaps more widely known in the United States was a review of 231 treatment studies published by Lipton, Martinson, and Wilks (1976). These authors, too, found that much of the research they reviewed was of unsatisfactory quality. Prior to the publication of their report, in a frequently cited article, Martinson (1974) argued that treatment could not be shown to add anything of value to the available network of criminal justice sentences, sanctions, or other formalized legal procedures. By "treatment" he meant any supplementary ingredient in criminal justice agencies or provided during the course of sentences, such as provision of counseling, education, vocational training, or psychological therapy.

In the wake of these exceedingly pessimistic conclusions, a number of fairly critical rejoinders appeared (for example, Palmer, 1975). The strongest challenge was issued by Ross and Gendreau (1980), who produced an edited book containing reports on effective services in which there was evidence of reductions in recidivism, demonstrating clearly the extent to which more positive evidence had been ignored (*see* also McGuire and Priestley, 1985; Thornton, 1987). But even before the end of the decade, the best-known name associated with the earlier gloomy reviews had been obliged to withdraw his initial conclusions (Martinson, 1979). Despite the very large volume of positive evidence now available in this field, the issue of treatment effectiveness continues to be disputed. The pessimism conveyed by the 1970s reviews appears to have been sufficient to convince many practitioners and policymakers that rehabilitation of offenders is not possible on any regular, methodical basis. Up to the present day, this remains a field in which it can be difficult to discern the boundaries between empirical evidence and underlying attitudes and values that may have pervasive effects on different observers' appraisal of that evidence.

Deterrence

Before turning to the current state of evidence regarding intervention programs, this author will use as a type of benchmark for what has been learned about punishment, which remains the predominant response in almost all societies to citizens who break the law. The process of sentencing offenders in courts of law is in many respects a symbolic one in which the community registers its disapproval of an offender's actions. Some indeed advocate use of punishment primarily or even solely on the basis of retribution, which is not concerned with its instrumental effects. But on a more concrete level, it is also a declared intention that underpins the sentencing process that it should alter criminal behavior by attempting to manage its consequences. This is the core of what is variously called the *utilitarian* or *consequentialist* approach to crime and punishment (Walker, 1991). It is founded on the idea that legal sanctions will have an impact on those so dealt with.

The traditional, virtually taken-for-granted expectation of sentencing practices, that they should deter individuals from committing crimes, is not well founded, however, on any consistent findings either in official criminal statistics or research studies. Several types of evidence are potentially relevant to the question of whether deterrent measures in criminal justice have an impact on recidivism (*see* McGuire 2002a, for review). They include studies of the relationship between imprisonment and crime rates; on the effects of capital punishment; on the outcomes of enhanced and intermediate punishments ("smart sentencing"); and self-report studies concerning undetected crime (criminology's "dark figure") and the perceived effect of sanctions. There is also a small quantity of literature reporting controlled studies of deterrence.

Although it is not focused directly on the correctional system, there is a very large collection of behavioral research literature on the effectiveness of punishment as a method of behavior change. The net finding from this, in a nutshell, is that punishment is only likely to be effective when certain very specific conditions are met (Axelrod and Apsche, 1983; McGuire, 2002a; Moffitt, 1983; Sundel and Sundel, 1993). The required conditions, however, are very unlikely to be met in the correctional system.

The Advent of Meta-analysis

By contrast to the largely negative findings concerning the outcomes of punitive sanctions, a large volume of evidence now has accumulated showing that other types of interventions can reduce offender recidivism. A crucial element in bringing about recognition of this has been the use of methods of statistical review or *meta-analysis* in detecting and consolidating trends across the findings of large numbers of primary outcome studies.

Some method of integrating the findings from different research studies was initially developed by the statistician Karl Pearson as long ago as 1904 (Glass, 1976). Glass, McGaw, and Smith (1981) used the method to resolve the long-standing dispute over the hypothesized relationship between class size and the educational attainment of young people. Until the advent of meta-analysis, despite a sizable volume of research, there was no clear pattern of findings discernible. Glass and his colleagues used meta-analytic techniques to review the research published between 1900 and 1978. They found 300 documents relevant to this, with a total of seventy-seven studies that had a direct bearing on the question. These studies, in turn, were based on data from an aggregate sample of 900,000 students from twelve countries over a seventy-year period. Altogether, the studies yielded 725 effect-size tests. Approximately 100 of the tests were from well-controlled experiments, in which students were randomly assigned to different sized classes. Plotting their findings in graph form, with other variables controlled, a clear relationship emerges between class size and educational performance. It is now an article of British government policy to reduce the size of classes or pupil-teacher ratio.

Given any selected research field, the available "primary studies"—the initial research reports—may differ in numerous ways including: their date of completion; whether they are published or unpublished; country and language of origin; sample size and composition; data provided on participants; nature of the study design and its methodological quality; the degree of detail given on procedures used; types of outcome measure employed; and types of data analysis undertaken. Unless the number of initial primary studies is small, these variations present formidable challenges when attempting a review. The traditional method of narrative review, while performing a useful function in the research process, may generate errors when applied to a large body of literature.

To conduct a meta-analytic review, certain steps should be followed, and several authors have specified the nature of this work together with procedures for ensuring its thoroughness and for maintaining quality control (Cooper and Hedges, 1994; Lipsey and Wilson, 2000). Durlak and Lipsey (1991) summarize the process as follows:

(1) Formulate the research question(s), clarify aims, and define literature to be reviewed.

(2) Locate relevant studies, using several methods of search; estimate the "fail-safe" or file-drawer number; that is, the number of unpublished studies showing no effects that would be needed to undermine a positive effect calculated from published studies.

(3) Code extracted critical information from studies; establish criteria on how information is to be recorded.

(4) Define the index of effect size, and select methods of analysis, making all procedures explicit.

(5) Conduct statistical analyses; record adjustments and variations in effect-size estimates; specify weighting procedures, and conduct comparisons for design quality and methodological rigor to eliminate or reduce methodological artifacts.

(6) Prepare conclusion and interpretation, noting relevant limitations; present findings in summary tables.

The findings of meta-analyses are usually reported in terms of a general outcome variable called the *mean effect size*. In outcome studies, this is an indicator of the overall relative impact on the dependent variable of the experimental (for example, treatment) and control (for example, no treatment) conditions, respectively. There are several different effect-size measures and numerous specific ways of reporting such data. In the reviews of correctional outcome research, three main types of effect size measures have been used (Rosenthal, 1994; Wilson, 2001). They are the following:

(a) *The standardized mean difference*, sometimes called Cohen's d statistic, and related measures. This compares changes in the means of experimental and control samples from pretest to posttest as a function of pooled variance expressed in standard deviation units.

(b) *Correlation coefficients*, such as Pearson's r, or the phi coefficient (ϕ). Here the researcher allocates outcomes of experimental and control samples across studies within "success/failure" or "improvement/no improvement" categories in a 2 x 2 matrix, and computes coefficients accordingly.

(c) The *odds ratio*, used in some recent reviews, expresses the odds of one of two dichotomous outcomes (for example, recidivism) for the experimental (intervention) group relative to the comparison group (occasionally, the reverse direction is used).

Meta-analysis has now been so widely employed as an approach to integrating research findings that even by ten years ago, there were more than 300 such analyses in the behavioral sciences literature alone (Lipsey and Wilson, 1993). *Systematic review*, usually employing meta-analytic techniques applied to carefully designed literature search strategies, has meanwhile become an engine of progress in many fields of inquiry. The largest expansion in such activity has been in the field of health care, where the international Cochrane Collaboration has set standards for research synthesis and acted as a central register for ongoing reviews and as holder of databases of outcome studies. In a parallel development, the Campbell Collaboration has now been established to work towards integration of research findings in the fields of educational and social and criminological interventions. In coming years, there are likely to be significant advances made due to the activities of the Campbell Crime and Justice Group (Farrington and Petrosino, 2001).

Interpreting Outcome Studies and Large-scale Reviews

Where the results of research purportedly show that an intervention has been successful in reducing recidivism, there are many interpretative hurdles to be overcome before that conclusion can be endorsed. The following are some of the issues to be considered.

Research design limitations. The quality of research in outcome studies of criminal justice interventions is extremely variable, and much of it suffers from a number of deficiencies. They may include: the non-equivalence of comparison groups; the limited length of follow-up in many studies; small size of participant samples, furnishing limited statistical power and restricting statistical conclusion validity; sizable levels of attrition at posttest or follow-up. It has also been argued that positive outcomes are predominantly a product of selection effects: offenders participating in programs change mainly because they are motivated to do so (Simon, 1998). To address these problems, schemes have been developed in some reviews for coding design quality in the analyses (for example, Lipsey, 1992; Lipton, Pearson, Cleland, and Yee, 1997), an approach also used in traditional narrative or tabulation approaches (MacKenzie, 1997).

Publication bias. It is widely acknowledged that some biases operate within the routine publication process and that studies obtaining zero effect sizes (demonstrating absence of treatment effect) may be less likely to be submitted or accepted for publication than those with statistically significant effects. To counter this to some extent, meta-analysts make every possible effort to locate unpublished studies; and to compute the file-drawer or fail-safe number, that is, the number of unpublished studies with zero or negative effect sizes that would be needed to undermine an observed positive mean effect size.

Internal versus external validity. There is an inherent tension between internal and external validity in research studies (Cook and Campbell, 1979). Internal validity refers to the extent to which we can justifiably infer that a relationship between two variables within a research study is causal; given that other potentially explanatory variables have been controlled. External validity refers to the extent to which any such relationship can be generalized across different populations, locations, or times. This presents a dilemma when interpreting research. The more tightly controlled is any given study, permitting clear conclusions, the less likely it is that the findings can be generalized elsewhere.

Efficacy versus effectiveness. Even when studies satisfactorily meet research design criteria, another criticism may be adduced. This is illustrated in disputes from an adjacent field, that of mental health. In the early 1990s, the American Psychological Association instigated a major review of the effectiveness of psychological therapy. The findings of this review led to the publication of a series of proposals concerning empirically supported treatments (Chambless and Hollon, 1998; Dobson and Craig, 1998). This is part of developing recognition of what works best for which types of problem (Department of Health, 2001; Nathan and Gorman, 1998). However, some commentators argue that the strongest types of evidence judged in purely scientific terms, such as randomized controlled trials, are often the least suitable for informing practical settings where operative variables are less well controlled (Persons 1991; Persons and Silbersatz, 1998).

These two standards of judging outcome are called efficacy and effectiveness, respectively. Paradoxically, for correctional research, the problem of extrapolating from one to the other may be less acute. Given its reputedly poorer design quality, "real world" research in our field may have greater utility as it often more closely reflects the complexities and the difficulties of correctional services, making it potentially easier to extrapolate from the results.

Lipsey (1999), using different nomenclature, calls this the difference between *demonstration* and *practical* programs, and has urged that there be much more research on the latter. Typically, evaluations of such programs yield effect sizes lower than those found in the former. Interventions being carefully evaluated for research purposes are usually allocated extra resources such as more intensively trained staff. Bridging the gap to everyday, busy, and sometimes chaotic correctional settings poses a major unresolved problem in applying an evidence-based practice agenda.

Meta-analytic Reviews of Interventions with Offenders

Table 1 summarizes findings from a total of thirty-four meta-analytic reviews published between 1985 and 2002, in chronological order of appearance, showing the designated review field, the number of outcomes subsumed in each, and the mean effect sizes so obtained. Some of the reviews overlap with each other in that they include portions of the same subsets of studies.

Table 1: A Summary of Meta-analytic Reviews of Tertiary Prevention (adapted from McGuire, 2002)

Source: Author (date)	Number of computed outcomes (k)	Mean Effect Size (ES)	Descriptive information
Garrett (1985)	Total k = 121; 34 on recidivism	+0.18	Survey of 111 studies conducted in the period 1960-1984, describing residential treatment programs for juvenile offenders. Cumulatively, 13,055 individuals were involved in the studies (mean age 15.8). Just under 50 percent of studies had random allocation or matched-group designs. Reports effects of programs on adjustment in institutions and community in addition to recidivism outcomes. Largest ES for recidivism were obtained from life-skills and behavioral programs.
Gensheimer, Mayer, Gottschalk, and Davidson (1986)	31	+0.26 weighted mean ES	Reviewed 44 studies of diversion schemes for young offenders (mean age 14.6 years) published in the period 1967-1983; 43 percent entailed random allocation. Of these studies, 31 involved comparisons between experimental and control groups with a combined sample size of 10,210. There were highly significant relationships between numbers of contact hours and outcome effect sizes.
Mayer, Gensheimer, Davidson, and Gottschalk (1986)	17	+0.33 weighted mean ES	A review of studies of the effects of interventions based on social learning principles published 1971-1982. A set of 34 studies yielded 39 effect sizes but only 17 were controlled experimental studies with recidivism as an outcome variable. Positive effect sizes were shown for behavioral, recidivism, and attitude change measures.
Gottschalk, Davidson, Gensheimer, and Mayer (1987a)	61	+0.22	Addressed the impact of community-based programs for young offenders. From an initial pool of 643 research studies, 163 were extracted; 38 percent involved random assignment. For recidivism as an outcome variable cumulative sample size = 11,463. However, CIs for most ES reported also included zero; authors interpreted positive findings cautiously.
Gottschalk, Davidson, Mayer, and Gensheimer (1987b)	14	+0.25	Focused on behavioral programs for young offenders. From the same database as employed in the preceding review, 25 studies were identified yielding 30 tests of treatment effects; 40 percent employed random assignment; however, only 14 addressed recidivism as the outcome variable.

Table 1 (con't)

Source: Author (date)	Number of computed outcomes (k)	Mean Effect Size (ES)	Descriptive information
Lösel and Koferl (1989)	16	+0.12	A study of the impact of German "socio-therapeutic" prison regimes designed for serious, recidivistic adult offenders. Patterns of effects were studied among 16 studies evaluating 11 prisons operating such regimes. A main focus of the review was the association between regime characteristics and recidivism outcomes.
Whitehead and Lab (1989)	50	+0.13	A review of juvenile offender treatment studies published in the period 1975-1984. Majority dealt with diversion programs. A wide range of effect sizes was noted with few positive results, though strict limits were set concerning what was regarded as constituting a significant finding (ES>0.2).
Andrews, Zinger, Hoge, Bonta, Gendreau, and Cullen (1990)	154	+0.10 $d = 0.53$ for appropriate treatment	Subjected a series of 154 outcome effects from studies with both adult and juvenile offenders to analysis. Studies were classified according to the extent to which the respective interventions adhered to principles of correctional intervention derived from earlier research. The pattern of findings supported the hypothesis that services which applied the principles of "human service" (risk, need and responsivity) produced larger effect sizes than those which did not do so.
Izzo and Ross (1990)	46	Cog > non-cog 2.5/1	Review designed to compare offender programs with and without cognitive-training elements. Rather than computing a mean effect size, the authors reported the ratio of relative effectiveness of the two types of program.
Roberts and Camasso (1990)	46	Range +0.06 to 0.81 (No mean ES given)	Review of treatment programs for young offenders published between 1980 and 1990. The mean age of the samples studied was 15.1 years; some interventions were targeted on offenders in the 9-12 age range and entailed primary prevention.
Lipsey (1992, 1995)	397	+0.10	Largest published meta-analytic review encompassing 443 studies of treatment of offenders in the age range 12-21; 65 percent of the studies obtained positive ES findings. Significant positive ES obtained for multimodal, behavioral and skill-oriented programs; negative effect sizes for deterrence-based interventions; conflicting evidence on employment-focused programs dependent on agency setting.

Table 1 (con't)

Source: Author (date)	Number of computed outcomes (k)	Mean Effect Size (ES)	Descriptive information
Hall (1995)	12	+0.12	Integrated findings from studies of the treatment of sexual offenders, both adolescent and adult. For this meta-analysis only 12 studies were located, with a total sample size of 1,313. There was a wide range of types of sexual offense. The mean effect size was + 0.12. The author calculated the "file drawer" sample size as 88.
Wells-Parker, Bangert-Drowns, McMillen, and Williams (1995)	215	8 percent-9 percent	Remedial interventions with offenders convicted of driving while intoxicated. Multi-modal interventions combining education, psychotherapy or counseling, and probation follow-up had the most positive effects in reducing drunk-driving recidivism and alcohol-related accidents. Some single modalities used alone had negative effect sizes (psychotherapy and AA).
Gendreau and Goggin (1996)	138	0.00	Meta-analytic review focused exclusively on effects of deterrence-related procedures. Integrated results from 138 outcome studies focused on intermediate punishment or "smart sentencing" (use of enhanced punishment, surveillance, random drug testing, intensive probation supervision, and other criminal sanctions or court-mandated procedures).
Pearson, Lipton, and Cleland (1997)	822	No mean ES given	Unpublished report given as a conference presentation. Part of a larger review known as the Correctional Drug Abuse Treatment Effectiveness (CDATE) project. Final project includes 1,600 studies.
Redondo, Garrido, and Sánchez-Meca (1997)	57	+0.12	Integrative survey of studies conducted in European countries between 1980 and 1993; 49 studies were included, based on a total sample of 7,728 participants. Mean ES for behavioral (0.23) and cognitive-behavioral (0.26) programs were each double that for programs as a whole.
Lipsey and Wilson (1998)	200	Institutions: +0.10 Community: +0.14	Studies of treatment of serious, persistent young offenders (age range 14-17); located 117 studies of community-based interventions; 83 based in institutions. Approximately half of the studies were randomized controlled trials. ES were computed in a number of ways: findings shown are "observed" ES. Numerous interaction effects were noted in the data. Largest and most consistent effects across settings were obtained with interpersonal skills training; for institutions, teaching family homes; for community, structured individual counseling and behavioral programs.

Table 1 (con't)

Source: Author (date)	Number of computed outcomes (k)	Mean Effect Size (ES)	Descriptive information
Alexander (1999)	79	+0.10	A review of outcome studies of interventions with sex offenders published between 1943 and 1996; cumulative sample size 10,988. The results were analyzed by age, offense type, setting, and treatment type. Included range of method/design quality. Recidivism rates generally low; positive treatment effects found for most categories of sexual offenses against children but no differences observed for rapists.
Dowden and Andrews (1999a)	24	Not applicable	A review to test the hypothesis that principles of "human service" (risk, need and responsivity), which have emerged from meta-analyses in studies of male offenders, applied to women offenders also. The authors located 6 studies yielded 45 tests, 24 on samples composed exclusively of female offenders, confirming that similar trends appeared for female as for male offender samples.
Dowden and Andrews (1999b)	229	+0.09	A study of outcomes of interventions with young offenders; 134 primary studies; effect sizes ranged from -0.43 to +0.83. Supplementary analyses reported effect sizes associated with different treatment targets, distinguished criminogenic and non-criminogenic targets, and tested hypotheses regarding "human service principles" in design of services.
Gallagher, Wilson, Hirschfield, Coggleshall, and MacKenzie (1999)	25	d = +0.43	Review of treatment of sex offenders; 22 studies. Most used cognitive-behavioral methods; only two employed random allocation; most reported positive ESs. Mixed results obtained for chemical/hormonal treatments; largest observed ES in a single study (for surgical castration) was thought to be compounded by motivational factors.
Polizzi, MacKenzie, and Hickman (1999)	13	No mean ES given: ES range from -0.23 to +0.70	A review of 21 studies of treatment of sex offenders dealing with interventions in both prison and community settings. Only 13 of the studies met acceptable design criteria; 50 percent showed effect sizes in favor of treatment. Four of the six studies showing positive treatment effects used cognitive-behavioral methods. Effect sizes were larger in community settings. Research did not allow any conclusions to be drawn about specific types of sexual offending.

Table 1 (con't)

Source: Author (date)	Number of computed outcomes (k)	Mean Effect Size (ES)	Descriptive information
Redondo, Sánchez-Meca, and Garrido (1999)	32	d = +0.24 r = +0.12	Second meta-analysis of European programs focused solely on recidivism. Highest ES obtained were for behavioral and cognitive-behavioral programs; ES were higher with juvenile offenders. Largest ES noted were with violent offenders and larger effect sizes for community than institutional programs.
Dowden and Andrews (2000)	52	+0.07	A review of studies focused on reduction of violent recidivism; 34 studies were located yielding 52 tests; 30 percent of the comparisons were based on young offender samples. CI for the mean ES does not include zero; mean ES for deterrence-based interventions just below zero; for "human service interventions", mean ES +0.19. Highly significant correlation (0.69) found between ES and number of criminogenic needs targeted.
Petrosino, Turpin-Petrosino, and Finckenhauer (2000)	9	-0.01	Review of randomized experimental evaluations of "scared straight" programs, including visits by youth to prisons, meetings with adult prisoners, education, and confrontational sessions in institutions. Conclusion drawn that their net effects were either negligible or potentially harmful.
Wilson, Gallagher, and MacKenzie (2000)	53	Odds ratio: 1.52	Meta-analysis of 33 studies of educational, vocational training, and allied programs for adult offenders. Highest effect sizes for postsecondary education programs (OR 1.74), corresponding to respective recidivism rates for comparison and intervention groups of 50 percent and 37 percent; lowest for a mixed group of multicomponent studies (1.33). Differences due to methodological variables were nonsignificant.
Wilson and Lipsey (2000)	22	+0.18	Review of 28 studies of "wilderness challenge" or outdoor-pursuit programs for young offenders. Of 60 effect-size tests, 22 focused on recidivism. Positive effects sizes were associated solely with intensity of physical exercise and inclusion of distinct therapeutic components.
Gendreau, Goggin, Cullen, and Andrews (2001)	140	0.00	Comparison between effect sizes for institutional and community sanctions and respective control samples. Total sample n = 53,614. Reviewed studies of intensive supervision, arrest, fines, restitution, boot camps, Scared Straight, drug testing, and electronic monitoring. Only fines yielded a small effect in reduced recidivism. All other interventions were associated with zero effects or marginally increased recidivism.

Table 1 (con't)

Source: Author (date)	Number of computed outcomes (k)	Mean Effect Size (ES)	Descriptive information
Lipsey, Chapman, and Landberger (2001)	14	Odds ratio: 0.66	Review of cognitive-behavioral programs: only studies with relatively strong randomized (8) or quasi-experimental (6) designs were included. The mean effect size represents a recidivism rate for participants approximately two-thirds of that for control samples. Larger effect sizes were found for "demonstration" than for "practical" programs.
MacKenzie, Wilson, and Kider (2001)	44	Odds ratio: 1.02	Review of evaluations of correctional boot camps. Applied detailed assessment of design quality, 19 (43 percent) of studies judged to be methodologically solid. Wide range of effect sizes noted; 9 studies favored boot camps, 8 favored comparison conditions, 17 obtained no difference. The only factor associated with the positive effect sizes was presence of an aftercare component for adult programs.
Lipton, Pearson, Cleland, and Yee (2002a)	42	Adult: +0.14 Juvenile: +0.14	Subset of CDATE studies on therapeutic communities and milieu therapy; 35 independent comparisons with adults and 7 with juveniles, from 37 studies. Also included re-analysis of German socio-therapeutic prisons (ES=+0.12; see Lösel and Koferl [1989] above).
Lipton, Pearson, Cleland, and Yee (2002b)	68	Overall: +0.11 Beh: +0.06 Cog-beh: +0.14 SST: +0.17	Subset of CDATE studies on impact of behavioral and cognitive-behavioral interventions on recidivism. Used method quality rating; 24 studies were allocated as "good" or "excellent" quality. Studies were also analyzed according to specific types of therapies; data shown are for behavioral studies using reinforcement; cognitive behavioral; and social skills training interventions.
Redondo, Sánchez-Meca, and Garrido (2002)	23	+0.21	Meta-analysis of European studies bringing period up to 1998. Median follow-up period 24 months; 8 studies focused on serious recidivism (ES=+0.22). ES were higher in community settings; highest for educational followed by cognitive-behavioral programs. By offense type, highest ES were for sexual offenses (+0.30), lowest for drug-trafficking offenses (+0.12).
Salekin (2002)	3	+0.62 across all outcomes; for recidivism, +0.22, +0.43, +0.63	A review of 42 outcome studies on treatment of psychopathy. A large proportion were single case studies and only 8 used control groups; mean level of change across the latter was used as a baseline for comparison with other treatment samples; file drawer n=160. Only three studies used reoffending as an outcome variable.

Occasionally, authors enter material that was reviewed earlier into a later, updated review; or publish separate meta-analyses covering different sectors of a field of literature preceding a larger, all-encompassing review. Even allowing for this, the total number of separate studies by 1996 exceeded 1,600 and a number of reviews published since then have incorporated more recent studies. Hence the grand total of primary research reports is probably approaching 2,000.

Also, in most instances, the number of studies or research reports reviewed does not correspond to the number of outcome effects used to calculate the mean effect size. We saw this, for example, in the Glass et al. (1981) meta-analysis of class size discussed earlier. In some cases, published studies contained more than one investigation. For example, 10 of the 111 studies reviewed by Garrett (1985) examined the effects of more than one treatment, so producing a total of 121 effect size tests. Conversely, in other reviews, not all studies that were located included recidivism as a dependent (outcome) variable. In the second review listed, by Gensheimer, Mayer, Gottschalk, and Davidson (1986), thirteen out of forty-four studies that were found had no control sample and entailed pre-post comparisons only.

Note that the reviews listed here are all concerned with "tertiary level" intervention, in other words, studies of work with individuals arrested for or convicted of criminal acts, and in which the focus was on recidivism as an outcome variable. Petrosino (2000) has compiled an annotated listing of meta-analyses in criminology and allied disciplines including others addressing primary and secondary prevention, and which focus on a wider range of outcome variables such as drug use, school vandalism, and sexual abuse.

The majority of the reviews, and also the primary studies on which they are based, originate from the United States or Canada. For the most part, they are focused on interventions with younger offenders (juveniles in the age range fourteen through seventeen and young adults aged eighteen through twenty-one). However, four reviews have dealt exclusively with European studies, and the largest review so far (the CDATE meta-analysis) includes studies from countries in many parts of the world.

In the overwhelming majority of the primary studies, the samples studied consisted entirely of male offenders. Of course, that is partly a reflection of the pattern in most official statistics of recorded crime, where males considerably outnumber females. In Lipsey's (1992, 1995) meta-analysis, only 3 percent of published studies focused on samples of female offenders. A recent review by Dowden and Andrews (1999a) was designed to counterbalance this and explore whether similar patterns of effects as found with men would emerge from studies with women offenders. While many primary studies report data concerning the proportions of offenders from different ethnic groups, the pattern of this is inconsistent, and it is not often coded in meta-analyses.

Principal Findings

In contradiction to the earlier reviews discussed at the outset of this paper, the overall finding shown across all meta-analyses is that the impact of "treatment" is on average positive. That is, it results in a reduction in recidivism in experimental relative to comparison samples. Treatment, however, can be defined in numerous ways and we will return to this point in a moment.

Secondly, however, the mean effect taken across a broad spectrum of treatment or intervention types is relatively modest. It is estimated on average to be approximately 9 or 10 percentage points (Lösel, 1995). Note, however, that this is across all types of "treatment." This may include criminal sanctions, which have been shown to have zero or negative-effect sizes. If these findings were removed from the overall calculation, the mean effect for remaining nonpunitive treatments would be higher than observed.

Given its apparently unspectacular overall scale, the question inevitably arises as to whether this finding has any meaningful policy significance. Rosenthal (1994) among other authors has drawn attention to an important distinction between statistical and practical significance. The mean effect sizes obtained, while typically small to mid-range, compare reasonably well with those found in other fields. Indeed, some health care interventions that are generally regarded as producing worthwhile benefits have lower mean effect sizes. Others with mean effects only marginally higher are in regular and unquestioned receipt of considerable public investment (Lipsey and Wilson, 1993; McGuire, 2002a).

The average effect size is fairly uninformative, and potentially even a misleading figure, in conveying the impact of interventions with offenders. All studies have found substantial variability in outcomes that depend on a range of other factors, and most researchers agree that this variability is of much greater interest than the average finding in itself. There are, of course, several sources of the variation observed in outcome effects, including the type of design used in evaluation studies (Lösel, 2001).

A principal implication of this is that there is no single solution to the problem of offending behavior or to the attempt to help individuals reduce its frequency or severity. No single approach can be designated a panacea or "cure all." Methods that work well in one context, with one selected sample, may work less well in others. Decisions regarding the approach best adopted in a given setting for a given group, therefore, need to take a number of factors into account. Bearing this caveat in mind, there remains a general accord among the reviews on a number of key points.

Ineffective Approaches

We saw earlier that the use of deterrence-based interventions has most frequently been shown to have nonexistent or negative effects on subsequent recidivism. There are also several other approaches that receive little or no support as effective interventions from the evaluation research that is available.

They include vocational training activities without associated links to real prospects of employment, which are also associated with increased recidivism (Lipsey, 1992, 1995) though the number of studies relevant to this finding is fairly small. There are conflicting results for wilderness or outdoor challenge programs, which have yielded mainly weak or absent effects, unless they include high-quality training or therapeutic elements (Lipsey, 1992, 1995; Lipsey and Wilson, 1998; Wilson and Lipsey, 2000). The average outcome for so-called "scared straight" programs is a slight increase in recidivism (Gendreau, Goggin, Cullen, and Andrews, 2001), and some authors have found them to be potentially damaging (Petrosino, Turpin-Petrosino, and Finckenauer, 2000). For young offenders, there is little support for the use of milieu therapy in institutional settings (Lipsey and Wilson, 1998) though there is more positive evidence regarding therapeutic communities with both adolescents and adults (Lipton, Pearson, Cleland, and Yee, 2002a).

Certain targets of change, though they may be deemed valuable for other purposes, are not promising as a focus in programs designed to reduce offending behavior. For that reason, they are sometimes called noncriminogenic needs. They include: hazily defined emotional or personal problems; individual self-esteem; physical activity viewed as an end in itself; increasing cohesiveness among antisocial peers; showing respect for offenders' antisocial thinking (Dowden and Andrews, 1999b). Dwelling on these targets in an intervention program is associated, on average, with increases in recidivism, which in some instances are not small (Andrews, 2001).

Perhaps, surprisingly, the evidence relating to substance abuse treatment and drug abstinence programs as a means of reducing recidivism among young offenders is weak. Criminological research generally shows the two kinds of problem to be closely associated. In two pertinent meta-analyses, the effects obtained were only mildly positive and not significantly different from zero (Dowden and Andrews, 1999b; Lipsey and Wilson, 1998).

Other Key Trends

There are sizable differences in effect sizes related to the age range of the target population of offenders. Cleland, Pearson, Lipton, and Yee (1997) analyzed age trends in effect sizes across a set of 659 studies with a cumulative sample size of 157,038. All the effect sizes obtained were significantly different from zero. The average mean effect size for offender samples below fifteen years of age was 0.09; for those aged fifteen to eighteen, 0.04; and for adults, 0.05. When values for "appropriate treatment" were computed, the respective mean effect sizes for the same three age groups were 0.16, 0.11 and 0.17.

Given the multitude of factors known to contribute to criminal behavior, there is virtual unanimity among researchers and reviewers concerning the need for interventions to entail several different ingredients and to target a spectrum of risk factors. This has led to the development of what are known as multimodal programs. This also has been called the "breadth principle" (Palmer, 1992).

Of possible significance for readers, several sets of results indicate that on balance, community-based interventions have larger effect sizes than those delivered in institutions (for example, Andrews et al., 1990; Lipsey and Wilson, 1998; Redondo, Garrido, and Sánchez-Meca, 1997; and Redondo, Sánchez-Meca, and Garrido, 2002). When similar programs were compared in their relative effects in institutional or community settings, the latter outperformed the former in terms of reduced recidivism in the ratio of approximately 1.75/1, though in other reviews the differential was somewhat lower than this at 1.33/1 (40 percent versus 30 percent reduction in recidivism). This is an important point, as analysis of crime statistics suggests that there is no differential outcome between custodial and community sentences as such (McGuire, 2002a).

However, there are crucial interaction effects to be noted in this respect. If interventions are poorly designed or use inappropriate methods, they emerge as ineffective regardless of the criminal justice setting in which they are delivered. Better-designed services are of maximum benefit when provided in a noncustodial setting. Moreover, even well-designed intervention programs may have zero and possibly even negative effects if the quality of delivery is poor. This highlights the importance of the relationship between program and organizational dimensions as defined by Bernfeld, Blase and Fixsen (1990). There are no known treatment or training materials that will achieve their goals in the absence of skilled, committed, and adequately resourced staff.

There is fairly strong support for the relationship between the level of risk of future offending (assessed using predictive tools of several sorts) and the intensity of services. This has not emerged consistently from all reviews (Antonowicz and Ross, 1994). But for the most part, larger effect sizes usually are obtained from work with more persistent offenders (Andrews et al., 1990). That may seem counterintuitive given an expectation that those groups would be more resistant to change. Intervention programs for more serious young offenders generally need to be of longer total duration, probably not less than twenty-six weeks on average, though not necessarily requiring a higher level of weekly contact (Lipsey, 1995).

A further frequently obtained finding is that effect sizes for acquisitive crimes (theft, burglary, robbery, and drug trafficking) are generally lower than those obtained for personal (violent and sexual) crimes (for example, Redondo et al., 1999, 2002). This may be a function of the larger part played by economic and environmental factors in crimes against property, which only can be addressed at a larger-scale social or macroeconomic level. Some approaches appear promising, but much more research is needed regarding this issue (McGuire, 2001a).

Most studies support the suggestion that intervention is more likely to be effective if it focuses on certain areas that have been shown to be risk factors for criminal activity. The evidence-base for the potential usefulness of a risk factors approach is very wide and includes large-scale studies adopting a longitudinal approach to the development of delinquency, alongside group-comparison studies of nonoffender and persistent offender populations (Andrews and Bonta, 1998; Farrington, 1996; McGuire, 2000b; Rutter, Giller and Hagell, 1998).

Such research highlights a range of psychosocial and individual factors that include the following: poor parental supervision or low attachment to families; experiencing difficulties in relation to school and employment prospects; having a network of associates involved in delinquency; manifesting antisocial attitudes; having distorted or biased patterns of information processing; possessing or exercising limited coping, problem-solving, and social skills; displaying low levels of self-control or a propensity towards impulsiveness. These factors can be described as criminogenic as they are theoretically and empirically associated with offending behavior. In marked contrast to the findings for noncriminogenic needs described above, targeting them, where possible, in intervention services is associated with substantial reductions in recidivism (Andrews, 2001).

Comparative Effectiveness of Interventions

Using meta-analysis, it also has been possible to examine the respective effect sizes observed when different types of interventions are evaluated separately. This and other dimensions of variability has enabled some researchers to conclude that effect sizes can be maximized by combining a number of elements in offender programs (Andrews, 1995, 2001; Gendreau, 1996a, b; Hollin, 1999). Effective interventions are thought to possess certain common features, which Andrews and his colleagues (1990) called "principles of human service." The list of features included within this framework has been steadily expanded and elaborated upon. The following series of recommendations is adapted from a compilation by Andrews (2001).

1. Base intervention efforts on a psychological theory of criminal behavior.
2. Within this, adopt a personality and social learning approach, which has provided an extensive evidence base on risk factors for criminal behavior.
3. Introduce human service strategies; avoid strategies based on retribution, restorative justice, or deterrence.
4. Make use of community-based services, where possible, in natural settings such as family; where custodial settings are required for other reasons, they should be as community-oriented as possible.
5. Assess risk levels and allocate individuals to different levels of service accordingly.

6. Assess dynamic risk factors (criminogenic needs) and target interventions towards their remediation.

7. Employ multimodal approaches: focus on a range of criminogenic needs in recognition of the multiple factors associated with offending.

8. Use the best-validated methods for assessment of risk and need factors.

9. General responsivity: attempt to match services to the learning styles, motivations, and aptitudes of participants within high-quality interpersonal relationships.

10. Specific responsivity: adapt intervention strategies to accommodate difference and diversity (age, gender, ethnicity/race, and language) among participants and recognize their strengths.

11. Assess specific responsivity and strengths using specially developed approaches and methods.

12. Develop coordinated strategies of monitoring continuity of services and care, including relapse prevention elements.

13. Identify and clarify areas in which staff may exercise personal discretion regarding application of principles.

14. Develop and make available a service plan or set of policies and guidelines regarding application of these principles.

15. Establish procedures for monitoring program and treatment integrity and for responding to departures from it; specify the elements within this including staff selection, training, supervision, and recording of information on all aspects of service delivery.

16. Staff: focus attention on detailed development of staff skills, including abilities in developing relationships, motivating others, and structuring programs and sessions.

17. Management: ensure managers have foregoing staff competencies and in addition, extensive knowledge of background principles, and ability to coordinate processes of program and site accreditation.

18. The most effective agencies will locate programmatic interventions within broader social arrangements, giving attention to variations in local contexts and client groups and adapting services accordingly.

Structured Programs

A key set of findings to have emerged from the research literature relates to what are known as structured programs of intervention. Much of the recent interest in these research findings, and investment in strategies that flow from them, has centered on the use of such programs. There is no formally agreed definition of what exactly the word "program" means, and different authors reviewing the field have devised various schemes for classifying criminal justice interventions.

At its simplest, a program can be defined as a structured sequence of opportunities for learning and change (McGuire, 2001b). Providing an activity of this kind involves some advance planning and preparation. It also means that the product of such preparatory work can be made explicit to others and that some aspects of practice can be standardized. That, in turn, offers opportunities for dissemination of good practice, and accountability of services to all those who have a legitimate interest in how they are designed, delivered, managed, and financed.

The following ingredients normally would be expected to be present in contemporary correctional programs. First, a program has a specified objective and it should be possible for this to be clearly stated by its designers, users, evaluators, and preferably also its participants. There may be intermediate objectives that in practice are only distantly connected to the goal of reducing recidivism, but the nature of that connection should be explained in supporting program documentation. Second, there is a planned sequence of activities; this might be called a "curriculum": a series of sessions or a timetable. It is the physical representation of what is involved in trying to operationalize the program's objectives. Third, it has internal coherence, in the sense that there is a clear and demonstrable link between the two foregoing elements. In other words, the activities that are planned can be shown to be justifiable for achieving the objectives. This should hold both theoretically (there is a sound model on which the design of the program is based) and empirically (there is evidence concerning its effectiveness, either as a totality or in terms of its components).

At first sight, this may appear highly prescriptive. Regrettably, the concept of programming risks alienating some staff who misperceive it as a mechanized attempt to brainwash or simply control offenders. Others confuse it with the idea of programmed learning, in which specially prepared texts or interactive computer software is used to guide individuals through a knowledge-acquisition process. Methods designed in this way could form a part of some interventions; but this is distinct from what is usually referred to as correctional programming.

Researchers and practitioners alike are interested in programs which, based on the literature to date, yield the highest effect sizes with the highest degree of consistency across different studies. For adult offenders, the methods that emerge as most reliably effective entail the use of structured cognitive-behavioral programs focused on risk factors for criminal recidivism (McGuire, 2000a). Variants of this approach have been well validated primarily for individuals with patterns of violent, sexual, and substance-related offending (Henning and Frueh, 1996; Hollin, 2001; Motiuk and Serin, 2001; Robinson, 1995).

For serious or persistent young offenders, interventions in the most consistently effective category have been shown to have an average impact in reducing recidivism by 40 percent in community settings and 30 percent in custodial settings (Lipsey and Wilson, 1998). Programs in this category, for the most part, employ the following types of methods: (a) interpersonal skills training; (b) behavioral interventions such as modeling, graduated practice, and role-playing; (c) cognitive skills training; (d) mentoring linked to individual counseling with close matching of young people and mentors on key background variables; (e) structured individual counseling within a reality therapy or problem-solving framework; (f) teaching family homes which involve specially trained staff acting in a parental role (Dowden and Andrews, 1999b; Lipsey and Wilson, 1998).

It is an undoubted advantage that all the forms of intervention in the foregoing list can be described in detail, and a systematic rationale can be provided for their use. Although this variable is not examined directly in outcome research, there appears to be a strong relationship between clarity of objectives, theoretical base, and methods employed within a program, and its overall effects. These are features of what has been called program integrity. For this to be present, it should be possible first to provide a coherent account of the program itself (Bernfeld, 2001; Hollin, et al., 1995).

Most of the programs which achieve consistent high effect sizes also are described as adhering to the principle of responsivity. This is conceptualized in two ways. General responsivity refers to the use of active, engaging, and participatory program ingredients, usually entailing the use of behavior change or skills development methods. There is likely to be a mixture of methods within program sessions that will serve to maintain the interest of participants. Specific responsivity refers to the provision of programs in a flexible manner that will address variations between participants in age or level of maturity, learning styles, cultural background, or other factors (Gendreau and Andrews, 1990; Andrews, 2001).

Contextual Factors

The interventions discussed so far focus on the individual offender and his or her risks and needs. In other words, their primary objective is to address aspects of offenders related to the difficulties they may have in respect of attitudes, peer influences, behavioral or cognitive skills, or attainment in terms of education or employment. An important supplementary finding concerns the extensiveness of interventions and the degree of involvement of services across a range of contexts of an individual's life, most importantly that of the family. As a guideline, the more areas of a person's life on which it is possible to have an influence, even if an indirect one, the greater the likelihood of securing and maintaining change.

In work with young offenders, effect sizes have been shown to be larger when a significant other person in the young person's life works alongside him or her and also attends individual programs of the types cited above. This may be a close relative with whom they have a positive relationship, or a mentor who is also familiar with the nature of the program (Goldstein, Glick, Carthan, and Blancero, 1994).

Effect sizes as high as 60 percent have been obtained from functional or behavioral family therapy, family empowerment, and allied therapeutic approaches, which involve working with young offenders and their families. For the most part, such programs have been provided for young people at the higher range of offense seriousness. Some of these programs also have reported lengthy follow-ups (Dembo, Ramírez-Garnica, Rollie, and Schmeidler, 2000; Gordon, 2002; Gordon, Graves, and Arbuthnot, 1995).

Effective programs involving young offenders and their families usually entail a specific focus on selected aspects of the family's functioning. Notably, they address areas such as parental supervision, training in negotiation and conflict resolution skills, and affectional bonds (Dowden and Andrews, 1999b). Such programs do not revolve around the provision of general family support. Approaches that involve diffuse, poorly defined work with families have been associated with increased recidivism (Dowden and Andrews, 1999b).

When elements of program-based intervention reach out yet further into other spheres of young offenders' activity, the strongest effect sizes to date have been obtained. This emerges from evaluative studies of Multi-Systemic Therapy (MST) in which work is done with the young person, his or her family, and school staff in addition (Borduin, Mann, Cone, and Henggeler, 1995; Henggeler, Schoenwald, Borduin, Rowland, and Cunningham, 1998). Obviously, programs of this type are comparatively resource intensive.

Benefit-cost Analysis of Offender Programs

The question of what resources are required to deliver effective interventions in criminal justice settings is not a central theme of this presentation. But it is worth noting that recent studies indicate that intervention programs with offenders are also relatively cost-effective. One review of seven studies of tertiary intervention found benefit-cost ratios ranging from 1×13/1 to 7×14/1 (Welsh and Farrington, 2000, 2001a). Another wider-ranging review has adduced evidence of significant cost-efficiency in evidence-based correctional programs, as compared with negative economic returns for punitive sanctions (Brown, 2001). Previous studies of the latter had already suggested that initial short-term savings from reduced incarceration rates were reversed by further expenses incurred later on, as a result of technical violations (Gendreau and Goggin, 1996; Gendreau, Paparozzi, Little, and Goddard, 1993).

Dissemination of Research Findings

The meta-analytic studies have been the subject of extensive discussion in the criminal justice field. The publication of several edited collections of reviews has assisted the process of dissemination of some of the principal findings (Bernfeld, Farrington, and Leschied, 2001; Crow, 2001; Harland, 1996; McGuire, 1995, 2002b; Ross, Antonowicz, and Dhaliwal, 1995). A review commissioned by the U.S. National Institute of Justice examined these types of interventions alongside other approaches to crime prevention (Sherman, Gottfredson, MacKenzie, Eck, Reuter, and Bushway, 1997). In the United Kingdom, Home Office researchers considered the role the findings could play in practical policies for correctional services (Goldblatt and Lewis, 1998; Vennard, Sugg, and Hedderman, 1997).

Implementation

The findings on reduction of recidivism summarized here have begun to have an impact on the direction of both practice and policy with offenders in a number of countries. Many policymakers have been impressed by the fact that it is possible to identify with some confidence those features of treatment interventions that contribute to higher levels of effectiveness. Both research and practice in the field have advanced considerably beyond their initial preoccupation with whether or not offender rehabilitation "works." Their focus is now, much more often, on more complex questions of what works when, where, and with whom; and why the various combinations of such elements form the patterns that they do. To optimize their chances of being effective, programs should be planned with reference to those who will participate in them, and in the organizational and societal context in which they are delivered (Bernfeld et al., 1990; Harris and Smith, 1996).

Unfortunately, there is no doubt, as several experts have commented, that the question of how programs are implemented in practical settings has been comparatively, perhaps dismally, neglected in research (Gendreau, Goggin, and Smith, 1999, 2001; Harris and Smith, 1996; Leschied, Bernfeld, and Farrington, 2001). Programs in themselves are merely the potential vehicles of change. Their impact is vitally influenced by the manner and setting in which they are delivered. It is therefore crucial that attention is paid to aspects of this in any attempt to provide high quality services (Goldstein and Glick, 2001; Leschied, Bernfeld, and Farrington, 2001; Lösel, 2001). The factors which may influence program delivery are numerous. They include the extent to which the objectives and contents of a program are understood and endorsed by the management and staff of a correctional agency; by their level of training and ability to deliver it; and by their resource capacity and its relationship to other aspects of their work (Gendreau, Goggin, and Smith, 1999; Gendreau, Goggin, Smith, and Paparozzi, 2002).

Effective implementation is also influenced by issues such as targeting of a program towards appropriate offender groups, and the installation and usage of procedures for assessment and selection. This is particularly applicable in community settings (Gendreau, Goggin, and Paparozzi, 1996; Lipsey and Wilson, 1998). Also, given the experience of high attrition rates, programs with larger effect sizes entail additional mechanisms for improving attendance by young people. This has included such strategies as inducements to attend by linking participation to other benefits (Goldstein, Glick, Carthan, and Blancero, 1994); provision of transport and other practical arrangements for ensuring young people arrive at a program site (Henggeler, Schoenwald, Borduin, Rowland, and Cunningham, 1998); or delivery of programs at locations where they will be accessible to participants (Edwards, Schoenwald, Henggeler, and Strother, 2001).

It has generally been found that the extent of monitoring of a program to ensure integrity of delivery is correlated with better outcomes. This is another aspect of program integrity. Where procedures are in place to ensure that a program is delivered as planned—adhering to the proposed theoretical model, and using the designated methods well—effect sizes tend to be higher. This finding emerges from several meta-analyses (Lipsey, 1995). It has also been confirmed by some research from Her Majesty's Prison Service in relation to cognitive skills programs (Friendship, Blud, Erikson, and Travers, 2002), though findings have also been somewhat inconsistent (Cann, Falshaw, Nugent, and Friendship, 2003).

Impact of Research Findings on Practice and Policy

During 1996, the Prison Service (England and Wales) embarked on a major initiative to increase the number of prison establishments providing programs and activities designed to reduce rates of recidivism following release. As with many other agencies, the process of management in the Prison Service has been linked to the use of Key Performance Indicators (KPIs), which are measures of the achievement of core objectives of the service. In 1996, the provision of programs designed to reduce recidivism was established as an indicator of this kind (KPI-7). Two independent specialist panels were appointed; one for accrediting programs for sex offenders, the other dealing with general offending behavior programs. The panels published sets of criteria for evaluating the design and delivery of prison-based interventions.

Programs designed to meet these criteria, and which have been accredited as doing so by the consultative panels, are now in use in more than eighty of England and Wales' 150 penal institutions. The introduction of these processes into the Prison Service in England and Wales from 1996 onwards has been described in more detail by Lipton, Thornton, McGuire, Porporino, and Hollin (2000). Similar developments have occurred in the Scottish Prison Services; in the Correctional Service of Canada; and at the time of writing, such initiatives are being pursued by prison services in several other countries.

To sustain an initiative of this kind is a substantial undertaking and has involved the deployment of significant additional resources. It has entailed an extensive program of staff training events; creation of a system of monitoring and audit; and associated mechanisms for administration and information management, both within individual prisons and on a service-wide scale. For example, all sessions of cognitive-skills programs are videotaped for scrutiny (on a sampling basis) by external assessors. Procedures have been put in place for the systematic evaluation of programs in respect of both short-term effects on intervening variables, and long-term impact on criminal recidivism.

The research findings outlined earlier also have had a marked impact on community agencies for offenders, principally the probation service (and more recently, youth justice services also). During 1997-1998 in England and Wales, the Probation Inspectorate, which monitors the working standards of probation nationally, conducted a focused or "thematic" inspection to examine the extent to which probation staff employ practices based on research evidence. The main report on this work (Underdown, 1998) proposed a series of new initiatives to extend the usage of evidence-based practice in probation work. This subsequently led to the selection of a number of programs designated as Pathfinder projects that were earmarked for further development. In late 1999, a new accreditation process was established to operate jointly for prison and probation services. Programs satisfactorily meeting accreditation criteria have now been delivered at a large number of sites, and by the end of 2003 nearly 20,000 offenders had attended such programs.

For a program to be accredited for use in prison or prison settings, a proposal must be submitted to the Joint Prison Probation Accreditation Panel, which like its predecessors in the Prison Service, consists of independent experts and consultants. A submission should include copies of all relevant materials such as a description of the program's theoretical rationale and evidence base; session manuals; staff training manuals; assessment and evaluation measures; and ideally, some preliminary indications of effectiveness. These are then judged against a pre-agreed set of accreditation criteria that define the minimal requirements for approval of a program (Home Office Probation Unit, 1999). The criteria are as follows.

1. **Model of change.** There should be a clear, evidence-based theoretical model underpinning the program which explains how what is proposed will have an impact on factors linked to offending behavior.

2. **Dynamic risk factors.** Program materials should identify factors linked to offending, specified in the model, and which if changed will lead to a reduction in risk of reoffending, and the program contents should reflect these objectives.

3. **Range of targets.** Multimodal programs with a range of treatment targets have yielded the largest effect sizes in research reviews. Program manuals specify an appropriate range of targets and the nature of their interrelationships.

4. **Effective methods.** The methods of change used in the program should have empirical support concerning effectiveness and be coordinated in an appropriate way.

5. **Skills orientated.** Programs targeting skills that will enable offenders to avoid criminal activities have yielded higher effect sizes in outcome studies. The skills targeted by the program should have explicit links to risk of reoffending and its reduction.

6. **Intensity, sequencing, duration.** The overall amount of programming (numbers of contact hours), the mode of delivery of sessions, and total program duration should be appropriate in the light of available evidence, the program's objectives and contents, and the risk level of the targeted offender groups.

7. **Selection of offenders.** The population of offenders for whom the program is designed should be explicitly and clearly specified. There should be agreed and realistic procedures for targeting and selecting, and for excluding inappropriate referrals.

8. **Engagement and participation.** This criterion refers to the principle of responsivity. Information should be provided concerning how this will be addressed, and how offenders will be encouraged and motivated to take part in and adhere to the program.

9. **Case management.** In prison settings, offenders are allocated a personal officer with responsibility for overseeing their individual sentence plans. On probation, they are supervised by a case manager. To be effective, programs should be interlinked with these processes, and guidelines provided for implementation within services.

10. **Ongoing monitoring.** To safeguard the integrity of a program and the treatment methods used, procedures should be in place for collection and monitoring of quality-of-delivery data, and systems established for review of this, and for taking action on the basis of it.

11. **Evaluation.** Finally, program materials should include assessment and evaluation measures and a framework for evaluation of its overall delivery, short-term, and long-term impact.

With regard to each criterion, a program may score 0 (not met), 1 (partially met), or 2 (fully met). Some of the criteria (items 1, 2, 7, 9, 10 and 11) are mandatory; in other words, it is essential that the requirements be fully met. To be accredited, a program must achieve a minimum score of 19/22 points, including full marks on all mandatory items.

In addition to program accreditation, each location in correctional services (such as an individual prison, probation office, or other unit) must also satisfactorily meet criteria for site accreditation. This is part of a process of certifying program and treatment integrity at that site. Systems for collecting information on quality of delivery (program integrity) also must be in place, and the data so collected made available for an annual site audit. Audit reports are then scrutinized both by correctional agency staff and by members of the independent accreditation panel.

Several correctional programs have successfully passed through this process, although others are still in development. The final product could be described as a national portfolio of offending behavior programs. Some are "generic" and include scope for working on multiple types of offenses, as the focus is on dynamic risk factors that may contribute to different criminal acts. Programs of cognitive-skills training have been developed for use either in group formats (Reasoning and Rehabilitation, Enhanced Thinking Skills, ThinkFirst) or individually (One-to-One). Those attending may have committed a variety of offenses with no single type dominant. Other programs are "offense specific" and are designed for individuals with a pattern dominated by one type of offense. Thus, there are specialized programs focused on violence (Aggression Replacement Training, Focus on Violence), sexual offending (Sex Offenders Treatment Program), domestic violence (Duluth), substance abuse (Addressing Substance-related Offending), and alcohol-impaired driving (Drink-Impaired Drivers). General cognitive-skills programs and those designed for work with sex offenders are available in separate versions for use in prison and probation settings, respectively. Studies are in progress both for intensive monitoring of the implementation process and for evaluating the overall impact of programming on rates of recidivism.

Recent Outcomes

The development and dissemination of practical programs of the kind just exemplified has been grounded in the findings from large-scale systematic reviews of the research literature. In recent years, positive outcomes have been reported from a number of practical programs focused on a variety of offenses. They have included projects for car crime (Wilkinson, 1997); sex offender treatment programs in probation settings (Beech, Erikson, Friendship, and Ditchfield, 2001); and interventions for domestic violence (Dobash, Dobash, Cavanagh, and Lewis, 1996).

While the process of implementing programs for delivery on a national scale is still ongoing, preliminary results have been encouraging. For example, preliminary analyses suggest that reductions in recidivism have been obtained following participation in prison-based cognitive skills programs (Friendship, Blud, Erikson, and Travers, 2002) and community-based use of Aggression Replacement Training (McGuire and Clark, 2003). Evaluations are in progress of a wide spectrum of community-based Pathfinder programs delivered within probation services (Hollin, McGuire, Palmer, Bilby, Hatcher, and Holmes, 2002).

An Agenda for Future Research

The accumulated set of findings that has emerged from the meta-analyses listed earlier has led to recognition that some interventions can be successful, and it has significantly consolidated our knowledge-base in the field of work with offenders. It also has enabled us to discern more from less effective interventions, both with regard to key program elements and types of approaches, and to aspects of the agency context in which methods are applied. Yet, many questions remain unanswered. The following are among the most important of them and are recommended as an agenda for future research, potentially forming part of continuing progress towards evidence-based practice in tertiary crime prevention (Welsh and Farrington, 2001b).

(a) As mentioned before, although the number of primary studies conducted in this field is fairly large, when the total sample is subdivided by different variables potentially relevant to any specific outcome, the number remaining in some "cells" of the overall matrix can be disappointingly low (Lösel, 2001). An obvious and vital first gap identified by many reviewers, therefore, is the sheer need for more and better-conducted research on certain kinds of intervention, including replication studies of those interventions, which in previous research have produced the most positive effects. At the same time, room must be left for exploratory studies of innovative approaches and new departures.

(b) There is a need for more careful study of the kinds of variations required in programs to accommodate diversity among participants. We do not know enough about the importance of gender, ethnicity, culture, and age as factors in program design. There are also large gaps in our ability to adapt materials, in appropriate ways, for people with literacy problems, communication problems, or learning disabilities.

(c) Little is known about the degree of appropriateness of programs delivered on either a group or individual basis, respectively. Research outcomes suggest the largest effect sizes are obtained when programs are matched closely to individual needs and designed accordingly. This does not preclude the possibility that an individual may attend a group program as an element in a larger "package" of activities. But to date, there is no firm basis for providing advice to agencies concerning a choice between one-to-one or group programs, other than on exclusion principles informed by their own experience.

(d) We have begun to learn a great deal about the importance of the context in which programs are delivered, with particular reference to differences between community and institutional settings; but also in relation to the organizational elements that provide support for new departures, maintain quality of delivery, and increase the likelihood of programmatic interventions being sustained. But there is much still to be learned concerning the extent of variations needed to take account of all the factors required for sound implementation. This should focus, for example, on whether there is a best timeframe during the course of a sentence for the delivery of programs and their links to other services; what are the best delivery formats and levels of intensity or distribution of multiple sessions; and which management structures are most effective and efficient.

(e) With reference to the distinction between generic and specific offense-focused programs depicted earlier, research is needed which will clearly delineate which of these approaches may be the preferable option, under which circumstances. The current position is one in which it is widely accepted that specialized programs are needed for those who have committed sexual offenses, have committed violent assaults, or have major problems of substance abuse. We need a clearer model of relationships between types of programs and types of offense beyond these fairly broad categories, and addressing other specific offense types in addition.

(f) There continues to be a major problem of attrition in community-based programs and this both weakens their potential effectiveness and diminishes their credibility in the eyes of sentencers and the public. Research is needed on factors influencing attrition and how to address it. Some of the findings may indicate a need for improved selection and targeting of participants, while others may highlight changes that could be introduced to program delivery or other factors that influence uptake and retention.

(g) There is pressure on policymakers towards incarceration on the grounds of retribution and perceived public safety; but simultaneous pressure away from it due to its much higher costs than community-based programming. This has led to the innovative use of some sentences that entail both custodial and community penalties in varying combinations. Systematic research is required on the likely impact of programs that are undertaken partly in institutional and partly in community settings, and of how to maximize the value of institutional-community linkages.

(h) Many staff working in agencies in which correctional programs are now being delivered were initially trained in a model of work in which much more emphasis was placed on the "working alliance" between a practitioner and an offender. There is a perception that the advent of structured programs has made this element redundant. The relative importance of the working alliance in engagement is felt to have been marginalized. There is some very important work to be done to illuminate the aspects of the working alliance that can be retained in correctional settings and that are essential for engaging and motivating offender participants (Florsheim, Shotorban, Guest-Warnick, Barratt, and Hwang, 2000). This could be linked to studies of other aspects of the relationship between "internal" and "external" motivations in securing program participation and completion, as has been discussed in relation to the use of coercion in drug treatment (Farabee, Prendergast, and Anglin, 1998).

Each of the above problems is important in itself. Each is also part of a bigger picture and a greater challenge: that of translating efficacy in well-designed demonstration programs into effectiveness in practical programs that are an integral feature of correctional services.

References

Alexander, M. A. 1999. Sexual Offender Treatment Efficacy Revisited. *Sexual Abuse: Journal of Research and Treatment.* 11: 101-116.

Andrews, D. A. 1995. The Psychology of Criminal Conduct and Effective Treatment. In J. McGuire, ed. *What Works: Reducing Re-offending: Guidelines from Research and Practice.* Chichester: John Wiley and Sons.

——. 2001. Principles of Effective Correctional Programs. In L. L. Motiuk and R. C. Serin, eds. *Compendium 2000 on Effective Correctional Programming.* Ottawa, Ontario: Correctional Service Canada.

Andrews, D. A. and J. Bonta. 1998. *The Psychology of Criminal Conduct.* 2nd ed. Cincinnati, Ohio: Anderson.

Andrews, D. A., I. Zinger, R. D. Hoge, J. Bonta, P. Gendreau, and F. T. Cullen. 1990. Does Correctional Treatment Work? A Clinically Relevant and Psychologically Informed Meta-Analysis. *Criminology.* 28: 369-404.

Antonowicz, D. and R. R. Ross. 1994. Essential Components of Successful Rehabilitation Programs for Offenders. *International Journal of Offender Therapy and Comparative Criminology.* 38: 97-104.

Axelrod, S. and J. Apsche, eds. 1983. *The Effects of Punishment on Human Behavior.* New York: Academic Press.

Beech, A. R., M. Erikson, C. Friendship, and J. Ditchfield. 2001. *A Six-Year Follow-Up of Men Going Through Probation-Based Sex Offender Treatment Programs.* Research Findings No.144. London: Home Office Research, Development and Statistics Directorate.

Bernfeld, G. A. 2001. The Struggle for Treatment Integrity in a "Dis-Integrated" Service Delivery System. In G. A. Bernfeld, D. P. Farrington, and A. W. Leschied, eds. *Offender Rehabilitation in Practice: Implementing and Evaluating Effective Programs.* Chichester: John Wiley and Sons.

Bernfeld, G. A., K. A. Blase, and D. L. Fixsen. 1990. Towards a Unified Perspective on Human Service Delivery Systems: Application of the Teaching-Family Model. In R. J. McMahon and R. DeV. Peters, eds. *Behavioral Disorders of Adolescence.* New York: Plenum Press.

Bernfeld, G. A., D. P. Farrington, and A. W. Leschied, eds. 2001. *Offender Rehabilitation in Practice: Implementing and Evaluating Effective Programs.* Chichester: John Wiley and Sons.

Borduin, C. M., B. J. Mann, L. T Cone, and S. W. Henggeller. 1995. Multi-systemic Treatment of Serious Juvenile Offenders: Long-Term Prevention of Criminality and Violence. *Journal of Consulting and Clinical Psychology.* 63: 569-578.

Brody, S. 1976. *The Effectiveness of Sentencing.* Home Office Research Study No.35. London: Her Majesty's Stationery Office.

Brown, S. L. 2001. Cost-effective Correctional Treatment. In L. L. Motiuk and R. C. Serin, eds. *Compendium 2000 on Effective Correctional Programming.* Ottawa, Ontario: Correctional Service Canada.

Cann, J., L Falshaw, F. Nugent, and C. Friendship. 2003. *Understanding What Works: Accredited Cognitive Skills Programmes for Adult Men and Young Offenders.* Findings 226. London: Home Office Research, Development and Statistics Directorate.

Chambless, D. L. and S. D. Hollon. 1998. Defining Empirically Supported Therapies. *Journal of Consulting and Clinical Psychology.* 66: 7-18.

Cleland, C. M., F. S. Pearson, D. S. Lipton, and D. Yee. 1997. Does Age Make a Difference? A Meta-Analytic Approach to Reductions in Criminal Offending for Juveniles and Adults. Paper presented at the Annual Meeting of the American Society of Criminology, San Diego, California.

Cook, T. D. and D. T. Campbell. 1979. *Quasi-Experimentation: Design and Analysis Issues for Field Settings.* Boston, Massachusetts: Houghton Mifflin.

Cooper, H. and L. V. Hedges, eds. 1994. *Handbook of Research Synthesis.* New York: Russell Sage Foundation.

Crow, I. 2001. *The Treatment and Rehabilitation of Offenders.* London: Sage Publications.

Dembo, R., G. Ramírez-Garnica, M. W. Rollie, and J. Schmeidler. 2000. Impact of a Family Empowerment Intervention on Youth Recidivism. *Journal of Offender Rehabilitation.* 30: 59-98.

Department of Health. 2001. *Treatment Choice in Psychological Therapies and Counselling: Evidence Based Clinical Practice Guideline.* Available from the Department of Health Website: http://www.doh.gov.uk/mentalhealth/treatmentguideline/index.htm

Dobash, R., R. E. Dobash, K. Cavanagh, and R. Lewis. 1996. *Re-Education Programs for Violent Men: An Evaluation.* Research Findings No.46. London: Home Office Research and Statistics Directorate.

Dobson, K. S. and K. D. Craig, eds. 1998. *Empirically Supported Therapies: Best Practice in Professional Psychology.* Thousand Oaks, California: Sage Publications.

Dowden, C. and D. A. Andrews. 1999a. What Works for Female Offenders: A Meta-Analytic Review. *Crime and Delinquency.* 45: 438-452.

———. 1999b. What Works in Young Offender Treatment: A Meta-Analysis. *Forum on Corrections Research.* 11: 21-24.

———. 2000. Effective Correctional Treatment and Violent Reoffending: A Meta-Analysis. *Canadian Journal of Criminology.* 42: 449-467.

Durlak, J. A. and M. W. Lipsey. 1991. A Practitioner's Guide to Meta-Analysis. *American Journal of Community Psychology.* 19: 291-332.

Edwards, D. L., S. K. Schoenwald, S. W. Henggeler, and K. B. Strother. 2001. A Multi-Level Perspective on the Implementation of Multisystemic Therapy (MST): Attempting Dissemination with Fidelity. In G. A. Bernfeld, D. P. Farrington, and A. W. Leschied, eds. *Offender Rehabilitation in Practice: Implementing and Evaluating Effective Programs.* Chichester: John Wiley and Sons.

Farabee, D., M. Prendergast, and M. D. Anglin. 1998. The Effectiveness of Coerced Treatment for Drug-Abusing Offenders. *Federal Probation.* 62: 3-10.

Farrington, D. P. 1996. The Explanation and Prevention of Youthful Offending. In J. D. Hawkins, ed. *Delinquency and Crime: Current Theories.* Cambridge: Cambridge University Press.

Farrington, D. P. and A. Petrosino. 2001. The Campbell Collaboration Crime and Justice Group. *Annals of the American Academy of Political and Social Science.* 578: 35-49.

Florsheim, P., S. Shotorban, G. Guest-Warnick, T. Barratt, and W-S. Hwang. 2000. Role of the Working Alliance in the Treatment of Delinquent Boys in Community-Based Programs. *Journal of Clinical Child Psychology.* 29: 94-107.

Friendship, C., L. Blud, M. Erikson, and R. Travers. 2002. *An Evaluation of Cognitive-Behavioral Treatment for Prisoners.* Findings 161. London: Home Office Research, Development and Statistics Directorate.

Gallagher, C. A., D. B. Wilson, P. Hirschfield, M. B. Coggeshall, and D. L. MacKenzie. 1999. A Quantitative Review of the Effects of Sexual Offender Treatment on Sexual Reoffending. *Corrections Management Quarterly.* 3: 19-29.

Garrett, C. G. 1985. Effects of Residential Treatment on Adjudicated Delinquents: A Meta-Analysis. *Journal of Research in Crime and Delinquency.* 22: 287-308.

Gendreau, P. 1996a The Principles of Effective Intervention with Offenders. In A. T. Harland, ed. *Choosing Correctional Options that Work: Defining the Demand and Evaluating the Supply.* Thousand Oaks, California: Sage Publications.

———. 1996b. Offender Rehabilitation: What We Know and What Needs to Be Done. *Criminal Justice and Behavior.* 23: 144-161.

Gendreau, P. and D. A. Andrews. 1990. Tertiary Prevention: What The Meta-Analyses of the Offender Treatment Literature Tell Us About "What Works." *Canadian Journal of Criminology.* 32: 173-184.

Gendreau, P. and C. Goggin. 1996. Principles of Effective Correctional Programming. *Forum on Corrections Research.* 8: 38-41.

Gendreau, P., C. Goggin, and F. T. Cullen. 1999. The Effects of Prison Sentences on Recidivism. Report to the Corrections Research and Development and Aboriginal Policy Branch. Ottawa, Ontario: Solicitor General of Canada.

Gendreau, P., C. Goggin, F. T. Cullen, and D. A. Andrews. 2001. The Effects of Community Sanctions and Incarceration on Recidivism. In L. L. Motiuk and R. C. Serin, eds. *Compendium 2000 on Effective Correctional Programming.* Ottawa, Ontario: Correctional Service Canada.

Gendreau, P., C. Goggin, and M. Paparozzi. 1996. Principles of Effective Assessment for Community Corrections. *Federal Probation.* 60: 64-70.

Gendreau, P., C. Goggin, and P. Smith. 1999. The Forgotten Issue in Effective Correctional Treatment: Program Implementation. *International Journal of Offender Therapy and Comparative Criminology.* 43: 180-187.

———. 2001. Implementation Guidelines for Correctional Programs in the "Real World." In G. A. Bernfeld, D. P. Farrington, and A. W. Leschied, eds. *Offender*

Rehabilitation in Practice: Implementing and Evaluating Effective Programs. Chichester: John Wiley and Sons.

Gendreau, P., C. Goggin, P. Smith, and M. Paparozzi. 2002. The Common-sense Revolution and Correctional Policy. In J. McGuire, ed. *Offender Rehabilitation and Treatment: Effective Programmes and Policies to Reduce Re-offending.* Chichester: John Wiley and Sons.

Gendreau, P., M. Paparozzi, T. Little, and M. Goddard. 1993. Does "Punishing Smarter" Work? An Assessment of the New Generation of Alternative Sanctions in Probation. *Forum on Corrections Research.* 5: 31-34.

Gendreau, P. and R. R. Ross. 1987. Revivification of Rehabilitation: Evidence from the 1980s. *Justice Quarterly.* 4: 349-407.

Gensheimer, L. K., J. P. Mayer, R. Gottschalk, and W. S. Davidson. 1986. Diverting Youth from the Juvenile Justice System: A Meta-Analysis of Intervention Efficacy. In S. A. Apter and A. P. Goldstein, eds. *Youth Violence: Programs and Prospects.* Elmsford, New Jersey: Pergamon Press.

Glass, G. V. 1976. Primary, Secondary, and Meta-analysis. *Educational Researcher.* 5: 3-8.

Glass, G. V., B. McGaw, and M. L. Smith. 1981. *Meta-analysis in Social Research.* Newbury Park, California: Sage Publications.

Goldblatt, P. and C. Lewis. 1998. *Reducing Offending: An Assessment of Research Evidence on Ways of Dealing with Offending Behavior.* Home Office Research Study No.187. London: Home Office.

Goldstein, A. P. 2002. Low-level Aggression: Definition, Escalation, Intervention. In J. McGuire, ed. *Offender Rehabilitation and Treatment: Effective Programmes and Policies to Reduce Re-offending.* Chichester: John Wiley and Sons.

Goldstein, A. P. and B. Glick. 2001. Aggression Replacement Training: Application and Evaluation Management. In G. A. Bernfeld, D. P. Farrington and A. W. Leschied, eds. *Offender Rehabilitation in Practice: Implementing and Evaluating Effective Programs.* Chichester: John Wiley and Sons.

Goldstein, A. P., B. Glick, W. Carthan, and D. A. Blancero. 1994. *The Prosocial Gang: Implementing Aggression Replacement Training.* Thousand Oaks, California: Sage.

Gordon, D. A. 2002. Intervening with Families of Troubled Youth: Functional Family Therapy and Parenting Wisely. In J. McGuire, ed. *Offender Rehabilitation and Treatment: Effective Programmes and Policies to Reduce Re-offending.* Chichester: John Wiley and Sons.

Gordon, D. A., K. Graves, and J. Arbuthnot.1995. The Effect of Functional Family Therapy for Delinquents on Adult Criminal Behavior. *Criminal Justice and Behavior.* 22: 60-73.

Gottschalk, R., W. S. Davidson, L. K. Gensheimer, and J. P. Mayer. 1987a. Community-based interventions. In H. C. Quay, ed. *Handbook of Juvenile Delinquency.* New York: John Wiley and Sons.

Gottschalk, R., W. S. Davidson, J. Mayer, and L. K. Gensheimer, 1987b. Behavioral Approaches with Juvenile Offenders: A Meta-Analysis of Long-term Treatment Efficacy. In E. K. Morris and C. J. Braukmann, eds. *Behavioral Approaches to Crime and Delinquency.* New York: Plenum Press.

Guerra, N. G., P. H. Tolan, and W. R. Hammond. 1994. Prevention and Treatment of Adolescent Violence. In L. D. Eron, J. H. Gentry, and P. Schlegel, eds. *Reason to Hope: A Psychosocial Perspective on Violence and Youth.* Washington, D.C.: American Psychological Association.

Hall, G. C. N. 1995. Sexual Offender Recidivism Revisited: A Meta-Analysis of Recent Treatment Studies. *Journal of Consulting and Clinical Psychology.* 63: 802-809.

Harland, A. T., ed. 1996. *Choosing Correctional Options that Work: Defining the Demand and Evaluating the Supply.* Thousand Oaks, California: Sage Publications.

Harris, P. and S. Smith. 1996. Developing Community Corrections: An Implementation Perspective. In A. T. Harland, ed. *Choosing Correctional Options that Work: Defining the Demand and Evaluating the Supply.* Thousand Oaks, California: Sage Publications.

Henggeler, S. W., S. K. Schoenwald, C. M., Borduin, M. D. Rowland, and P. B. Cunningham. 1998. *Multisystemic Treatment of Antisocial Behavior in Children and Adolescents.* New York: Guilford Press.

Henning, K. R. and B. C. Frueh. 1996. Cognitive-behavioral Treatment of Incarcerated Offenders: An Evaluation of the Vermont Department of Corrections' Cognitive Self-Change Program. *Criminal Justice and Behavior.* 23: 523-542.

Hollin, C. R. 1995. The Meaning and Implications of Program Integrity. In J. McGuire, ed. *What Works: Reducing Reoffending: Guidelines from Research and Practice.* Chichester: John Wiley and Sons.

———. 1999. Treatment Programs for Offenders: Meta-analysis, "What Works," and Beyond. *International Journal of Law and Psychiatry.* 22: 361-371.

———, ed. 2001. *Handbook of Offender Assessment and Treatment.* Chichester: John Wiley and Sons.

Hollin, C. R., K. J. Epps, and D. J. Kendrick. 1995. *Managing Behavioral Treatment: Policy and Practice with Delinquent Adolescents*. London: Routledge.

Hollin, C. R., J. McGuire, E. Palmer, C. Bilby, R. Hatcher, and A. Holmes. 2002. *Introducing Pathfinder Programmes into the Probation Service: An Interim Report*. Home Office Research Study 247. London: Home Office.

Home Office Probation Unit. 1999. *What Works Initiative: Crime Reduction Program*. Joint Prison and Probation Accreditation Criteria. London: Home Office.

Izzo, R. L. and R. R. Ross. 1990. Meta-analysis of Rehabilitation Programs for Juvenile Delinquents. *Criminal Justice and Behavior*. 17: 134-142.

Kaufman, P. 1985. Meta-analysis of Juvenile Delinquency Prevention Programs. Unpublished Master's Thesis. Claremont Graduate University, Claremont, California.

Leschied, A. W., G. Bernfeld, and D. P. Farrington. 2001. Implementation Issues. In G. A. Bernfeld, D. P. Farrington, and A. W. Leschied, eds. *Offender Rehabilitation in Practice: Implementing and Evaluating Effective Programs*. Chichester: John Wiley and Sons.

Lipsey, M. W. 1992. Juvenile Delinquency Treatment: A Meta-analytic Inquiry into the Variability of Effects. In T. Cook, D. Cooper, H. Corday, H. Hartman, L. Hedges, R. Light, T. Louis, and F. Mosteller, eds. *Meta-analysis for Explanation: A Casebook*. New York: Russell Sage Foundation.

————. 1995. What Do We Learn from 400 Studies on the Effectiveness of Treatment with Juvenile Delinquents? In J. McGuire, ed. *What Works: Reducing Reoffending: Guidelines from Research and Practice*. Chichester: John Wiley and Sons.

————. 1999. Can Rehabilitative Programs Reduce the Recidivism of Juvenile Offenders? An Inquiry into the Effectiveness of Practical Programs. *Virginia Journal of Social Policy & the Law*. 6: 611-641.

Lipsey, M. W., G. L. Chapman, and N. A. Landenberger. 2001. Cognitive-behavioral Programs for Offenders. *Annals of the American Academy of Political and Social Science*. 578: 144-157.

Lipsey, M. W. and D. B. Wilson. 1993. The Efficacy of Psychological, Educational, and Behavioral Treatment: Confirmation from Meta-analysis. *American Psychologist*. 48: 1181-1209.

————. 1998. Effective Intervention for Serious Juvenile Offenders: A Synthesis of Research. In R. Loeber and D. P. Farrington, eds. *Serious and Violent Juvenile Offenders: Risk Factors and Successful Interventions*. Thousand Oaks, California: Sage Publications.

————. 2000. *Practical Meta-analysis*. Thousand Oaks, California: Sage Publications.

Lipton, D. S., R. Martinson, and J. Wilks. 1975. *The Effectiveness of Correctional Treatment: A Survey of Treatment Evaluation Studies*. New York: Praeger.

Lipton, D. S., F. S., Pearson, C. Cleland, and D. Lee. 1997. Synthesizing Correctional Treatment Outcomes: Preliminary CDATE Findings. Paper presented at the 5th Annual National Institute of Justice Conference on Research and Evaluation in Criminal Justice, Washington, July.

————. 2002a. The Effects of Therapeutic Communities and Milieu Therapy on Recidivism: Meta-Analytic Findings From the Correctional Drug Abuse Treatment Effectiveness CDATE Study. In J. McGuire, ed. *Offender Rehabilitation and Treatment: Effective Programmes and Policies to Reduce Re-offending*. Chichester: John Wiley and Sons.

————. 2002b. The Effects of Cognitive-Behavioral Treatment Methods on Offender Recidivism: Meta-Analytic Outcomes from the CDATE Project. In J. McGuire, ed. *Offender Rehabilitation and Treatment: Effective Programmes and Policies to Reduce Re-offending*. Chichester: John Wiley and Sons.

Lipton, D. S., D. Thornton, J. McGuire, F. Porporino, and C. R. Hollin. 2000. Program Accreditation and Correctional Treatment. *Substance Use and Misuse*. 35: 1705-1734.

Lösel, F. 1995. The Efficacy of Correctional Treatment: A Review and Synthesis of Meta-Evaluations. In J. McGuire, ed. *What Works: Reducing Re-offending: Guidelines from Research and Practice*. Chichester: John Wiley and Sons.

————. 2001. Evaluating the Effectiveness of Correctional Programs: Bridging the Gap between Research and Practice. In G. A. Bernfeld, D. P. Farrington, and A. W. Leschied, eds. *Offender Rehabilitation in Practice: Implementing and Evaluating Effective Programs*. Chichester: John Wiley and Sons.

Lösel, F. and P. Köferl. 1989. Evaluation Research on Correctional Treatment in West Germany: A Meta-analysis. In H. Wegener, F. Lösel and J. Haisch, eds. *Criminal Behavior and the Justice System: Psychological Perspectives*. New York: Springer-Verlag.

MacKenzie, D. L. 1997. Criminal Justice and Crime Prevention. In L. W. Sherman, D. Gottfredson, D. L. Mackenzie, J. Eck, P. Reuter, and S. Bushway. *Preventing Crime: What Works, What Doesn't, What's Promising*. Washington, D.C.: Office of Justice Programs.

MacKenzie, D. L., D. B. Wilson, and S. B. Kider. 2001. Effects of Correctional Boot Camps on Offending. *Annals of the American Academy of Political and Social Science*. 578: 126-143.

Martinson, R. 1974. What Works? Questions and Answers about Prison Reform. *The Public Interest*. 10: 22-54.

———. 1979. New Findings, New Views: A Note of Caution Regarding Sentencing Reform. *Hofstra Law Review*. 7: 243-258.

Mayer, J. P., L. K. Gensheimer, W. S. Davidson, and R. Gottschalk. 1986. Social Learning Treatment within Juvenile Justice: A Meta-Analysis of Impact in the Natural Environment. In S. A. Apter and A. P. Goldstein, eds. *Youth Violence: Programs and Prospects*. Elmsford, New Jersey: Pergamon Press.

Mayhew, P. and P. White. 1997. The 1996 International Crime Victimisation Survey. Research Findings No. 57. London: Home Office Research and Statistics Directorate.

McGuire, J., ed. 1995. *What Works: Reducing Re-offending: Guidelines from Research and Practice*. Chichester: John Wiley and Sons.

McGuire, J. 2000a. *Cognitive-Behavioral Methods: An Introduction to Theory and Research*. London: Home Office.

———. 2000b. Explanations of Offence Behaviour. In J. McGuire, T. Mason, and A. O'Kane, eds. *Behavior, Crime and Legal Processes: A Guidebook for Practitioners*. Chichester: John Wiley and Sons.

———. 2001a. Property Offences. In C. R. Hollin, ed. *Handbook of Offender Assessment and Treatment*. Chichester: John Wiley and Sons.

———. 2001b. Defining Correctional Programs. In L. L. Motiuk and R. C. Serin, eds. *Compendium 2000 on Effective Correctional Programming*. Ottawa, Ontario: Correctional Service Canada.

———. 2001c. What Works In Correctional Intervention? Evidence and Practical Implications. In G. A. Bernfeld, D. P. Farrington, and A. W. Leschied, eds. *Offender Rehabilitation in Practice: Implementing and Evaluating Effective Programs*. Chichester: John Wiley and Sons.

———. 2001d. Development of a Program Logic Model to Assist Evaluation. In L. L. Motiuk and R. C. Serin, eds. *Compendium 2000 on Effective Correctional Programming*. Ottawa, Ontario: Correctional Service Canada.

———. 2002a. Criminal Sanctions Versus Psychologically-based Interventions with Offenders: A Comparative Empirical Analysis. *Psychology, Crime & Law*. 8: 183-208.

———. ed. 2002b. *Offender Rehabilitation and Treatment: Effective Programmes and Policies to Reduce Re-offending*. Chichester: John Wiley and Sons.

McGuire, J. and D. Clark. 2003. A National Dissemination Program. In A. P. Goldstein, R. Nensen, M. Kalt and B. Daleflod, eds. *New Perspectives on Aggression Replacement Training.* Chichester: John Wiley and Sons.

McGuire, J. and P. Priestley.1985. *Offending Behavior: Skills and Stratagems for Going Straight.* London: Batsford.

Moffitt, T. E. 1983. The Learning Theory Model of Punishment: Implications for Delinquency Deterrence. *Criminal Justice and Behavior.* 10: 131-158.

Motiuk, L. L. and R. C. Serin, eds. 2001. *Compendium 2000 on Effective Correctional Programming.* Ottawa, Ontario: Correctional Service Canada.

Nathan, P. E. and J. M. Gorman, eds. 1998. *A Guide to Treatments that Work.* New York: Oxford University Press.

Palmer, T. 1975. Martinson Revisited. *Journal of Research in Crime and Delinquency.* 12: 133-152.

————. 1992. The *Re-emergence of Correctional Intervention.* Newbury Park, California: Sage Publications.

Pearson, F. S., D. S. Lipton, and C. M. Cleland. 1997. Rehabilitative Programs in Adult Corrections: CDATE Meta-analyses. Paper presented at the Annual Meeting of the American Society of Criminology, San Diego.

Persons, J. B. 1991. Psychotherapy Outcome Studies Do Not Accurately Represent Current Models of Psychotherapy: A Proposed Remedy. *American Psychologist.* 46: 99-106.

Persons, J. B. and G. Silbersatz. 1998. Are the Results of Randomised Controlled Trials Useful to Psychotherapists? *Journal of Consulting and Clinical Psychology.* 66: 126-135.

Petrosino, A. 2000. Crime, Drugs and Alcohol. In *Evidence from Systematic Reviews of Research Relevant to Implementing the Wider Public Health Agenda.* University of York: NHS Centre for Reviews and Dissemination. Available from website: http://www.york.ac.uk/inst/crd/ wph.htm

Petrosino, A. J., C. Turpin-Petrosino, and J. O. Finckenauer. 2000. Well-meaning Programs Can Have Harmful Effects! Lessons from Experiments of Programs Such as Scared Straight. *Crime and Delinquency.* 46: 354-379.

Polizzi, D. M., D. L. MacKenzie, and L. J. Hickman. 1999. What Works In Adult Sex Offender Treatment? A Review of Prison- and Non-prison-based Treatment Programs. *International Journal of Offender Therapy and Comparative Criminology.* 43: 357-374.

Redondo, S., V. Garrido, and J. Sánchez-Meca. 1997. What Works in Correctional Rehabilitation in Europe: A Meta-Analytical Review. In S. Redondo, V. Garrido, J. Pérez and R. Barberet, eds. *Advances in Psychology and Law: International Contributions.* Berlin: Walter de Gruyter.

Redondo, S., J. Sánchez-Meca, and V. Garrido.1999 The Influence of Treatment Programs on the Recidivism of Juvenile and Adult Offenders: An European Meta-analytic Review. *Psychology, Crime & Law.* 5: 251-278.

————. 2002. Crime Treatment in Europe: A Review of Outcome Studies. In J. McGuire, ed. *Offender Rehabilitation and Treatment: Effective Programmes and Policies to Reduce Re-offending.* Chichester: John Wiley and Sons.

Roberts, A. R. and M. J. Camasso. 1991. The Effect of Juvenile Offender Treatment Programs on Recidivism: A Meta-analysis of 46 Studies. *Notre Dame Journal of Law Ethics and Public Policy.* 5: 421-441.

Robinson, D. 1995. *The Impact of Cognitive Skills Training on Post-release Recidivism among Canadian Federal Offenders.* Ottawa, Ontario: Correctional Service Canada.

Rosenthal, R. 1994. Parametric Measures of Effect Size. In H. Cooper and L. V. Hedges, eds. *Handbook of Research Synthesis.* New York: Russell Sage Foundation.

Ross, R. R., D. H. Antonowicz, and G. K. Dhaliwal. 1995. *Going Straight: Effective Delinquency Prevention and Offender Rehabilitation.* Ottawa, Ontario: Air Training and Publications.

Ross, R. R. and P. Gendreau, eds. 1980. *Effective Correctional Treatment.* Toronto, Ontario: Butterworths.

Roth, A. and P. Fonagy. 1996. *What Works for Whom? A Critical Review of Psychotherapy Research.* New York: Guilford Press.

Rutter, M., H. Giller, and A. Hagell. 1998. *Antisocial Behavior by Young People.* Cambridge: Cambridge University Press.

Salekin, R. T. 2002. Psychopathy and Therapeutic Pessimism: Clinical Lore or Clinical Reality? *Clinical Psychology Review.* 22: 79-112.

Sherman, L. W., D. Gottfredson, D. MacKenzie, J. Eck, P. Reuter, and S. Bushway. 1997. *Preventing Crime: What Works, What Doesn't, What's Promising.* Washington, D.C.: Office of Justice Programs.

Simon, L. M. J. 1998. Does Criminal Offender Treatment Work? *Applied and Preventive Psychology.* 7: 137-59.

Sundel, S. S. and M. Sundel. 1993. *Behavior Modification in Human Services: A Systematic Introduction to Concepts and Applications.* Newbury Park, California: Sage Publications.

Thornton, D. M. 1987. Treatment Effects on Recidivism: A Re-Appraisal of the "Nothing Works" Doctrine. In B. McGurk, D. M. Thornton, and M. Williams, eds. *Applying Psychology to Imprisonment: Theory and Practice.* London: Her Majesty's Stationery Office.

Thornton, T. N., C. A. Craft, L. L. Dahlberg, B. S. Lynch, and K. Baer. 2000. *Best Practices of Youth Violence Prevention: A Sourcebook for Community Action.* Atlanta, Georgia: National Center for Injury Prevention and Control.

Underdown, A. 1998. *Strategies for Effective Offender Supervision: Report of the HMIP What Works Project.* London: Home Office.

Vennard, J., D. Sugg, and C. Hedderman, 1997. *Changing Offenders' Attitudes and Behavior: What Works?* Home Office Research Study No.171. London: Her Majesty's Stationery Office.

Walker, N. 1991. *Why Punish? Theories of Punishment Reassessed.* Oxford: Oxford University Press.

Wells-Parker, E., R. Bangert-Drowns, R. McMillen, and M. Williams. 1995. Final Results from a Meta-Analysis of Remedial Interventions with Drink/Drive Offenders. *Addiction.* 90: 907-926.

Welsh, B. C. and D. P. Farrington. 2000. Correctional Intervention Programs and Cost Benefit Analysis. *Criminal Justice and Behavior.* 27: 115-133.

————. 2001a. Evaluating the Economic Efficiency of Correctional Intervention Programs. In G. A. Bernfeld, D. P. Farrington, and A. W. Leschied, eds. *Offender Rehabilitation in Practice: Implementing and Evaluating Effective Programs.* Chichester: John Wiley and Sons.

————. 2001b. Toward an Evidence-based Approach to Preventing Crime. *Annals of the American Academy of Political and Social Science.* 578: 158-173.

Whitehead, J. T. and S. P. Lab. 1989. A Meta-Analysis of Juvenile Correctional Treatment. *Journal of Research in Crime and Delinquency.* 26: 276-295.

Wilkinson, J. 1997. The Impact of Ilderton Motor Project on Motor Vehicle Crime and Offending. *British Journal of Criminology.* 37: 568-581.

Wilson, D. B. 2001. Meta-analytic Methods for Criminology. *Annals of the American Academy of Political and Social Science.* 578: 71-89.

Wilson, D. B., C. A. Gallagher, and D. L. MacKenzie. 2000. A Meta-analysis of Corrections-based Education, Vocation and Work Programs for Adult Offenders. *Journal of Research in Crime and Delinquency*. 37: 568-581.

Wilson, S. J. and M. W. Lipsey. 2000. Wilderness Challenge Programs for Delinquent Youth: A Meta-Analysis of Outcome Evaluations. *Evaluation and Program Planning*. 23: 1-12.

Yoshikawa, H. 1994. Prevention as Cumulative Protection: Effects of Early Family Support and Education on Chronic Delinquency and Its Risks. *Psychological Bulletin*. 115: 28-54.

Using an Integrated Model to Implement Evidence-Based Practices in Corrections

4

Lore Joplin
Deputy Director
Crime and Justice Institute
Boston, Massachusetts

Brad Bogue
Project Director
Justice System Assessment
and Training
Boulder, Colorado

Nancy M. Campbell
Affiliate Associate Professor
University of Washington
Bainbridge Island, Washington

Mark Carey
Warden
Minnesota Correctional Facility-
Shakopee
Shakopee, Minnesota

Elyse Clawson
Executive Director
Crime and Justice Institute
Boston, Massachusetts

Kate Florio
Project Assistant
Crime and Justice Institute
Boston, Massachusetts

Billy F. Wasson
Former Director
Marion County Department of
Corrections
Salem, Oregon

William Woodward
Director, Training and Technical
Assistance
Center for Study and Prevention
of Violence
Boulder, Colorado

Overview

Criminal justice system costs have grown exponentially during the last twenty years, yet they have failed to keep pace with the burgeoning offender population. Most of the increase in system costs can be attributed to the growth in prison and jail capacity during the 1980s, but these institutions continue to operate at or over capacity; and budget cuts have left policymakers without the resources to build more institutional beds. Therefore, many states are focusing on community corrections as they search for more effective and efficient methods of managing offenders without compromising public safety.

The leaders of community corrections agencies, faced with their own shrinking agency budgets, are being called on to alleviate systemic pressures by managing this growing number of offenders in the community while maintaining public safety. Meeting this challenge requires that corrections leaders make effective use of resources and provide services that work to reduce offender recidivism.

Until recently, the criminal justice field has suffered from a lack of research that identified proven methods of reducing offender recidivism. Recent research efforts based on meta-analysis (the syntheses of data from many research studies) have broken through this barrier and provided the field with concrete and scientifically proven indications of how to better reduce offender recidivism (McGuire, 2002; Sherman et al., 1998; Henggeler et al., 1997; Meyers et al., 2002). This research indicates that criminal justice agencies can significantly reduce offender recidivism by implementing a series of evidence-based practices.

An Integrated Model of Implementation

Implementation of these evidence-based practices requires corrections agencies to change the way they operate and rethink the way they do business, which is no easy task. This level of change requires dynamic and committed leadership with the ability and willingness to place equal focus on evidence-based practices, organizational development, and collaboration. These three components, when implemented together, form an integrated model for system reform. Each component of this integrated model is essential:
- Evidence-based principles provide the content for the provision of effective services.

- Organizational development is required to successfully implement systemic change. To implement evidence-based practices, organizations must rethink their missions and values, gain new knowledge and skills, adjust their infrastructure to support this new way of doing business, and transform their organizational culture.
- Collaboration enhances internal and external buy-in of the change process, supporting successful implementation in the complex web of public safety agencies, service providers, and other stakeholders.

As a part of their strategy for facilitating the implementation of effective interventions, the National Institute of Corrections, Community Corrections Division entered into a cooperative agreement with the Crime and Justice Institute in 2002 to develop a model for implementing evidence-based practices in criminal justice systems. This integrated model emphasizes the importance of focusing equally on evidence-based practices, organizational development, and collaboration to achieve successful and lasting change. The scope of the model is broad enough so that it can be applied to all components of the criminal justice system and across varying jurisdictions.

The National Institute of Corrections and the Crime and Justice Institute have worked for decades to further the implementation of effective interventions in criminal justice. Their experience in the field of community corrections indicates that many organizations are able to successfully implement components of evidence-based principles, such as assessment tools or cognitive-behavioral programming. Unfortunately, very few organizations have successfully implemented or been able to sustain implementation of evidence-based principles throughout their operations. While some organizations may have developed a certain breadth of implementation, many have not managed to achieve the depth necessary to change the organizational culture and attain desired outcomes. As a result, change efforts often lose focus, stagnate, and are not institutionalized. An integrated approach to implementation provides the depth and breadth necessary to ensure lasting change.

Figure 1

**Implementing Evidence-based Practice:
The Integrated Model**

Evidence-based Principles

Alignment with Principles and Values

Building policy and service delivery collaboratively

Reducing Recidivism

Organizational Development

Interdependency

Collaboration

Many organizations are beginning to use or want to use evidence-based principles in their supervision practices and program design to better achieve reductions in recidivism. Most organizations have spent time on organizational development initiatives and collaborations. Few organizations, though, have focused their attention simultaneously on all three areas, to achieve full integration. In September 2004, The National Institute of Corrections and the Crime and Justice Institute began working with two pilot sites (Illinois and Maine) to implement this integrated model (Figure 2).

Evidence-based Practice

As stated earlier, recent research efforts based on meta-analysis have provided the criminal justice field with much needed information about how to better reduce offender recidivism. This research indicates that certain programs and intervention strategies, when applied to a variety of offender populations, reliably produce sustained reductions in recidivism. Unfortunately, few criminal justice agencies are using these effective interventions and their related concepts/principles.

Figure 2

Integration Continuum

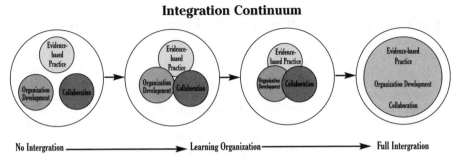

The conventional approach to supervision in this country emphasizes individual accountability from offenders and their supervising officers without consistently providing either the skills, tools, or resources that science indicates are necessary for risk and recidivism reduction. Despite the evidence that indicates otherwise, officers continue to be trained and expected to meet minimal contact standards which emphasize rates of contacts. These standards largely ignore the opportunities these contacts provide for reinforcing behavioral change.

The biggest challenge in adopting these evidence-based practices is to change our existing systems to appropriately support the new innovations. Identifying interventions with good research support and realigning the necessary organizational infrastructure are both fundamental to evidence-based practice.

Evidence-based practice is a significant trend throughout all human service fields that emphasize outcomes. Interventions within corrections are considered effective when they reduce offender risk and subsequent recidivism and therefore make a positive long-term contribution to public safety.

The evidence-based principles component of the integrated model highlights eight principles for effective offender interventions. The organization or system that is most successful in initiating and maintaining offender interventions and supervision practices consistent with these principles will achieve the greatest recidivism reductions.

The following framework of principles is listed in developmental order, and they are all highly interdependent. For example, offender assessments must consider both risk to reoffend and criminogenic needs, in that order. Research indicates that resources are used more effectively when they are focused on higher-risk rather than lower-risk offenders, therefore considering offenders' risk to reoffend prior to addressing criminogenic needs allows agencies to target resources on higher-risk offenders.

Eight Evidence-based Principles for Effective Interventions

1. Assess Actuarial Risk/Needs
2. Enhance Intrinsic Motivation
3. Target Interventions
   a. *Risk Principle:* Prioritize supervision and treatment resources for higher-risk offenders
   b. *Need Principle:* Target interventions to criminogenic needs
   c. *Responsivity Principle:* Be responsive to temperament, learning style, motivation, culture, and gender when assigning programs
   d. *Dosage:* Structure 40 to 70 percent of high-risk offenders' time for three-to-nine months
4. Skill Train with Directed Practice (use cognitive-behavioral treatment methods)
5. Increase Positive Reinforcement
6. Engage Ongoing Support in Natural Communities
7. Measure Relevant Processes/Practices
8. Provide Measurement Feedback

1. Assess Actuarial Risk/Needs

Develop and maintain a complete system of ongoing offender-risk screening/triage and needs assessments. Assessing offenders in a reliable and valid manner is a prerequisite for effective management (in other words, supervision and treatment) of offenders. Timely, relevant measures of offender risk and need at the individual and aggregate levels are essential for the implementation of numerous principles of best practice in corrections (for example, risk, need, and responsivity). Offender assessments are most reliable and valid when staff are formally trained to administer tools. Screening and assessment tools that focus on dynamic and static risk factors, profile criminogenic needs, and have been validated on similar populations are preferred. They also should be supported by sufficiently detailed and accurately written procedures.

Offender assessment is as much an ongoing function as it is a formal event. Case information that is gathered informally through routine interactions and observations with offenders is just as important as formal assessment guided by instruments. Formal and informal offender assessments should reinforce one another. They should combine to enhance formal reassessments, case decisions, and working relations between practitioners and offenders throughout the jurisdiction of supervision (Andrews et al., 1990; Andrews and Bonta, 1998; Gendreau et al., 1996; Kropp et al., 1995; Clements, 1996).

Questions to Ask

Does the assessment tool we are using measure for criminogenic risk and need?

How are officers trained to conduct the assessment interview?

What quality assurance is in place to ensure that assessments are conducted appropriately?

How is the assessment information captured and used in the development of case plans?

2. Enhance Intrinsic Motivation

Staff should relate to offenders in interpersonally sensitive and constructive ways to enhance intrinsic motivation in offenders. Behavioral change is an inside job. For lasting change to occur, a level of intrinsic motivation is needed. Motivation to change is dynamic, and the probability that change may occur is strongly influenced by interpersonal interactions, such as those with probation officers, treatment providers, and institution staff. Feelings of ambivalence that usually accompany change can be explored through motivational interviewing, a style and method of communication used to help people overcome their ambivalence about behavior changes. Research strongly suggests that motivational interviewing techniques, rather than persuasion tactics, effectively enhance motivation for initiating and maintaining behavior changes (Miller and Rollnick, 2002; Miller and Mount, 2001; Harper and Hardy, 2000; Ryan and Deci, 2000).

Questions to Ask

Are officers and program staff trained in motivational interviewing techniques?

What quality assurance is in place?

Are staff held accountable for using motivational interviewing techniques in their day-to-day interactions with offenders?

3. Target Interventions

a. **Risk Principle:** Prioritize supervision and treatment resources for higher-risk offenders.

b. **Need Principle:** Target interventions to criminogenic needs.

    c. **Responsivity Principle:** Be responsive to temperament, learning style, motivation, gender, and culture when assigning to programs.

    d. **Dosage:** Structure 40 to 70 percent of high-risk offenders' time for three-to-nine months.

    e. **Treatment Principle:** Integrate treatment into the full sentence/sanction requirements.

3a. Risk Principle

Prioritize primary supervision and treatment resources for offenders who are at higher risk to reoffend. Research indicates that supervision and treatment resources that are focused on lower-risk offenders tend to produce little if any net positive effect on recidivism rates. Shifting these resources to higher-risk offenders promotes harm-reduction and public safety because these offenders have a greater need for prosocial skills and thinking, and are more likely to be frequent offenders. Reducing the recidivism rates of these higher-risk offenders reaps a much larger bang-for-the-buck.

Successfully addressing this population requires smaller caseloads, the application of well developed case plans, and the placement of offenders into sufficiently intense cognitive-behavioral interventions that target their specific criminogenic needs (Gendreau and Goggin, 1997; Andrews and Bonta, 1998; Harland, 1996; Sherman et al., 1998; McGuire, 2001, 2002).

3b. Criminogenic Need Principle

Address offenders' greatest criminogenic needs. Offenders have a variety of needs, some of which are directly linked to criminal behavior. These criminogenic needs are dynamic risk factors that, when addressed or changed, affect the offender's risk for recidivism. Examples of criminogenic needs include criminal personality; antisocial attitudes, values, and beliefs; low self-control; criminal peers; substance abuse; and a dysfunctional family. Based on an assessment of the offender, these criminogenic needs can be prioritized so that services are focused on the greatest criminogenic needs (Andrews and Bonta, 1998; Lipton et al., 2000; Elliott et al., 2001; Harland, 1996).

3c. Responsivity Principle

Responsivity requires that we consider individual characteristics when matching offenders to services. These characteristics include, but are not limited to, culture, gender, motivational stages, developmental stages, and learning styles. These factors influence an offender's responsiveness to different types of treatment.

The principle of responsivity also requires that offenders be provided with treatment that is proven effective with the offender population. Certain treatment strategies, such as cognitive-behavioral methodologies, have consistently produced reductions in recidivism with offenders under rigorous research conditions.

Providing appropriate responsivity to offenders involves selecting services in accordance with these factors, including matching treatment type to offender; and matching style and methods of communication with the offender's stage of change readiness (Miller and Rollnick, 2002; Gordon, 1970).

3d. Dosage

Providing appropriate doses of services, prosocial structure, and supervision is a strategic application of resources. Higher-risk offenders require significantly more initial structure and services than lower-risk offenders. During the initial three-to-nine months postrelease, 40 to 70 percent of their free time clearly should be occupied with a delineated routine and appropriate services (for example, outpatient treatment, employment assistance, education, and so forth). Certain offender subpopulations (for example, severely mentally ill, chronic dual diagnosed, and so forth) commonly require strategic, extensive, and extended services. However, too often individuals within these subpopulations are neither explicitly identified nor provided a coordinated package of supervision/services. The evidence indicates that incomplete or uncoordinated approaches can have negative effects, often wasting resources (Palmer, 1995; Gendreau and Goggin, 1995; Steadman, 1995).

3e. Treatment Principle

Treatment, particularly cognitive-behavioral types, should be applied as an integral part of the sentence/sanction process. A proactive and strategic approach to supervision and case planning that delivers targeted and timely treatment interventions will provide the greatest long-term benefit to the community, the victim, and the offender. This does not necessarily apply to lower-risk offenders, who should be diverted from the criminal justice and corrections systems whenever possible (Palmer, 1995; Clear, 1981; Taxman and Byrne, 2001; Currie, 1998; Petersilia, 1997, Andrews and Bonta, 1998).

Questions to Ask

How do we manage offenders assessed as low risk to reoffend?
Does our assessment tool assess for criminogenic need?
How are criminogenic risk and need information incorporated into offender case plans?
How are offenders matched to treatment resources?
How structured are our case plans for offenders, especially during the three-to-nine-month period in the community after leaving an institution?
How are staff held accountable for using assessment information to develop a case plan and then subsequently using that case plan to manage an offender?

4. Provide skills training using cognitive-behavioral treatment methods

Provide evidence-based programming that emphasizes cognitive-behavioral strategies and is delivered by well trained staff. To successfully deliver this treatment to offenders, staff must understand antisocial thinking, social learning, and appropriate communication techniques. Skills are not just taught to the offender, but are practiced or role-played and the resulting prosocial attitudes and behaviors are positively reinforced by staff. Correctional agencies should prioritize, plan, and budget to predominantly implement programs that have been scientifically proven to reduce recidivism (Mihalic et al., 2001; Miller and Rollnick, 2002; Lipton et al., 2000; Lipsey and Wilson, 1993; McGuire, 2001, 2002).

Questions to Ask

How are social-learning techniques incorporated into the programs we deliver?
How do we ensure that our contracted service providers are delivering services in alignment with social-learning theory?

Are the programs we deliver and contract for based on scientific evidence of recidivism reduction?

5. Increase Positive Reinforcement

When learning new skills and making behavioral changes, individuals respond better and maintain learned behaviors for longer periods of time when approached with carrots rather than sticks. Sustained behavioral change is better achieved when an individual receives a higher ratio of positive to negative reinforcements. Research indicates that a ratio of *four positive to every one negative* reinforcement is optimal for promoting behavior changes. These rewards do not have to be applied consistently to be effective (as negative reinforcement does) but can be applied randomly.

Increasing positive reinforcement should not be done at the expense of or interfere with the administration of swift, certain, and real responses for negative and unacceptable behavior. Offenders having problems with responsible self-regulation generally respond positively to reasonable and reliable additional structure and boundaries. Offenders may initially overreact to new demands for accountability, seek to evade detection or consequences, and fail to recognize any personal responsibility. However, with exposure to clear rules that are consistently (and swiftly) enforced with appropriate and graduated consequences, offenders will tend to comply in the direction of the most rewards and least punishments. This type of extrinsic motivation often can be useful for beginning the process of behavior change (Gendreau and Goggin, 1995; Meyers and Smith, 1995; Higgins and Silverman, 1999; Azrin, 1980; Bandura et al.,1963; Bandura, 1996).

Questions to Ask

Do we model positive reinforcement techniques in our day-to-day interactions with our coworkers?
Do our staff understand and use the four-to-one theory in their interactions with offenders?

6. Engage Ongoing Support in Natural Communities

Realign and actively engage prosocial supports for offenders in their communities. Research indicates that many successful interventions with high-risk populations (for example, inner-city substance abusers, homeless, dual diagnosed) actively recruit and use family members, spouses, and supportive others in the offender's immediate environment to positively reinforce desired new behaviors. This Community Reinforcement Approach (CRA) has been found effective for a variety of behaviors (for example, unemployment, alcoholism, substance abuse, and marital conflicts). Research also indicates the efficacy of twelve-step programs, religious activities, and restorative justice initiatives geared toward improving bonds and ties to prosocial community members (Azrin and Besalel, 1980; Higgins and Silverman, 1999; Meyers and Smith, 1997; Bonta et al., 2002; Meyers et al., 2002).

Questions to Ask

Do we engage community supports for offenders as a regular part of case planning?
How do we measure our community network contacts as they relate to an offender?

7. Measure Relevant Processes/Practices

Accurate and detailed documentation of case information, along with a formal and valid mechanism for measuring outcomes, is the foundation of evidence-based practice. Agencies must routinely assess changes in offenders' cognitive and skill development and recidivism, if services are to remain effective.

In addition to routinely measuring and documenting offender changes, staff performance also should be assessed regularly. Staff that are periodically evaluated for performance achieve greater fidelity to program design, service delivery principles, and outcomes. Staff whose performance is not consistently monitored, measured, and subsequently reinforced work less cohesively, more frequently at cross-purposes, and provide less support to the agency mission (Henggeler et al., 1997; Milhalic and Irwin, 2003; Miller et al., 1988; Meyers et al., 1995; Azrin et al., 1982; Meyers et al., 2002; Hanson and Harris, 1998; Waltz et al., 1993; Hogue et al., 1998; Miller and Mount, 2001; Gendreau et al., 1996; Dilulio, 1993).

Questions to Ask

What data do we collect regarding offender assessment and
case management?
How do we measure incremental changes in offenders while
they are under supervision?
What are our outcome measures and how do we track them?
How do we measure staff performance? What data do we use?
How is that data collected?

8. Provide Measurement Feedback

Once a method for measuring relevant processes/practices is in place
(principle seven), this information must be used to monitor progress and
change. Providing feedback to offenders on their progress builds
accountability, and is associated with enhanced motivation for change,
lower treatment attrition, and improved outcomes (for example, reduced
drink/drug days, treatment engagement, and goal achievement).

The same is true within an organization. Monitoring delivery of services and fidelity to procedures helps build accountability and maintain
integrity to the agency's mission. Regular performance audits and case
reviews with an eye toward improved outcomes keep staff focused on the
ultimate goal of reduced recidivism through the use of evidence-based
principles (Miller, 1988; Agostinelli et al., 1995; Alvero et al., 2001; Baer et
al., 1992; Decker, 1983; Ludeman, 1991; Zemke, 2001; Elliott, 1980).

Questions to Ask

How is information regarding offender change and outcomes
shared with officers? With offenders?
With whom do we share information regarding outcome
measures?
How is staff performance data used in the performance-
evaluation process?

Summary

Aligning these evidence-based principles with the operations of an
agency is difficult, but it will largely determine the impact the agency has

on sustained reductions in recidivism. To accomplish this shift to an outcome orientation, practitioners must be prepared to dedicate themselves to a mission that focuses on achieving sustained reductions in recidivism. The scientific principles presented in this document are unlikely to produce a mandate for redirecting and rebuilding an agency's mission by themselves. Leadership in organizational change and collaboration for systemic change are also necessary.

Organizational Development

The organizational development concepts and strategies highlighted in the integrated model mirror the evidence-based principles of effective offender supervision. Focusing on assessment, intervention, and monitoring/measurement, the same principles used to manage offender cases and change offender behavior can be used to manage organizations and change organizational behavior.

Shifting to an evidence-based agency-management approach may require significant changes in the way business is conducted. Some changes may include how staff are recruited and hired; how they conduct their job duties; how they receive performance feedback; and how they interact with each other, offenders, and system stakeholders. While the strategies that follow help guide leaders toward the goal of implementing evidence-based practices both in offender supervision and organizational management, leaders must be prepared for the inherent challenges of conducting such a transition process.

Organizational Development Strategies

1. Assess and Develop Leadership Capacity
2. Create and Communicate the Vision
        a. Creating the Vision
        b. Communicating the Vision
        c. Identifying Internal and External Stakeholders
        d. Developing Strategies for Achieving the Vision
        e. Overcoming Resistance
3. Manage Change
        a. Recognize History
        b. Assess Current Conditions
        c. Describe the Desired Future
        d. Develop Strategies to Achieve the Desired Future
        e. Implement, Monitor, and Provide Feedback
4. Develop Infrastructure

Figure 3   The Strategic Management
Triangle

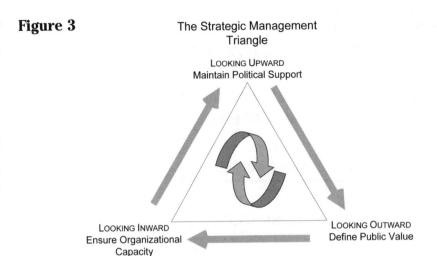

LOOKING UPWARD
Maintain Political Support

LOOKING INWARD
Ensure Organizational
Capacity

LOOKING OUTWARD
Define Public Value

Adapted from Mark Moore. 1995. *Creating Public Value: Strategic Management in Government.*
Cambridge, Massachusetts: Harvard University Press.

1. Assess and Develop Leadership Capacity

Strong and flexible organizational leadership is key to the success of
any change effort. It is especially true when implementing evidence-
based practices in corrections due to the complexity of the public safety
system. The complex nature of the system requires that leadership identify, create, and show value to internal and external stakeholders. In Mark
Moore's *Creating Public Value*, he emphasizes a key assumption for any
service provided by the public sector: the service or product must provide value for a variety of constituents. As illustrated in the Strategic
Management Triangle above, public sector leaders must focus on providing value outward, upward, and inward. They show it outward by defining the value their organization provides to the public; upward by building political support for the organization and its services as they align
with that value; and inward by ensuring the necessary organizational
capacity exists to achieve that value.

Implementing evidence-based practices in corrections and building
the corresponding value for constituents requires strong leadership
along with the capacity and willingness to practice outcome-oriented,
collaborative leadership styles, not the authoritarian and controlling
leadership styles more traditionally associated with corrections. Taking
the time to assess leadership capacity and styles prior to beginning the
implementation process will provide critical information on the strengths

Figure 4

The Diagonal Slice Group

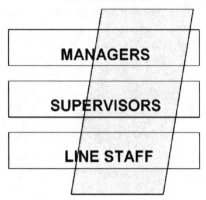

and weaknesses that must be addressed to support a successful change effort. The artistry of leadership exists in the ability to access leadership skills that are appropriate to the situation, recognizing that different situations require different leadership strategies. The ability to clearly articulate a vision for organizational change, while employing multiple leadership strategies, will help further the organizational change process, creating a shared desire for change among a variety of people in a variety of settings.

2. Create and Communicate the Vision

2a. Creating the Vision

Before the change process begins, there must be a clear vision of what the changed organization will look like. This vision should be articulated in a concise statement describing the changed organization and how it interacts with others, including service recipients, system partners, and employees.

Strong, visionary leadership is a must. The vision for change can be formed in numerous ways by various groups, including the leadership of the organization, policymakers, or a diagonal slice of organizational representatives, as shown in Figure 4. No matter how the vision is formed, leadership must embrace it and take responsibility for charting the direction and change process for the organization.

Once the leadership has crystallized the direction of change, it needs to look broadly throughout the organization and consider the many layers of change that will occur as a result of the process. The most progressive public policy direction for an organization is meaningless at the line staff and client level without leadership and strategic action to cultivate the change at all levels. True change happens at the top, at the bottom, and in between. It is up to the leadership to consider how change will occur within each of those layers.

Questions to Ask

Is there a story or metaphor for what the organization is trying to become?

Can you draw a picture of your vision for the organization?

If the organization achieves its goals for change—

what will clients say about their experience of this organization?

what will a member of the public say?

what will staff say?

What facets of the organization will be affected by the change?

2b. Communicating the Vision

Once leadership clarifies the organizational goals for change, the next step is communication of the vision. Involving staff in the development of the vision leads to greater commitment from and more effective communication with those staff. Effective communication is a critical ingredient in achieving successful and long-lasting change and is dependent on the ability of leadership to model openness and support ongoing dialog. Communication is key. The clearer a leader communicates the goals of organizational change, the more helpful staff, community, clients, and policymakers can be. Once they understand what leadership seeks to accomplish, they can begin striving for those same goals.

How an idea or goal is communicated can be as important as the goal or idea itself. Leaders attend to both process and outcomes. People will draw conclusions from how the message is communicated and from the content of the message. For example, if a leader directly and personally communicates an idea to the organization, the message has more impact and meaning than if it comes down to line staff through channels. If a leader convenes a staff focus group to discuss an issue, the importance of the issue is heightened, simply by the fact that the leader cared enough to gather a group to address it.

Leadership also must tailor communication strategies to the groups they seek to reach. Leaders need to think about their audience in advance, consider how they receive information, and strategize about how to best reach them. Communication must occur continually throughout the organization, both horizontally and vertically.

Leaders also need to pay close attention to the collective impact of seemingly minor decisions during the change process. For example, if leadership determines that those employees who actively participate and cooperate with the change process will be rewarded, that strategy must be consistent throughout the organization, even in seemingly minor decisions. One act in one part of the organization, such as the promotion of a line staff person who is still doing business the old way, might not seem like it could affect the change process. However, these seemingly independent, unrelated decisions collectively can send a message that undermines the change process.

Trust and confidence in the organization's vision and leadership is built through understanding and awareness of how decisions are made. Decisions and the process by which they are reached should be transparent to the members of the organization. Good leaders seek broad input into decision making and encourage consideration of different perspectives. Diverse perspectives build strength. Good leaders also ensure that decisions support the stated vision, values, and direction of the organization. This requires the leader to stay in touch with decision making at many levels in the organization to ensure that the organization walks its talk.

Questions to Ask

What is your personal communication style?

What are your strengths and weaknesses in this arena?

How is information communicated in your organization? Formally and informally?

Are there more effective communication strategies for reaching multiple audiences?

What are the greatest communication challenges for the organization?

What leadership, management, and staff behavior supports the vision? What behavior does not support the vision?

2c. Identifying Internal and External Stakeholders

Leaders seeking change must work closely with many stakeholders, and collaboration with those partners is critical and powerful. The partners, both internal and external, can be identified using various methods. Leadership can identify partners in consultation with others. Staff can conduct system mapping to identify unusual partners. The organization can convene planning circles where partners come together and identify more partners, who then identify more partners, and so forth. All of these strategies can be effective ways to identify important stakeholders in the change process.

Internal stakeholders: Internal stakeholder groups will be affected by organizational change, some more than others. It is important that those groups most affected have a voice in the process. Broad participation creates commitment. Leaders should consider the multiple levels of authority in the formal chain of command and classifications of employees, and then ensure that all of these groups understand the vision of change, and have a voice and a means with which to communicate their opinions. Diagonal slice work groups can help to achieve this goal by providing representation from throughout the organization.

Leaders also should consider more informal networks as they identify internal partners. While the organizational chart of an agency may show a vertical hierarchy, organizations are rarely so cleanly defined. Instead, organizations are webs, with information leaders and power brokers throughout the organization. Leadership should think beyond the formal hierarchy to ensure they reach out to all key partners.

Diagonal slice work groups can serve a variety of roles—as sounding boards, transition monitoring teams, steering committees with decision-making power, and implementation teams. Leadership must clearly define the roles and authority of each group. Each working group should develop a charter.

The charter will help guide the group's efforts, provide structure, describe outcomes, clarify decision-making authority, and codify organizational and leadership support for the group's work. Communication is a key function of these work groups and should be highlighted in their charter. A large part of their responsibility is ongoing communication with the larger organization about the change process. To enhance productivity and efficiency, all groups should be provided with a trained facilitator or be trained in the basics of group process and facilitation prior to beginning work.

Questions to Ask

What diverse groups are represented in your organization?
Who are the natural leaders in the organization?
What groups are forgotten or feel excluded?
Who can help create a buzz about the change process in your organization?

External stakeholders: The changes your organization undergoes also will affect external partners. Community corrections agencies are intertwined with a host of other criminal justice, social service, and community organizations and systems. This means that any significant, long-lasting change in your organization requires the participation of and acceptance by external entities. These organizations will need to be collaborative participants in this process every step of the way.

Partner organizations need to understand the value that participation in this change process has for them. Their leaders should know how supporting your change aids them in accomplishing their organizational mission. The impact that specific changes will have on their service delivery must be completely clear. Leaders need to consider these issues and craft specific plans for engaging their partners.

Questions to Ask

What partnerships currently exist in your system?
Where do new partnerships need to be forged?
How does participation in this change process assist partners in accomplishing their mission and/or vision?

2d. Developing Strategies for Achieving the Vision

The development of strategies moves the vision from concept into action. While strategies must be broad enough to encompass the work of many parts of the organization, they also must be specific enough that objectives, outcomes, and work plans can be developed to achieve the strategies. Leaders can use many different processes to develop strategies. Tools for developing strategies must balance broad participation in decision making with the creation of the most innovative strategies infused with best practice knowledge. The relative importance of these two issues in an organization's change process will drive the selection of the tool for strategy development.

Engaging the broadest number of internal and external partners in the development of the strategy is essential, and a system- or organizationwide development conference can be a helpful tool. This type of conference is a daylong or more meeting where the participants gain an understanding of the vision and then, in smaller groups, develop the strategies to accomplish this vision. Conference techniques often result in maximum participation and buy-in, and allow participants opportunities to understand best practices and expand their thinking to create an innovative new direction for the organization.

The diagonal slice group from your organization also can be charged with creating strategies. This method provides opportunities for input from a variety of levels and perspectives in a more controlled process. It also provides an opportunity for alternative perspectives to weigh more heavily in the process. In the conference model, minority voices may not be heard.

In another method, the management team can use stakeholder groups to review and refine strategies—including the diagonal slice group. This method does not allow for as much diverse input into the strategies. However, if the management team has been intensively schooled in innovative new practices, they still can create effective strategies that are informed by the literature. The strategies must be approved and supported by the policymakers in your jurisdiction, regardless of the method chosen.

Questions to Ask

> How much participation is required to build maximum trust in the organization?
>
> How much do various stakeholders know about evidence-based practices to incorporate them into strategies?
>
> How can you best incorporate diverse perspectives into strategies?
>
> How involved do policymakers wish to be in the strategy-development process?

Figure 5

The Integrated Model Organizational Change Process

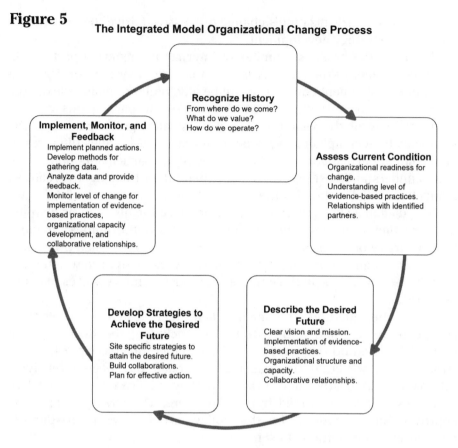

2e. Overcoming Resistance

Leadership and work teams need to plan strategies for overcoming resistance to change, as shown in Figure 5. Employee resistance may stem from the organization's failure to consider and eliminate barriers with changing work conditions, a lack of tools to do the new job, or an inadequate understanding of the need for change. Leadership must assess worker's needs in relation to the strategic implementation of change, structure the work, and provide the tools and the information required for success. For example, if leadership asks officers to spend more time out in the field and less time in the office, providing tools such as laptops, personal data assistants, and cell phones will facilitate that transition. Leadership must be empathetic and create a climate for success for the workers to do their job. Culture changes are difficult for workers to accommodate but can be made easier with responsive, responsible leadership.

Manage Change

The strategies and methods of implementing change in complex organizations have been used in the private sector for years and are just as valid in the corrections field. The following illustration of the change process highlights each of the change-process phases.

3a. Recognize History

Organizational members must reflect on where they come from as an organization, where they have been, and what they have experienced during that journey. This reflection enables organizations to clarify and articulate a collective narrative and a shared vision of history. This shared history then can become a launching pad for change rather than a warehouse for an uninterpretable array of artifacts and anecdotes.

Questions to Ask

How did we, as an organization, arrive at our current structure, technologies, and culture?
What do we value?
How do we operate?

3b. Assess Current Conditions

Assessment and documentation of the present condition assists the organizational members in determining where they are at the current time and what gaps remain. Participants must assess the degree to which the organization's beliefs, operational systems, technologies, policies, and practices are consistent with, and supportive of, evidence-based practices. Participants must pay attention to the organizational culture, as well as the quality and types of existing collaborations and partnerships with internal and external stakeholders.

Questions to Ask

What is our organization's level of change readiness?

How well are evidence-based practices understood and implemented in our system?

Who are our partners?

How well are we working with our partners?

3c. Describe the Desired Future

In expressing a vision for the future, the organizational members describe their ideal picture of the changed organization. The participants, along with leadership, articulate a vision for organizational change at all levels. By creating a vision of a learning organization, members become committed to the journey of change that provides value to employees, clients, and stakeholders.

Questions to Ask

What do we want our organizational future to look like?

What is our organizational vision and mission?

At what level do we envision the implementation of evidence-based practices?

What type of organizational structure is needed to best support evidence-based practices?

What collaborative relationships need to be developed to strengthen implementation?

3d. Develop Strategies to Achieve the Desired Future

Build collaborations of mutual interest. Correctional organizations relate to and are dependent on many partners throughout the public, private, and community-based sectors who share a commitment to achieving the outcomes of reduced recidivism and increased public safety.

Plan for effective action to reach the desired future. Develop a detailed, concrete plan of action that is time phased, measurable, politically and culturally competent, and includes effective, sustainable accountability and feedback loops. Clearly define the multiple roles of participants.

Questions to Ask

With whom does the organization partner and collaborate?

How do partnerships and collaborations help members successfully achieve their goals and further their unique corporate mission?

What steps does the organization need to attain its goals?

What are the specific activities needed to ensure an equal focus on evidence-based practices, organizational development and capacity building, and collaborative relationships?

3e. Implement, Monitor, and Provide Feedback

Carry out the implementation. Planning without action often leads to desperation and hopelessness for staff and stakeholders. Successful implementation results from a broad and deep commitment throughout the organization, relentless attention to the vision, support for the change process, removal of barriers, and careful monitoring and adjustment of the change process.

Feedback includes gathering, sharing, assessing, and constructing a valid and shared interpretation of the information. Successful implementation results from the availability and management of information that is meaningful, timely, and accurately represents the progress made on the change plan within the unique cultural and political context of the participating site.

Questions to Ask

How will we gather data?

What types of feedback are needed by which groups?

How will we monitor progress and make adjustments when necessary?

4. Develop Infrastructure

While leadership is moving the organization forward through the process of implementing evidence-based practices, contemporaneous changes in an organization's infrastructure must occur. These infrastructure changes are designed to align the organization's human resource management systems, policies and procedures, and operational standards with evidence-based practices. Aligning an organization's human resources management systems with evidence-based practices involves revising policies and practices for recruiting, hiring, writing job descriptions, training, using performance measurement, making promotional decisions, and using reward systems. All policies and procedures must be consistent with and supportive of the new way of doing business. They also must be put into practice—clearly articulated and shared throughout the organization, and used as the new standard to which staff are held accountable. Aligning the organization's infrastructure clarifies the commitment to organizational change and facilitates implementation of evidence-based practices. Maintaining a focus on these changes over time will produce a critical mass of employees well-versed in the tenets of a new philosophy, further limiting the possibility of slipping back into the old ways of doing business.

The subsequent transformation of organizational culture relies on this alignment of tasks, mission, and goals and a clear nexus throughout the organization's practices (Kreps and Baron, 1999). Combining the fundamental changes in these structural areas with the philosophical and policy shift of evidence-based practices enhances the opportunity to more effectively institutionalize changes.

Summary of Section One

Leading organizational change requires that corrections leaders evaluate their own strengths and weaknesses as well as those of their organizations. Prepared with this knowledge, leaders will be better equipped to engage in the challenges of changing organizational practice, infrastructure, and culture. Corrections' leaders who want to implement evidence-based practices must be willing and able to focus on all three components of the integrated model. They must have the content knowledge of evidence-based practices, the leadership skills required to lead such extensive organizational change, and the collaborative expertise necessary to engage stakeholders in the change process.

Collaboration

Collaboration is an equally important component of implementing systemic change within the complex web of public safety agencies, service providers, and other stakeholders. It is defined as "a mutually beneficial and well-defined relationship entered into by two or more organizations to achieve common goals" (Griffith, 2000). The collaborative process is intended to move participants away from the traditional definition of power as control or domination, toward a definition that allows for shared authority. This results in greater achievements than would be attained by one organization working alone. Since no public safety agency operates in a vacuum, engaging system stakeholders in change efforts helps eliminate barriers, increases opportunities for success, enriches the change process, educates stakeholders about the agency's work, and creates a shared vision that supports the systemic change efforts.

Public safety system stakeholders include a wide range of entities, from prisons and police agencies, to victim advocates and faith-based community organizations. Working collaboratively with all stakeholders in the planning and implementation of systemic change in corrections can result in a more coherent continuum of care, one that uses evidence-based principles to reduce recidivism. By collaborating with each other, public agencies and community-based providers jointly can provide a comprehensive and integrated array of services that could not be provided by a single agency or sector working alone. Access to a well-organized network of services and prosocial community connections can greatly enhance an offender's ability to succeed. The following strategies help make collaborative efforts more constructive and useful tools of social action and recidivism reduction.

Collaboration Strategies

1. Include the Right People/Agencies
2. Develop Sufficient Structure
3. Invest the Right Amount of Resources and Effort to Sustain Collaboration

1. Include the Right People/Agencies

As previously mentioned, a key concept in organizational development and the collaborative process is to ensure that those individuals and organizations most affected have a voice in the process of change. While organizational development focuses on the internal stakeholders, our collaboration work focuses on external entities. For collaboration to work, all relevant stakeholders must have a presence at the table. Since the actual number of participants must be somewhat limited to ensure efficiency, formal communication methods must be established to ensure that those unable to be at the table still have their views heard.

Leaders must assist stakeholders in understanding and appreciating the value that participation in the change process has for them. Involving external stakeholders not only increases their understanding of the system, but also can help to identify overlapping client populations and shared goals. For example, as corrections agencies implement evidence-based principles, they will shift their resources to focus onto higher-risk offenders. This shift in focus often results in decreased access to treatment resources for low-risk/high-need offenders. Involving human services agencies in the change planning process can help identify other treatment resources for these offenders.

The development of a policy-level committee that includes leaders from key stakeholder groups and helps to guide change is an essential component of implementing change in the public safety system. Members of the policy committee should include policymakers from key stakeholder organizations and community groups, including those supportive of the change and those who may pose potential barriers to implementation. Involving those who may not be entirely supportive of all planned changes ensures a richer policy development, educates those policymakers more fully about the system complexity, and may help to alleviate future barriers. The policy committee should be charged with guiding systemwide policy related to implementing evidence-based practices, implementing corresponding changes in their own organizations that support the system changes, and communicating with their own organization about the impact of system changes.

Questions to Ask

> What partnerships currently exist in your system?
> Where do new partnerships need to be forged?
> How does participation in the change process assist partners in accomplishing their missions?

2. Develop Sufficient Structure

Every collaboration needs some structure, but the degree of structure required for a collaboration to attain its goals may vary. Collaboration participants should choose a structure that supports their endeavors and fits their desired level of joint activity and risk. Methods of developing structure, such as charters, memoranda of understanding, and partnering agreements fulfill multiple purposes. For example, they can help clarify the authority and expectations of the group and roles/functions of all participants, focus parties on their responsibilities, and eliminate miscommunication and backtracking when the inevitable staff changes occur. These tools should clarify decision-making responsibilities and emphasize the concept that no single agency or individual is in charge in the familiar sense. Instead, collaboration participants are empowered to do work in their own center of expertise to the enhancement of the collective goal.

3. Invest the Right Amount of Resources and Effort to Sustain Collaboration

Collaboration and system change are very time-consuming and resource-intensive processes. They require constant attention and nurturing to maintain momentum. Acknowledging the inevitability of obstacles, admitting them when they reappear, developing collective strategies to overcome them, and having a sense of humor are all important in surviving the process (Feely, 2000).

Working collaboratively with system partners provides a greater opportunity for successful implementation of true system change. With a united and common vision, the combined efforts of stakeholders can achieve more than any one organization could achieve on its own. No organization exists in a vacuum; therefore, recognizing the inherent interdependence and including it in the development of change-implementation strategies greatly enhances the chance of success.

Questions to Ask

What are the goals of the collaboration?
Why are we collaborating?
How are we going to collaborate?
Who is going to do what?
What are the communication pathways within our collaboration?
Who has authority to make what decisions?
How do we consciously develop mutual respect within our collaboration?

A Collaborative Model for Implementing Change

Collaborative endeavors must develop a balance between broad participation and the need to make decisions and take action. The collaborative process has to be perceived as fair, not dominated by one interest

Figure 6

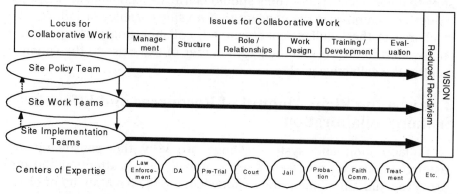

group, and accessible to all stakeholders (Carter, Ley, Steketee, Gavin, Stroker, Woodward, 2002). It should ensure that the number of participants is small enough to allow for productivity, but broad enough to achieve widespread support. The collaboration model above can be used to implement systemic change in criminal justice systems. As Figure 6 shows, it identifies multiple levels of systemic involvement, both internal and external to the targeted organization. The collaborative work takes place at all levels, including policy and implementation. Although each level may share an overriding vision of system change as reduced recidivism, each has different work to do. While the policy-level team focuses on policy development that supports the systemic change, implementation teams are responsible for the practicalities of making that change happen.

Mutual respect and understanding are key to sustaining shared authority in collaborative relationships. Borrowing from a concept developed by Michael Hammer in *Beyond Reengineering*, all partners are seen as centers of excellence, defined as a collective of professionals, led by a coach, who join together to learn and enhance their skills and abilities to contribute best to whatever processes are being developed. Each agency is an expert at performing its piece of the work of public safety (Carter et al., 2002).

In the above model, teams include representation from these centers of expertise, such as the court, prosecution, defense, corrections, law enforcement, probation, and parole. Each center may be a self-contained organization, but all are linked with the other centers through the public safety system. The collaboration participants work together toward the shared vision of an enhanced service provision and reduced recidivism.

Questions to Ask

Are key stakeholders/centers of expertise involved within each locus of collaborative work?
Do participants at all levels understand and buy in to the vision?
Do participants understand how collaboration works?

Essential elements of collaboration

Including the right people
Developing structure
Having a shared vision
Having a unique purpose
Having clear roles and responsibilities
Using healthy communication pathways
Having the right membership
Employing respect and integrity
Providing accountability to the collaboration and to the participating organizations
Using data-driven process
Using effective problem solving
Having sufficient resources, including staff
Developing an environment of trust and collaborative leadership

---

Conclusion

The research on evidence-based practices continues to emerge, and organizations around the world continue to work to translate this research into practice. The unique feature of this integrated model is its insistence that the systemic change required to do this cannot be fully implemented or sustained without an equal and integrated focus on evidence-based principles, organizational development, and collaboration. The model builds heavily on work already being done by corrections systems. While it may not require a heavy investment of new resources, it may require a change in the way existing resources are allocated, which can be just as challenging. Implementing this model requires strong leaders who are willing to challenge the status quo, advocate for better service provisions, and strive for better outcomes.

The financial crisis facing criminal justice systems is forcing policy-makers and administrators to rethink the old way of doing business and reexamine policies that favor institutional growth. The research is clear about which interventions result in reduced recidivism. Criminal justice leaders must be clear about whether they are willing to accept the status quo or take the steps necessary to make more effective use of the public resources allocated to corrections. If they opt for more effective use of resources and increased public safety, this model will guide corrections systems through the three components of successful implementation: evidence-based practices, organizational development, and collaboration.

Project Contact Information

Dot Faust, Correctional Program Specialist
National Institute of Corrections, Community Corrections Division
dfaust@bop.gov
(202) 514-3001
www.nicic.org

Elyse Clawson, Executive Director
Crime and Justice Institute
eclawson@crjustice.org
(617) 482-2520
www.cjinstitute.org

References

Agostinelli, G., J. M. Brown, and W. R.. Miller. 1995. Effects of Normative Feedback on Consumption among Heavy Drinking College Students. *Journal of Drug Education.* 25: 31-40.

Alvero, A. M., B. R. Bucklin, and J. Austin. 2001. An Objective Review of the Effectiveness and Essential Characteristics of Performance Feedback in Organizational Settings. *Journal of Organizational Behavior Management.* 21(1): 3-29.

Andrews, D. A. and J. Bonta. 1998. *The Psychology of Criminal Conduct.* Cincinnati, Ohio: Anderson Publishing Co.

Andrews, D. A, J. Bonta, and R. Hoge. 1990. Classification for Effective Rehabilitation: Rediscovering Psychology. *Criminal Justice and Behavior.* 17: 19-52.

Azrin, N. H. and V. A. Besalel. 1980. *Job Club Counselor's Manual*. Austin, Texas: Pro-Ed.

Azrin, N. H., R. W. Sisson, R. Meyers, and M. Godley. 1982. Alcoholism Treatment by Disulfiram and Community Reinforcement Therapy. *Journal of Behavioral Therapy and Psychiatry*. 13: 105-112.

Baer, J. S., A. G. Marlatt, D. R. Kivlanhan, K. Fromme, M. E. Larimer, and E. Williams. 1992. An Experimental Test of Three Methods of Alcohol Risk Reduction with Young Adults. *Journal of Consulting and Clinical Psychology*. 60: 974-979.

Bandura, A. 1996. Mechanisms of Moral Disengagement in the Exercise of Moral Agency. *Journal of Personality and Social Psychology*. 71: 364-374.

Bandura, A., D. Ross, et al. 1963. Vicarious Reinforcement and Imitative Learning. *Journal of Abnormal and Social Psychology*. 67: 601-607.

Baron, James and David M. Kreps. 1999. Strategic Human Resources. *Framework for General Managers*. Wiley.

Beckland, R. and W. Pritchard. 1992. *Changing the Essence: The Art of Creating and Leading Fundamental Change in Organizations*. Indianapolis, Indiana: Jossey-Bass.

Bennis, W. and B. Nanus. 1985. *Leaders: The Strategies for Taking Charge*. New York: Harper and Row.

Blake, R. R., J. Srygley Mouton, and A. Adams McCanse. 1989. *Change by Design*. Boston: Addison Wesley.

Block, P. 1981. *Flawless Consulting*. Tucson, Arizona: University Associates.

———. 1988. *The Empowered Manager*. Indianapolis, Indiana: Jossey-Bass.

Bonta, J., S. Wallace-Capretta, J. Rooney, and K. McAnoy. 2002. An Outcome Evaluation of a Restorative Justice Alternative to Incarceration. *Justice Review*. 54: 319-338.

Bridges, W. 1991. *Managing Transitions, Making the Most of Change*. Boulder, Colorado: Perseus Books.

Burns, J. 1982. *Leadership*. New York: Harpercollins.

Carter, M., A. Ley, M. Steketee, F. Gavin, R. Stroker, and W. Woodward. 2002. *Collaboration: A Training Curriculum to Enhance the Effectiveness of Criminal Justice Teams*. Washington, D.C.: State Justice Institute.

Clear, T. R. 1981. *Objectives-based Case Planning.* Washington D.C.: National Institute of Corrections.

Clements, C. B. 1996. Offender Classification: Two Decades of Progress. *Criminal Justice and Behavior.* 23: 121-143.

Covey, S. R. 1990. *Principle-Centered Leadership.* New York: Summit Books.

Currie, E. 1998. *Crime and Punishment in America.* New York: Metropolitan Books.

Decker, P. J. 1983. The Effects of Rehearsal Group Size and Video Feedback in Behavior Modeling Training. *Personnel Training.* 36: 763-773.

Dilulio, J. J. 1993. *Performance Measures for the Criminal Justice System.* Washington, D.C: Bureau of Justice Statistics.

Elliott, D. et al. 2001. *Youth Violence: A Report of the Surgeon General.* Washington, D.C.: U.S. Department of Health and Human Services.

Elliott, D. 1980. A Repertoire of Impact Measures. In *Handbook of Criminal Justice Evaluation.* Thousand Oaks, California: Sage.

Feely, K. 2000. *Pathways to Juvenile Detention Reform: Collaboration and Leadership.* Baltimore: Annie E. Casey Foundation.

Fuller, J. 2001. *Organizational Change from a Leadership Perspective.* Portland, Oregon: Multnomah County Department of Community Justice.

Gendreau, P. and C. Goggin. 1995. *Principles of Effective Correctional Programming with Offenders.* Center for Criminal Justice Studies and Department of Psychology, University of New Brunswick, New Brunswick, Canada.

Gendreau, P. and C. Goggin 1997. Correctional Treatment: Accomplishments and Realities. In P. V. Voorhis, M. Braswell, and D. Lester, eds. *Correctional Counseling and Rehabilitation.* Cincinnati, Ohio: Anderson.

Gendreau, P. et al. 1996. A Meta-analysis of the Predictors of Adult Offender Recidivism: What Works. *Criminology.* 34: 575-607.

Gordon, T. 1970. *Parent Effectiveness Training.* New York: Wyden.

Griffith, G. 2000. *Report to Planning Committee on Study of Three Collaboratives.* Portland, Oregon: Department of Corrections.

Hanson, R. K. and A. Harris.1998. Triggers of Sexual Offense Recidivism: Research Summary. *Corrections Research and Development.* 34: 1-2.

Harland, A. T. 1996. *Choosing Correctional Options that Work: Defining the Demand and Evaluating the Supply.* Thousand Oaks, California: Sage.

Harper, R. and S. Hardy. 2000. An Evaluation of Motivational Interviewing as A Method of Intervention with Clients in a Probation Setting. *British Journal of Social Work.* 30: 393-400.

Henggeler, S. W., G. B. Melton, M. J. Brondino, D. G. Scherer, and J. H. Hanley. 1997. Multisystemic Therapy with Violent and Chronic Juvenile Offenders and Their Families: The Role of Treatment Fidelity in Successful Dissemination. *Journal of Consulting and Clinical Psychology.* 65: 821-833.

Hesselbein, F., M. Goldsmith, and I. Somerville, eds. 1999. *Leading Beyond the Walls.* New York: Drucker Foundation.

Higgins, S. T. and K. Silverman, eds. 1999. *Motivating Behavior Change Among Illicit-Drug Abusers: Research On Contingency Management Interventions.* Washington, D.C.: American Psychological Association.

Hogue, A., H. A. Liddle, C. Rowe, R. M. Turner, G. A. Dakof, and K. Lapann. 1998. Treatment Adherence and Differentiation in Individual Versus Family Therapy for Adolescent Substance Abuse. *Journal of Counseling Psychology.* 45: 104-114.

Kropp, P., S. Hart, C. Webster, D. Eaves. 1995. *Manual for the Spousal Assault Risk Assessment Guide.* Vancouver, British Columbia: British Columbia Institute on Family Violence.

Lipsey, M. W. and D. B. Wilson. 1993. The Efficacy of Psychological, Educational, and Behavioral Treatment. *American Psychologist.* 48: 1181-1209.

Lipton, D. S., D. Thornton, et al. 2000. Program Accreditation and Correctional Treatment. *Substance Use and Misuse.* 35: 1705-1734.

Ludeman, K. 1991 Measuring Skills and Behavior. *Training and Development.* November; 61-66.

McGregor, D. 1960. *The Human Side of Enterprise.* New York: McGraw-Hill/Irwin.

McGuire, J. 2001. What Works in Correctional Intervention? Evidence and Practical Implications. In D. F. Gary Bernfeld, Alan Leschied, eds. *Offender Rehabilitation In Practice: Implementing and Evaluating Effective Programs.* New York: John Wiley and Sons.

———. 2002. *Evidence-based Programming Today.* Paper presented at the International Community Corrections Association Conference, Boston, Massachusetts, November.

Meyers, R. J, W. R. Miller, J. E. Smith, and S. Tonnigan. 2002. A Randomized Trial of Two Methods for Engaging Treatment-refusing Drug Users through Concerned Significant Others. *Journal of Consulting and Clinical Psychology*. 70: 1182-1185.

Meyers, R. J. and J. E. Smith. 1995. *Clinical Guide to Alcohol Treatment: The Community Reinforcement Approach*. New York: Guilford Press.

———. 1997. Getting Off the Fence: Procedures to Engage Treatment-resistant Drinkers. *Journal of Substance Abuse Treatment*. 14: 467-472.

Mihalic, S. and K. Irwin. 2003. *Blueprints for Violence Prevention: From Research to Real World Settings—Factors Influencing the Successful Replication of Model Programs*. Boulder, Colorado: Center for the Study and Prevention of Violence.

Mihalic, S., K. Irwin, D. Elliott, A. Fagan, and D. Hansen. 2001. *Blueprints for Violence Prevention*. Washington, D.C.: U.S. Department of Justice.

Miller, W. R. and K. A. Mount. 2001. A Small Study of Training in Motivational Interviewing: Does One Workshop Change Clinician and Client Behavior? *Behavioural and Cognitive Psychotherapy*. 29: 457-471.

Miller, W. and S. Rollnick. 2002. *Motivational Interviewing: Preparing People for Change*. New York: Guilford Press.

Miller, W. R., G. R. Sovereign, and B. Krege. 1988. Motivational Interviewing with Problem Drinkers: II. The Drinker's Check Up As a Preventive Intervention. *Behavioral Psychotherapy*. 16: 251-268.

Moore, M. 1995. *Creating Public Value*. Boston: Harvard University Press.

Nanus, B. 1992. *Visionary Leadership*. Indianapolis, Indiana: Jossey-Bass.

Osborne, D. and T. Gaebler.1992. *Reinventing Government*. Boston: Addison Wesley.

Palmer, T. 1995. Programmatic and Non-Programmatic Aspects of Successful Intervention: New Directions for Research. *Crime and Delinquency*. 411: 100-131.

Petersilia, J. 1997. Probation in the United States: Practices and Challenges. *National Institute of Justice Journal*. 233: 2-8.

Project Match Research Group. 1997. Therapist Effects in Three Treatments for Alcohol Problems. *Psychotherapy Research*. 84: 455-474.

Rees, F. 1991. *How to Lead Work Teams: Facilitation Skills*. Hoboken, New Jersey: Pfeiffer and Co.

Ryan, R. M. and E. L. Deci. 2000. Self-determination Theory and the Facilitation of Intrinsic Motivation, Social Development, and Well-Being. *American Psychologist*. 55: 68-78.

Senge, P. 1990. *The Fifth Discipline: The Art and Practice of the Learning Organization*. New York: Currency Doubleday.

Sherman, L. W., D. C. Gottfredson, D. L. Mackenzie, J. Eck, P. Reuter, and S. D. Bushway. 1998. *Preventing Crime: What Works, What Doesn't, What's Promising*. Washington, D.C.: National Institute of Justice.

Steadman, H. et al. 1995. The Diversion of Mentally Ill Persons from Jails to Community-based Services: A Profile of Programs. *American Journal of Public Health*. 85: 1630-1635.

Taxman, F. and J. Byrne. 2001. Fixing Broken Windows Probation Together. *Perspectives*. Spring: 23-29.

Valentine, K. 2001. *How to Make Partnerships Work: Suggestions from the Field*. Washington, D.C.: National Institute of Corrections.

Waltz, J., M. E. Addis, K. Koerner, and N. S. Jacobson. 1993. Testing the Integrity of a Psychotherapy Protocol: Adherence and Competence Ratings. *Journal of Consulting and Clinical Psychology*. 61: 620-630.

Weisebord, M. R. 1987. *Productive Workplaces*. Indianapolis, Indiana: Jossey-Bass.

Weisebord, M. R. and S. Janoff. 1995. *Future Search*. San Francisco: Berrett-Koehler.

Wheatley, M. J. and M. Kellner-Rogers. 1996. *A Simpler Way*. San Francisco: Berrett-Koehler.

Woodward, W. 2001. *Collaboration: What It Takes*. Washington, D.C.: National Institute of Corrections.

Zemke, R. 2001 Systems Thinking. *Training*. February: 39-46.

PUBLIC SAFETY AND THE SEARCH FOR A STRATEGIC CONVENER

5

Peggy McGarry
Principal
Center for Effective Public Policy
Silver Spring, Maryland

> *"Justice is not programs, justice is a way of life."*
> — Leo Hayden, president and CEO,
> Center for Violence Interruption, Chicago, Illinois

If justice is a way of life, then clearly it cannot belong to the criminal justice system. And if programs are not the way to achieve it, then its origins must lie outside of any official system. What role, then, does the criminal justice system have to play in achieving and ensuring justice?

This paper will argue that a significant portion of justice is achieved when people in every neighborhood, in every small community, are free to go about their lives in safety and without fear, and when their safety is itself free from unwarranted intrusions on their liberties in its name. The criminal justice system as we know it can be and is a partner in achieving that combination of safety and freedom. Some within the criminal justice system have begun a process of democratization that offers all of our communities the tools and the opportunities to bring about this portion of justice.

This process of democratization is still in its earliest development, but already some lessons are emerging:

1. First, the community—all of those who live, work, study, or frequent, a definable area—must be a partner in criminal justice system efforts: not the site of our efforts, not a consumer to be satisfied (or not) with our services, but a partner in creating safety, opportunity, and justice for all of us.

2. Second, we, the criminal justice system, publicly entrusted and empowered to protect and ensure justice and safety, must have a strategic convener: a platform from which strategic decisions and choices can be made about the deployment of collective resources and through which the criminal justice system can function as the partner with which the community can work.

3. Third, the role of strategic convener is best played by a policy team representing all of the entities, agencies, and offices of the criminal justice system.

The Shift in the Criminal Justice System Focus

The last twenty years in criminal justice have seen any number of changes in our philosophies and approaches. Many of these changes have been made possible by the startling progress in the availability of electronically stored data, and by our ability to use this information for analysis in ways that would have seemed unimaginable even ten years ago. What continues to startle is how much these new capabilities change our notions of what we ought to be doing and how this causes us to redefine our roles and responsibilities.

Looking across the various parts that make up the criminal justice system, the change that is common to all, and arguably the most compelling, is the shift in focus from an efficient processing of cases through the system to a relentless questioning of the outcomes of our work overall. What are the outcomes that we want? Who decides what they are? How are we measuring them? And once measured, how are we doing?

Because of this shift to an outcome focus, a second profound change is beginning to be felt across the board. As we look at how we are doing, we are increasingly asking hard questions about what we are doing. A current truism is, "If you always do what you've always done, you'll always get what you've always gotten." That examination is leading to the realization of how many resources we devote to reacting to crime after the fact, and how little we have devoted to preventing it in the first place. As we examine and determine with increasing confidence criminogenic factors in offenders, characteristics of high crime neighborhoods, crime patterns in certain blocks or areas, some have had the corollary realization that we can change those things that produce crime in the first place. And the profound change is that we are seeing criminal justice agencies— from police, to prosecutors and corrections—taking on responsibility for preventing crime. This is occurring not just by catching bad guys, not just by shutting down drug houses, but by looking at positive activities related to young people, to the quality of housing stock in a neighbor- hood, to the nature of the bond developed between a mother and her newborn and saying, "These are OUR business."

This change has had an impact on even the G-men of the FBI—those storied paragons of hard crime-busting have changed their focus: They now agree that it is more important to prevent acts of terrorism than to go after every charge and every prosecution. Their question has gone from, "What can we get this guy on?" to "What does this guy know?" From "Let's set up a situation where we got him cold," to "What is he planning and how can we stop him, even if that means we forego the evidence for a good prosecution?"

It was the police, the part of the system most in touch with the impact of crime on families and neighborhoods, who first advocated using their power and resources in new ways. In the 1970s, they developed new approaches that attack crime as a problem to be solved and prevented rather than as a series of incidents whose perpetrators have to be pros- ecuted, adjudicated, and punished. The latter are tools of problem solv- ing and prevention, not ends in themselves.

Police departments, in pursuing this approach, realized their depen- dence on the rest of the system to make their strategies work. They have teamed with probation and parole agencies to monitor likely reoffenders and persuaded prosecutors to create neighborhood-based prosecution teams. Together, these agencies have gone to regulatory agencies to enlist their enforcement power and to health and social service agencies for their resources to attack crime and safety on many different fronts.

For the courts, it was drug and domestic violence cases overwhelm- ing dockets, crowding jails, and crying out for a different notion of justice that led judges to reexamine the limits of traditional approaches and to seek a broader analysis and response than that afforded solely by the adjudication and punishment process. First with drug courts and later with domestic violence courts, the court has reached out not only to prosecutors, defense attorneys, and corrections, but also to public and private treatment and social service providers to form partnerships to address complex medical, social, and behavioral problems that nonetheless pose significant threats to the safety and well-being of communities.

Whatever their pressure points or reasoning, more and more, the individual parts of the criminal justice system have grown weary at the ineffectiveness or frustration of the conveyor-belt notion of justice. As one probation official in Kalamazoo, Michigan, put it, "We used to look for the case file/offender to come over the wall into our cubicle from the preceding one; do what we did to it, and then stand up and put it over the wall to the next cubicle." The case comes down the chute, we do what we can, and send it on. React to individual behavior, see what punishment or deterrence, occasionally rehabilitation, could be effected, and move it on, hoping for the best.

"If you always do what you've always done, you'll always get what you've always gotten." For most of us, it has taken awhile to realize that what we have always gotten isn't much! But the public has had that realization for some time. It was the public's loss of confidence in the system and their demand for more safety for their tax dollars that have prompted many parts of the criminal justice system to look for new ways to address problems, to ask whether our reactive, after-the-crime, adversarial approach to justice and law enforcement continues to make sense as our only or even primary response to crime. The success of things like Proposition 36 in California, and the many counties that have had jail building and related bond issues fail, are powerful testimonies to public frustration with "what we've always done."

The question is being asked, and the shift in our focus grows steadily. Our definition of success, whether we are a parole agent or a prosecutor, a judge, or a police officer, is less and less, "How did I do with this case?"—did I solve it, did I win a conviction, was my sentence appropriate, are the parolees on my caseload staying off the police docket—and more and more, "How safe are the communities, the people, the neighborhoods that I am sworn to serve and protect?" As Ronnie Earle, Travis County (Texas) District Attorney, put it, "I got tired of waiting for something terrible to happen before I could do anything. Tough prosecution is not enough by itself; you've also got to have smart prevention" (Center for Court Innovation, 2000).

One former corrections commissioner tells this story about his own awakening: "Every day I would get up and quickly scan the morning paper for the 'crime news' section. There would be the usual assortment of reports: robberies, break-ins, rapes, murders—the usual stuff. I would look to see if any of the suspects caught were on probation or parole. If they weren't, it was going to be an okay day. One day, it hit me, 'I wonder what the citizens of my state would think if they knew that that was what I thought, that that was the extent of my worry.' And I didn't think they would have thought much of it or of me." As we change our notion of success, as the focus of our efforts moves into an acceptance of a broader responsibility for public safety in its widest meaning, this cannot help but also change the way we view the jobs of individuals and agencies. No longer can we view our task as "doing whatever it is we do with the cases that have come over the wall to us today."

The Evidence of this Change

It would be easy to characterize this change as simply a different way to do the same job: those agencies are moving from a reactive to a proactive posture, but their work remains the same. A corollary characterization would be that in being more proactive, criminal justice agencies are being more inclusive of community members: seeking their help as volunteers, listening to their concerns. A review of how these changes have played out in various segments of the system reveals some things more fundamental at work.

Problem-oriented Policing

As indicated, problem-oriented policing, advanced out of Wisconsin by Herman Goldstein, is likely the earliest widespread venture by traditional agencies of the criminal justice system to change their focus from reaction to proactivity. Problem-oriented policing uses an analysis of crime patterns to address crime-prevention (Goldstein, 1990). The fundamental position of this approach is that most crime happens for knowable reasons. Crime can be rationally examined as a problem to be understood and solved, in other words, prevented. At the time many in corrections were deep in "nothing works," our brothers and sisters in policing were busy trying to understand how crimes happen, the situations that lead to the vulnerability of a place or a victim, and the often simple forces that bring a motivated offender into contact with that vulnerable victim in an undefended place (Scott, 2001).

The police who engaged this approach defined their job as understanding which places in their area were undefended and why; which groups of people were especially vulnerable, and under what circumstances, and what conditions prompted someone to offend. As police, their efforts were not directed at understanding where that offender came from on the road to becoming an offender, but rather what prompted him or her on this particular occasion to offend—and how to create a different kind of circumstance for the next would-be criminal that happened along.

Car thefts, for example, are approached both in terms of what made that car a target, and also what made that garage, that lot, or that block a likely place where car theft might happen. Responses will include reminding car owners to lock their cars, but might also include forcing lot owners to install better lighting and establish clearer fields of vision to the street. When violent convenience store robberies are demonstrated to occur most frequently in stores with only a single staff person on duty, local ordinances can be adopted requiring higher staffing levels during vulnerable periods.

At root here is a fundamental shift in the notion of what the job of policing is. No longer is it enough to solve a crime after it happens, no longer is it enough to understand vulnerability and help citizens and businesses to be less vulnerable; police have set about to take action to prevent crime by creating change. Police have taken on the job of analyzing what causes problems and of working with whomever it takes to solve or mitigate those problems. They have done research on crime patterns in their own and other cities; they have consulted with research organizations (like the National League of Cities); they have met with community residents to learn both what was going on when they were not there, and what residents thought ought to be done; they have done the same with business groups, social service agencies, and university campuses. And they have turned around and enlisted the help of all of those groups in creating solutions (*see* Community Oriented Policing Services, 2002).

These kinds of findings and responses led to the realization that prosecution of individual cases was often not the most effective use of the legal resources at the disposal of a municipal or county police department. Lawyers are useful in more proactive ways: the corporation counsel of a city can draft new ordinances that specify the lighting requirements of new parking garages or lots, or they can negotiate agreements with downtown business owners to help pay for increased lighting in the alleys behind stores and restaurants where bar patrons are frequently victimized.

Community Prosecution

These advances in policing helped precipitate the movement toward so-called community prosecution. "So called" because so much of what the lawyers engaged in this enterprise do is "lawyering" for sure, but not necessarily prosecution.

Community prosecution might well also be called "problem-oriented public lawyering." The city attorneys and county prosecutors who operate under its mantle are as likely to be found trying to enforce city housing codes or to take the owner of a drug house to court for operating a nuisance property as they are to be prosecuting a drug dealer or car thief (*Community Prosecution Profiles*, 2000).

Community prosecution as a distinct initiative originated in the office of Michael Schrunk, the district attorney of Multnomah County, Oregon (Goldkamp et al., 2001). As it has spread across the country, 23 percent of state court prosecutors' offices reported having community prosecution units or attorneys in 2001, and that does not include city and county attorneys' offices (Bureau of Justice Statistics, 2002). Community or neighborhood prosecution has been nurtured by two related but distinct ideas. The first has its roots in the "broken windows" theories of George Kelling. Responding to disorder to all crimes in any area, even low-level, quality-of-life crimes, can help reduce the overall level of criminality in an area. The second is more closely tied to problem-oriented policing. Focusing a prosecutor's (or a unit's) attention on the problems and crimes of a particular area will enable the prosecutor's office, working closely with police, to have better intelligence about what is going on in that community, and to identify more readily the sources of crime (persons, situations, businesses, buildings) that require attention beyond the apparent seriousness of any one incident.

The practical result of these two strategies may look the same on the ground, but they have differences. Among other things, the latter approach often means that prosecutors are just as likely to take on the homicides and major drug busts in a community as they are low-level cases (Boland, 2001).

Perhaps the biggest change to the way that all prosecutors, regardless of the category of cases they pursue, have made to their business in this approach is the very different way that they think about and use their legal and moral authority. As mentioned above, community-based or problem-oriented prosecutors do not just prosecute individual criminal cases. They may be doing broader legal research on noncriminal legal areas, pursuing code enforcement cases in civil court, writing new codes or ordinances, or providing legal advice to police and community organizations. They may spend far more time intelligence gathering—on the street, in community meetings, in meetings with police and other agencies—than in preparing cases. Their hours are long and varied, and they may well not work out of a conventional office, but in a storefront or a police station, or, as in Kalamazoo, Michigan, in a church basement. Their efforts are aimed at the resolution of broad problems that increase the level of criminal activity in an area: abandoned buildings and cars that become refuges for drug dealing; overgrown and untended parks that invite transient camping and provide cover for street crime; a bar that sells to minors or serves the already-intoxicated; the slumlord who preys on illegal immigrants (Criminal Justice Research Institute, 2001).

In some places, however, the prosecutors' efforts have not stopped there. In Denver, for example, the district attorney's office employs community organizers who provide skills, information, and training to neighborhood residents through Community Justice Councils. As one member of the Globeville Community Justice Council said, "This is not about the DA taking over our neighborhood; this is about us taking over our neighborhood" (Cleo Valdez, remarks, October 28, 2002). In Kalamazoo, the senior neighborhood district attorney, Karen Hayter, has become an expert on housing law in all its forms, with the expressed aim of working with residents and nonprofit groups to improve the housing stock and the number of resident owners in poor neighborhoods in that city. These kinds of efforts point to the power of the prosecutor—both legal and moral—to support community-building as a vehicle of promoting public safety (personal conversation, May 2002).

In Indianapolis, the neighborhood DA's are called "Street Level Advocates," making explicit their role in communities. Scott Newman, the district attorney of Indianapolis, defines the future of these efforts as the promotion of "community efficacy" to counter disorder and promote safety—a far cry from "taking the next case from over the wall" (Scott Newman, remarks, October 7, 2002).

Drug Courts

While drug courts started out as a way to impose greater account-ability on low-level drug addicts (Drug Court Clearinghouse and Technical Assistance Project, 1999), the goal of drug courts, as developed by its practitioners over time, has become much broader. These judges, prosecutors, defense attorneys, and probation officers want nothing less than the elimination of addiction—and thus a massive reduction in all kinds of crime—among a broad swath of their eligible population. In a report to Chief Judge Judith Kaye, the New York State Commission on Drugs and the Courts (June, 2000), after reviewing the efforts and out-comes of drug courts and related initiatives around the state, recom-mended that:

> *[T]he Office of Court Administration launch a systematic, statewide approach to the delivery of "coerced" drug treatment to non-violent addicts in every jurisdiction. . . . his approach should not be limited to criminal cases, but should be extended throughout the state's Family Courts. . . . If this treatment could be made to work on a broad scale, the benefits could be signif-icant. . . . the eventual savings in jail and prison costs could be in the tens of millions of dollars per year, and the . . . savings in court, social services and other costs could be higher still . . . to say nothing about the benefits to the offenders and their communities that could result from a reduction in addiction and recidivism.*

From its beginnings in Miami, Florida, in 1989, the drug court move-ment has spread with such alacrity that there are now drug courts in operation or in planning in forty-nine states, the District of Columbia, in many tribal courts, and several territories (Drug Court Clearinghouse and Technical Assistance Project, 1999). Judges with experience in these courts have become advocates for the creation of other specialized courts that focus on particular social problems with an eye to long-term prevention. Domestic violence, mental health, and homeless courts are now in operation around the country. They now have their own name: problem-solving courts. As with the drug courts, these newer courts are looking to use their authority over adjudication, sanctioning, and super-vision to force those in need to remain in compliance with their court-ordered regimen of treatment and/or intensive supervision. Such interventions in these cases have little to do with imposing punishment or deterrence. Often the level of supervision is out of proportion to the level of risk of harm that they represent, but rather the conditions imposed are aimed squarely at preventing future harm to the offenders themselves as well as to others (Berman and Feinblatt, 2001).

Through Hamilton County's Mental Health Court, for example, a combination of local public and private funding has enabled the county to screen defendants at booking, to seek further assessment if the screening indicates a problem, to secure the assistance of mental health case managers in finding an appropriate treatment placement, to ensure that the defendant has both needed medications and a link to treatment before release from jail, and a separate docket where the results of all of these can be considered before and at adjudication and sentencing (meeting in Hamilton County, Ohio, August, 2001).

A similar process, with screening done through social workers at the Public Defenders Office, is at work in Davidson County, with even more intense case management available to the most chronic, mentally ill offenders (meeting in Davidson County, Tennessee, June, 2002). These courts and their supporting services are set up to address one of the most intractable problems in criminal justice: chronic offending, usually nonviolent, by mentally ill persons. The solution is treatment and case management—often denied or unavailable without court adjudication, and often not enforced without specialized court supervision.

In domestic violence cases, the desire is not just to prevent further harm to the assaulted partner, but also to provide safety and stability to children and the extended family who are so often involved.

Juvenile Probation—Youth Accountability Boards

Youth accountability boards as a tool for responding in a meaningful way to low-level offending by juveniles have been in use for many years. They vary widely in their level of formal affiliation with criminal justice system case processing, from informal referral by the district attorney or judge, to part of a formal diversion program (as they are in many counties in Washington State.) But all of them are operated on the principle that community members who live in the neighborhood or town where the offense was committed, who may know the youngster's parents or other family members, who may be on the staff at his or her school, are in the best position to help the juvenile to understand the implications of his actions, devise an appropriate sanction, and supervise its completion.

Over time, however, these programs, too, have moved beyond their original scope. In Boise County, Idaho, community members who have participated in the boards (called the Idaho City Accountability Network) have been so moved by the life situations and stories of the juvenile offenders, that they have organized themselves to provide needed recreational and other opportunities for children and teens in their poor, rural county (personal conversations at various community meetings, 1998-2001). In Missoula, Montana, the juvenile prosecutor, working with the probation department, realized that most of the teens in their program, the Community Youth Justice Council, had younger siblings at home who faced similar risks in terms of the family's situation. She applied for and received a grant for the county's health department for a nurse to call on the parents of the teens in the program to offer prevention services for the rest of the family (meeting with Dori Brownlow, assistant prosecutor, Missoula County, May, 2000).

Community Corrections

The community corrections field long ago rejected the idea of the "offender" as their chief client, and has embraced the notion of the community as customer. Its largest membership organization promotes the idea of probation and parole contributing to public safety and forging community partnerships (*see* the American Probation and Parole Association's vision statement; Arola and Lawrence, 2000). Unfortunately, faced with budget cuts and reductions in force, many still lack the resources to provide the type of assessments advocated by the International Community Corrections Association, much less the programming that the assessments might call for.

Two states, however, have tried to examine this issue systematically. In 1997, the Governor's Task Force on Sentencing and Corrections in Wisconsin issued a report that called for a dramatic rethinking of the way corrections resources are deployed and the purposes they were to serve. Although the Task Force's recommendations were never adopted, the co-chairs of that body wrote about them in the *Corrections Management Quarterly* (Smith and Dickey, 1998). The seven principles described in that article and articulated in the Task Force's recommendations speak to the use of corrections as an essential tool for producing public safety; for deploying correctional resources in a locally based, problem-solving manner that is responsive to the combination of risks presented by individual offenders and neighborhoods. These principles were subsequently adopted by law in 1999 in the state of Washington through the Offender Accountability Act. Here is how the Washington State Department of Corrections, the agency responsible for community corrections in Washington, describes its implementation of some of those principles:

Active Community Involvement: Effective management of offenders under the jurisdiction of the Department includes active community involvement. Community safety requires collaboration and mobilization of resources at the neighborhood level. Research shows that social controls are more powerful than the coercive authority of the criminal justice system. In other words, "We can't do it alone." Communities, including victims, law enforcement, offenders, and families, will be involved in defining problems, seeking solutions, and developing community standards for managing offenders.

Guardians: Guardians are at the core of the new community-oriented supervision model. Guardians are individuals who have the capacity to influence the behavior of offenders. They can also influence the safety of victims or potential victims and the safety of places in our neighborhoods and communities. Victims, citizens, treatment providers, family members, and law enforcement will be asked to play a special role in managing offender risk.

Community Risk and Safety: There is a growing awareness . . . that public safety is more than having convicted felons closely monitored, or seeing a reduction in crime or recidivism rates. Public safety . . . is a condition found in places where people are free to live their lives without threat of criminal acts against their person or property. Making safe communities is not . . . the responsibility of one agency or one volunteer organization. It is something, however, in which the department has a vital role to play. By collaborating with others in high-risk neighborhoods, be they criminal justice agencies or concerned citizens and citizen organizations, the Department can be part of the problem solving that can lead to a broader sense of community justice.

The Department of Corrections has started recruiting individuals and organizations to serve as guardians, has created "community justice centers" to offer needed services to offenders in the community in a single location, and placed its agents in community-based offices that are co-located with other agencies. While this initiative in Washington State is still very new, and its implementation still in process, it represents a wholesale rethinking of how probation and parole do their job.

Community Courts

Jurisdictions across the country have created community courts because they "seek a court process that imposes immediate, meaningful sanctions on offenders, is visible to the community, and has the capacity to address the social problems that underlie minor crimes" (Bureau of Justice Assistance, 1999). In some ways, community courts resemble the magistrate courts that used to be common in cities and larger towns in decades past: lower-level crimes were handled near where they occurred, sometimes right at the police station; they were dealt with immediately and removed from the system. Jail space was more plentiful then and crimes of all kinds were fewer.

Court reform efforts of the sixties and seventies caused many jurisdictions to both centralize courts "downtown" or at the county seat, and to seat judges rather than magistrates at initial proceedings. The huge increases in crime of recent decades and the subsequent overwhelming of judicial and correctional resources caused New York to rethink their so-called reform and to create the Midtown Community Court in 1993 (Feinblatt and Berman, 1997). They did not, however, recreate the magistrate court of an earlier day. They sought to create an institution that would not simply process cases into and out of the system quickly and more efficiently, but would address the underlying issues that brought so many low-level offenders into the system—while also creating value for the community surrounding the court (Berman and Feinblatt, 2001). There was a concerted effort to understand who the offenders were, why they offended, and what would offer a positive impact for the community: social, employment, medical, and treatment services for offenders and community service work that makes sense for and contributes to the immediate midtown community.

Far from Midtown Manhattan, other jurisdictions around the country have sought to replicate the principles of Midtown, tailoring their location, services, and sanctions to their own problems and needs.

Some Observations on These Developments

It is possible to draw two major conclusions from the descriptions of these efforts and their development over time.

First, the criminal justice system is in the process of radically changing its notion of how it delivers public safety.

Second, democracy has invaded the criminal justice system.

But before we can draw those conclusions, we should look a little more closely at some of the details of what we have seen associated with these developments:

1. The closer agents and agencies of the criminal justice system get to problems, the more likely they are to turn their efforts to prevention. As police get out of their cars, prosecutors and probation agents get out of their offices, and judges interact with individual offenders, their attention becomes focused on defining the conditions, situations, or needs that have prompted offending in the first place, and then onto remedying those. Individual cases, while never lost, become sources of information and learning and the criminal justice system becomes the tool of social intervention and social change.

2. The prevention that we seek to do, in the name of doing good, can be enormously intrusive. Both problem-solving courts and drug courts bring the full weight and authority of the criminal justice system apparatus to bear on defendants and offenders whose actual offenses, in themselves, would probably not have earned such a response. Community prosecutors, conducting community meetings or locating their offices in a house on a residential block (as they do in Kalamazoo) are likely to see and learn about offending or take action against violators that might never have come to their attention or have warranted their attention earlier. Problem-oriented policing can bring a level or kind of surveillance to an area that is unwelcome by law-abiding people who frequent a particular area or business.

3. The intrusiveness of problem-solving and prevention is usually justified by referencing "what the community wants." What remains unclear in all of this author's work in this arena, all of her reading and site visits, is: Who gets to define this so-called "community" and who decides who speaks for them? Leo Hayden, president of the Center for Violence Interruption in Chicago, describes this as the problem of "the chosen few." Put

another way, who is it that we are not talking to? Who is it that does not come to community meetings, does not serve on an accountability board, or is not represented on the staff of local nonprofits, or the membership rolls of the local churches, synagogues, or mosques?

4. These initiatives are costly and often poorly understood by local governments who pay for them. Police officers who are spending time doing research, conducting focus groups or community meetings, or meeting with business owners are not patrolling the streets. (And patrolling the streets is what most people—including taxpayers and the people they elect—think the police should be doing.) Drug and other specialized courts are enormously resource intensive in the short-run; not only do they make sometimes costly assessment and treatment services available to those who could not afford them, they also take up the time of court and corrections staff, including prosecutors, defense attorneys, court administrators, bailiffs, and probation agents. Devoting the time of prosecutors to neighborhoods, where most of their time will not be spent on individual cases, is a significant expense to a prosecutor's office.

5. There are many jurisdictions where some version of all of these efforts is going on simultaneously, often at enormous cost. In recent years, a flurry of federal support, usually coming from separate federal agencies, has encouraged local courts and agencies to develop these programs at a rapid rate. Since different federal agencies work with or fund different local counterparts (for example, the Office of Community Oriented Policing Services (COPS) funds police departments, the Drug Court Program Office funds courts, and so forth), these initiatives frequently have been developed without consideration for one another. These federal funds, however, are temporary, and many programs will soon have no source of federal support.

To go back, then, to our two conclusions:

1. **A changing notion of how to deliver public safety.** Our answer to that has to be yes—and no. Yes, many police departments, prosecutors' offices, corrections departments, courts, and other agencies are questioning the way we have always done things. They are using their enhanced information and data capacities to approach crime and criminals, victims and

locations as problems that can be analyzed, understood, and, if not solved, at least mitigated. These agencies, and the individuals within them, are willing to make themselves uncomfortable—they are discarding their early training, taking risks, trying new approaches.

The answer is no on several counts. First, too many departments and offices are not implementing these strategies at all, are implementing them piecemeal, or are only paying them lip service (MacDonald, 2002).

In the case of policing, a community liaison officer by herself does not add much value to the delivery of public safety in a neighborhood. If the information she develops is not sought by her department, taken up, combined with other information, analyzed and acted upon, she is really a public relations officer. If a community prosecutor does little more than attend community meetings, or act on individual complaints that residents bring to him, then, he too has not added much value.

Second, across disciplines we are not learning from one another, nor integrating what is known in one area into another. For example, juvenile delinquency prevention research has produced many promising leads on primary and secondary prevention of violence and delinquency (the Blueprints Project, for example, out of the University of Colorado). That research has demonstrated the value of fostering parent-child bonds in the first few months of life, and of continuing there kinds of learning in the first three years of life, especially when delivered by a loving and connected caregiver. But how many corrections departments (in jails or prisons or in the community) are using that information in programs where most of their clients are parents? How many drug courts are extending their efforts to include civil cases of child neglect or abuse due to drug or alcohol abuse by parents?

Third, within most jurisdictions, these efforts are being undertaken and carried on without coordination. For all of the resources being spent on them, there seems to be little attempt to make strategic decisions about which problems loom most significantly in an entire city or county, and therefore, which initiatives should be implemented, with what kind of priority, and how might they be integrated. Even resources for the same problem, drug abuse, for example, are not deployed strategically. In some jurisdictions, an offender's access to treatment depends completely on which court he appears in and not on his level of risk or addiction, much less some combination of the two. In one jurisdiction, misdemeanor drug possession cases are sent to twenty-eight days of residential drug treatment, while felony cases get probation.

Fourth, the emphasis of police and prosecutors on particular neighborhoods or on particular problems in a neighborhood can result in the simple displacement of crime to another neighborhood. This is more likely to happen when the approach to the problem is too simplistic or it has not been analyzed enough to understand all of its implications. For example, a common problem identified by both downtown business districts and residential neighborhoods is streetwalking. The response is likely to be focused on how we get those prostitutes off this street. But unless we take the time to understand why the prostitutes are on the street, why this street or area is attractive, and how to keep the "customers" away, and then respond to what we learn about all three, we will simply move the problem to another part of town and start over. A lack of comprehensive analysis and problem solving can lead to unwanted displacement (as opposed to desirable displacement), but it can also result from the lack of strategic planning that goes beyond one area.

2. **Democracy is invading the criminal justice system.** It seems that the answer here is much more unequivocally a "yes"—but with some serious caveats. First, these efforts are not democratic when they are allowed to be a cover for enforcing one group's notion of propriety on everyone else (Dickey and McGarry, 2001). The criminal justice agency or system has an obligation to explore who is speaking for a particular community and who remains unrepresented. The unrepresented may simply be those whose work and family obligations keep them too busy to participate and to voice their concerns—or it might be recent immigrants with a pervasive distrust of law enforcement brought with them from their home country.

Second, public safety is justice, and government is charged with delivering both. However, we must exercise caution when the focus of our "public safety" efforts is simply criminalizing the poor and the homeless (Police Officer Desiree Small, Austin Police Department, remarks, October 29, 2002). We all recognize why street prostitution and public urination are problems. "Indoor" prostitution is as much a crime—yet we round up street prostitutes. If public places refuse to let the homeless use their facilities, where are they supposed to go?

Third, in the poorest communities, community members may lack the resources and the skills that they need to serve as effective advocates and voices for their community's needs (Dickey and McGarry, 2001). As the Denver District Attorney's Office has done, criminal justice system agencies have some obligation to recognize the inherent differences in power that exist between their officers and community members, and to address the lack of skills and resources that only enhance it.

Fourth, as described above, many problem-solving, public safety efforts are or become efforts to provide primary prevention services to individuals, families, and neighborhoods. While the services are desperately needed, and the criminal justice system agency may be in a position to provide them, one has to ask whether this is the most appropriate use of agencies with all of the power and authority of the criminal justice system. A corollary question might also be why are the appropriate "civilian" agencies (health, mental health, education, housing, and so forth) not providing these essential services to those who need them?

Conclusions

First, there is a need for a "strategic convener." We have the technology, the know-how, and the capacities that we need to approach public safety as a series of problem to be solved. Our various agencies have begun to take this approach. What is required at this moment is the capacity to collect the intelligence and information developed by these agencies, to create systemic strategies for addressing the problems they reveal, and to deploy the collective resources of the criminal justice system to address them.

Because of the way that our criminal justice system is structured, across all levels and branches of governments, no one agency has the authority, the mandate, or the capacity to perform this function. The agencies of the system must come together to form a policy council or team to take on this role. This is not the traditional "coordinating council" that so many of us are familiar with; this is a body of policymakers who have agreed to accept the collective responsibility of "steward" of the system and overall guardian of public safety from the government's side.

In a policy team, the system's leaders, drawn from different agencies, different branches of government, perhaps different political parties or beliefs, can function as a true management body, working together on jointly identified goals, addressing problems that have an impact on the entire system, and using the collective wisdom of their varied experiences and perspectives to deliver safety and justice. This is, after all, their mutual responsibility.

Together, these leaders are smarter, know more, and have more resources at their disposal than any one individual. Together, they are in a better position both to anticipate the risks of any decisions and actions, and to stand firm with one another when one or more of those decisions and actions fails or produces unanticipated results. Together, they have access to more information, of more kinds, than any one of their agencies has alone. Together, their access to and contact with a broad cross-section of constituent groups and private organizations is greatly expanded. Together, they are far better at delivering safety and justice.

Second, there is the need for this body to engage communities as partners. Our concepts of communities as, first, sites of activities (the original concept of "community corrections"), or later, as customers of our services, are no longer adequate. What we have learned is that if public safety is a "condition of life," the everyday freedom to live and work and raise families without fear, then the criminal justice system cannot create public safety by itself. Communities must, and have shown their willingness to, get involved in efforts of all kinds. They will form community justice councils and youth accountability boards; they will mentor young people and advocate for and organize greater opportunities for their young people; they will show up for community meetings and pack courtrooms; they will convene press conferences and announce that they have had it with the drug markets outside their front doors. And, like Angel Dawson in Baltimore, some are willing to risk everything.

As the research coming out of Chicago is demonstrating, helping communities to gain a sense of their own power and efficacy is probably one of the most effective things we can do in seeking public safety.

In a way, we do not have a choice. Communities in many places will no longer accept simply being "the eyes and ears" of the police, or being given flashlights and vests and given "permission" to patrol their own block. They want a say in what you are doing and how you are doing it.

Sharing power among ourselves is difficult; sharing it with the community may seem out of the question. However, with the experience of collaborating and sharing information, resources, and decisions among ourselves through the policy team, it will be easier. Through the policy team we are also more likely to recognize the wealth of diverse communities within our jurisdictions, to find ways to reach them and to bring them into the ongoing dialog about public safety.

Third, as the strategic convener, with the communities of your jurisdiction as partners, the policy team can serve as a broker to bring prevention services to those who need them. One of the undeniable functions of the criminal justice system is to serve as the monitor and barometer of the dysfunction of our families and neighborhoods. This is why its agencies so often get involved in providing services outside of their core mandate. It is the "default option" of individual officers and their agencies that are on the frontline in responding to disorder and dysfunction.

The policy team can serve to convene parties beyond the criminal justice system, both public and private agencies, businesses, universities, faith-based groups, and powerful individuals, to put what it has learned about community problems on the table, and to brainstorm solutions with all of these stakeholders.

The National Institute of Corrections

The National Institute of Corrections was created by Congress in 1974 to be a center for correctional knowledge, and to offer leadership and assistance to the field of corrections. For more than twenty-six years, the Institute has conducted national projects, training events, and provided technical assistance in countless jurisdictions across the country. The challenges to creating a body that is prepared and willing to function as a strategic convener are formidable. It has been the experience of the National Institute of Corrections, with more than twenty years of working on this issue, that the creation of a policy team committed and prepared to engage in a process of criminal justice system planning is the only way that these challenges can be met and overcome.

For many years, the National Institute of Corrections' training and technical assistance efforts focused on single parts of the criminal justice system, like jails or prisons, or on decision making in limited areas, like parole release or responses to probation violations. But all of those efforts added critical learning experiences that inform the National Institute of Corrections' knowledge about systemic criminal justice collaboratives, and ultimately inspired the Criminal Justice System Project (CJSP) and its resulting document, *An Operator's Manual for the Criminal Justice System*.

The manual is in its final stages of completion. It incorporates the lessons learned and the strategies developed during the Criminal Justice System Project and the many other National Institute of Corrections' projects that preceded it. It is very much a how-to guide for system policymakers at any level who want to create the kind of vehicle or platform from which to partner with other agencies and communities.

This process and the work needed to support it are comprised of very different types of tasks, requiring a range of skills and approaches. What follows are the key principles on which this process rests. The remainder of the manual will address each one in more detail, including specific instructions for achieving it.

The Policy Team Is the Steward of the Criminal Justice System

We have made the point that the criminal justice system has evolved as a series of separate and distinct specialty tasks: arrest, prosecution, pretrial release, trial, sentencing, corrections, parole, and probation, to name a few. Many of these agencies have achieved excellence within their own areas of responsibility. They have hired specialized staff, developed first-rate skills, and excelled in their area. What is missing is an overall mission for the entire criminal justice system that is larger than the goals of any of its component parts. Further, the criminal justice system lacks a quality control manager or steward—a group or individual who can develop that mission and oversee how the entire system is engaged in meeting it.

This manual argues that such a steward is essential to the success of the system, and, because there is no manager of the entire system, it is critical that the key policymakers come together in a policy team to play this vital role. Without a policy body to look across all parts of the criminal justice system, there is little chance that we can forge a shared vision of the system, or that even our most passionately held hopes for the future can become a reality.

Collaborate

One of the hallmarks of a systemic approach to criminal justice is collaboration across the traditional boundaries of agency, branch, and level of government. Indeed, because ownership of various portions of the system resides in so many agencies and different levels and branches of government, a systems approach requires collaboration among key stakeholders. Collaboration can be difficult and time consuming because of the many criminal justice agencies involved, but the distribution of responsibility and discretion among different agencies also makes collaboration essential. In jurisdictions that have made a commitment to a systemic, collaborative approach to criminal justice, we observe a marked change in the ways they conduct the business of criminal justice. In some jurisdictions, agencies or policy team members share agency resources to achieve a common benefit; they have altered individual schedules, court dockets, and inconvenienced themselves to achieve a higher goal or common vision of the criminal justice system. Agency directors have signed joint memoranda of understanding agreeing to consensual decision making on all criminal justice policy matters. The jurisdictions who have been involved in the Criminal Justice System Project and related efforts have succeeded in using a radically different method to attack the difficult challenges within the criminal justice system—they have begun to collaborate.

Provide the Process with Support

A comprehensive, collaborative criminal justice system planning process is not possible without the availability of staff and other resources to support the work of the policy team. Staff are needed to take care of routine administrative tasks, prepare for meetings, collect and present data and information, prepare reports, and manage communication among the team members. Other resources are needed to support the costs of extended meetings, facilitators for some meetings, and costs connected with data collection. These staff and other resources can be supplied in a variety of ways, but it is not possible to move forward productively without them. In fact, beginning the process without some commitment of staff time and resources is likely to lead to failure as policymakers feel that their time is being wasted.

Focus on Outcomes

One result of the evolution of the criminal justice system as a network of distinct areas of specialized responsibilities and skills is that each area has come to define and judge success according to how each defines its job. Courts have focused on timely and efficient case processing and case management; the police on crime clearance rates; and the pretrial agency on failure to appear rates. What has often been missing is a focus on a vision for the entire criminal justice system. It is a very costly and powerful part of government. What is it that we expect it to produce for us? What are the outcomes we should look for as a result of its work overall?

If we can agree on that vision and articulate specific goals, then we can deconstruct the system and look at how each agency contributes to those. We can spell out the outcomes we should look for, and identify how responsibility for achieving those outcomes should be apportioned. We can measure how we are doing, and identify gaps and needs.

Research on private-sector businesses reinforces the importance of having an articulated and shared vision for the future. In studying many companies, Collins and Porras (1966) found that some firms' stock appreciated fifteen times more than the average company that stayed in business from 1926 to 1990. They found that one of the major characteristics of these visionary companies was that they had Big, Hairy, Audacious Goals, and a clear purpose and vision. Big, Hairy, Audacious Goals must be doable and readily applied by each employee, but also challenge the abilities of the organization. This can be risky since the organization channels all of its efforts to achieve a core vision and purpose. The firms studied exhibited a drive for progress and a core ideology of values beyond simply making money. Finally, these organizations were so imbued with their core values that employees received a consistent set of signals reinforcing behavior that supported the Big, Hairy, Audacious Goals, and the purpose and values of the company.

Get All the Information

Public agencies have resisted the idea that they ought to operate on the same kinds of standard as private businesses. They have been reluctant, in many cases, to articulate goals, set targets, and measure performance.

This has been especially true with criminal justice agencies. Because the criminal law is secular society's effort to codify standards of behavior, to spell out right from wrong, there is resistance in many quarters to basing criminal justice policy or its implementation on empirical information. Many policymakers have been content to make policy—whether in the form of new laws, budgets, or common practice—on the basis of beliefs and assumptions. So, it is not a surprise that the system has not valued good information, nor invested in the kind of automated data capacity that might have supplied that information.

However, once the policy team has begun focusing on a larger vision for the system and on defining specific outcomes, good information becomes an essential next step—perhaps even the first step. The policy team needs to know the full range of the system's activities, what each agency does and how it does it, the numbers of people the system takes in, the kinds of cases it handles, and how those cases are disposed. The team will want to understand where resources go and to what end. They will want to assess how well things work, in terms of both operations and outcomes, as measured against the vision and goals they have taken as their own. This is information in the service of understanding and analyzing your system; in that way it is distinguished from information for purposes of measuring or evaluating the success of a program or initiative.

Listen to the Data

Once you have good system information, the next step is to gather data that enable you to measure and evaluate your activities. As in many other areas, the police have led the way on the analysis and use of good data. Once police departments decided to stop simply reacting to crime, but to try to understand and control it, they realized they needed hard numbers. Increasingly, police departments across the country are developing sophisticated crime mapping capabilities that allow them to do real-time analysis of crime patterns. Other parts of the system are beginning to appreciate the value of this type of capacity. The routine and ongoing collection and analysis of data permit agencies to understand who is in the system, why, and for how long. It is possible then to identify the areas where even small changes to operations might yield large impacts, and where the investment of new resources would be most productive. Further, if such changes are implemented, it is possible afterward to monitor and evaluate whether they are achieving the desired ends.

Connect with the Community

Establishing strong connections with agencies and leaders from the community through or as part of this process serves several interests. First, they represent important resources to the criminal justice system: intelligence, information, support, and assets. As we have seen, the criminal justice system goes from being the place of last resort to being an essential player in our response to all types of personal, social, familial, neighborhood, and other problems. It is vital that the system identify and ally with the organizations and individuals who can reconnect people with more appropriate resources. These people and agencies are also important sources of information about neighborhoods, conditions, and problems that need addressing in the interests of public safety.

Second, community members are the primary constituents and customers of the criminal justice system—it is, after all, their safety that you are charged with securing. It is helpful to have their perspective present or available as the policy team discusses issues and options. Third, by including them in some way, you are educating community members to the issues you struggle with, and building a constituency for your decisions and needs.

Adopt a Problem-solving Orientation

An essential part of the change in the way the system does its business is a fundamental shift from a reactive posture to an active, problem-solving approach to issues of crime and safety. The shift may take time for leaders who are used to acting after something has happened, to trying to catch people who are committing or have committed a crime. In approaching the crime problem, our systems tend to rely on after-the-fact strategies rather than seeking to prevent or ameliorate the problems, conditions, or situations that encourage or facilitate crime. This shift will get easier once policymakers have identified and committed themselves to specific outcomes. With clear goals and good information, the policy group more readily will take problems and issues apart to seek true understanding before leaping ahead to solutions.

Exert Leadership

No policymaker in any criminal justice system lacks for things to do. Persuading them to take on a process that will be hard and time consuming is not easy. Keeping them involved, committed, and working is even harder. The advantages of this process may seem distant while the costs are immediate. The process requires leaders who can stand back and see the payoffs, who are willing to take risks, and are willing to use their personal credibility and stock with their peers to get this effort off the ground and keep it going.

Develop Policy, Procedure, and Programs

If you have identified the outcomes you expect from the system and from each agency; if you have taken the time to gather good information about the system, and to assess how well it is doing; if you have been thoughtful about understanding the problems and issues that assessment has revealed, then you are positioned to see your policies, procedures, and programs as the tools and strategies that you can employ to achieve your goals. You are less likely to look at these as the discrete and immutable possessions of individual agencies, and more likely to view them as collective resources to be used for common ends. For example: How might the specialized staff of one agency be deployed to solve the larger problem common to several? Do the procedures of another agency get in the way of an approach that the policy team has agreed to try? Lastly, if you have taken the time to go through the process as described, the implementation of policies, procedures, and programs to effect outcomes is often much more efficient, and you will be prepared to handle unexpected glitches that may occur.

References

Arola, T. and R. Lawrence. 2000. Broken Windows: The Next Step in Fighting Crime. *Perspectives*. 24(1): 26-33.

Berman, G. and J. Feinblatt. 2001. *Problem-solving Courts: A Brief Primer. Law and Policy*. April.

Boland, B. 2001. *Community Prosecution in Washington*, D.C. Washington, D.C.: National Institute of Justice.

Bureau of Justice Assistance. 1999. *Overcoming Obstacles to Community Courts*. Washington, D.C.: U.S. Department of Justice.

Bureau of Justice Statistics. 2002. *Prosecutors in State Courts, 2001*. Washington, D.C.: U.S. Department of Justice.

Center for Court Innovation. 2000. *Community Prosecution Profiles*. New York: Center for Court Innovation.

Collins, J. and J. Porras. 1966. *Building Your Company's Vision*. Harvard Business Review. September-October: 65-77.

Community Oriented Policing Services. 2002. *Problem-solving Tips: A Guide to Reducing Crime and Disorder through Problem-solving Partnerships*. Washington, D.C.: U.S. Department of Justice, Office of Community Oriented Policing Services.

Criminal Justice Research Institute. 2001. *Community Prosecution Strategies*. Washington, D.C.: Criminal Justice Research Institute.

Dickey, W. and P. McGarry. 2001. *Community Justice in Rural America: Four Examples and Four Futures*. Washington, D.C.: Bureau of Justice Assistance.

Drug Court Clearinghouse and Technical Assistance Project. 1999. *Looking at a Decade of Drug Courts*. Washington, D.C.: Drug Court Program Office, Office of Justice Programs.

Feinblatt, J. and G. Berman. 1997. *Community Court Principles: A Guide for Planners*. New York: Center for Court Innovation.

Goldstein, H. 1990. *Problem-oriented Policing*. New York: McGraw-Hill.

Goldkamp, J., C. Irons-Guynn, and D. Weiland. 2001. *Community Prosecution Strategies: Measuring Impact*. Philadelphia: Crime and Justice Research Institute.

MacDonald, J. 2002. Effectiveness of Community Policing in reducing Urban Violence. *Crime and Delinquency*. 48(4): 592-618

Scott, M. 2001. *Problem-oriented Policing: Reflections on the First 20 Years*. Washington, D.C.: U.S. Department of Justice, Office of Community Oriented Policing Services.

Smith, M. E. and W. J. Dickey. 1998. What If Corrections Were Serious about Public Safety? *Corrections Management Quarterly*. 2(3): 12-30.

MEETING THE CHALLENGES OF PRISONER REENTRY

6

Joan Petersilia, Ph.D.
Professor of Criminology, Law, and Society
University of California, School of Social Ecology
Irvine, California

> *"Never doubt that a small group of thoughtful committed people can change the world. Indeed, it's the only thing that ever has!"*
> —Margaret Mead

Recognizing that prisoner reentry is a critically important public safety issue and that there is much to be done to improve the prospects of prisoners' success when they return to our communities, this paper outlines the data surrounding prisoner release and reentry and makes recommendations about how best to reform parole and prisoner reentry.

More Than 600,000 Prisoners Released Each Year

Never before in U.S. history have so many individuals been released from prison. About 600,000 people were released in 2002 alone, a number nearly equal to the population of Washington, D.C., and greater than the state of Wyoming. This number is expected to grow in future years, as more inmates complete long prison terms.

Just 7 percent of all prisoners are facing death or life sentences, and only a fraction of inmates—about 3,000 each year—die in prison. Thus, 93 percent of all prisoners eventually come home. And although the average prison term served is now two and a half years (seven months longer on average than a decade ago), many prison terms are short enough that 44 percent of all state prisoners will be released within the year. If the capacity to manage reintegration had kept pace with the flow of prisoners, and the characteristics of prisoners had remained the same, the reentry phenomenon today would be no different than in times past. Inmates have always been released from prison, and officials have long struggled with reintegration, but the current situation is decidedly different for several reasons:

The sheer numbers of releasees dwarf anything in our history.
The problems of parolees appear to be more serious than in the past.
The corrections system retains few rehabilitation programs.

The way in which we plan for an inmates' transition to free living—including the way in which they spend their time during confinement, the process by which they are released, and the way in which they are supervised after release—is critical to public safety. This process is called "prisoner reentry," and simply defined, it includes all of the activities and programming conducted to prepare ex-convicts to return safely to the community.

Who Is Coming Home?

Serious Social and Medical Problems. Most inmates released from prison today have serious social and medical problems. About three-fourths of all prisoners have a history of substance abuse, and one in six suffers from mental illness. Yet fewer than one-third of exiting prisoners have received substance abuse or mental health treatment while in prison. Although some states have provided more funding for prison drug treatment, the percentage of state prisoners participating in such programs has been declining—from 25 percent a decade ago to about 10 percent in 2002. It is not that the number of programs or number of participants has declined, as much as it is that the prison population has increased so dramatically that the percentage participating has declined significantly.

Infectious Disease. A significant share of the prison population also lives with an infectious disease. Two percent to 3 percent of state prisoners are HIV-positive or have AIDS, a rate five times higher than that of the U.S. population. According to the Centers for Disease Control and Prevention, about 25 percent of all individuals living with HIV or AIDS in the United States had been released from a prison or jail. Public health experts believe that HIV will continue to escalate within prisons and that it will eventually affect prevalence rates in the general community as we incarcerate and release more drug offenders, many of whom engage in intravenous drug use, share needles, or trade sex for drugs.

Few Marketable Skills. Few inmates have marketable skills or sufficient literacy to become gainfully employed. A third of all U.S. prisoners were unemployed at the time of their most recent arrest, and just 60 percent of inmates have a GED credential or high school diploma, compared with 85 percent of the U.S. adult population.

Mental Impairment. The National Adult Literacy Survey established that 11 percent of inmates have a learning disability, compared with 3 percent of the general population, and 3 percent are mentally retarded.

Declining Participation in Prison Education or Vocational Programs. Again, despite evidence that inmates' literacy and job readiness have declined in the past decade, fewer inmates are participating in prison education or vocational programs. Today, just over one-fourth of all those released from prison will have participated in vocational training programs, and about one-third of exiting prisoners will have participated in education programs—both figures down from a decade ago.

Declining Use of Transitional Facilities. The use of transitional facilities and halfway houses has also declined. Although all states legally permit work and educational furloughs, and most states operate halfway houses or reentry facilities, the vast majority of prisoners being released do not participate in such programs. Today, just 7 percent of all prison releasees initially live in a halfway house or other community facility—

despite the fact that every study group has strongly recommended that such programs be expanded.

Declining Use of Work and Educational Furloughs. Work and educational furloughs are almost nonexistent in many states, having been particularly hard hit by our get-tough policies and bad national publicity. Who can forget Willie Horton? The rape he committed while on furlough had the effect of shutting down many excellent programs. In the Federal Bureau of Prisons, for example, fewer than 1 percent of inmates are now allowed furloughs. In California, no furloughs were granted in 2001—despite a massive program in the 1970s, when 15,000 furloughs were granted each year. Currently, about one-third of prisons report operating furlough programs, but fewer than 3 percent of inmates participate in them.

How We Help, How We Hinder

So, the needs of inmates are more serious than in the past, and the programs to meet those needs have declined. Why?

Part of the Problem Is Money. Part of the problem is money—and, certainly, it is even more of a problem in 2004, with the economy struggling. State and federal prisons continue to consume an increasing share of tax dollars. We spend about $31 billion a year to operate the nation's prisons. If we add in jail, probation, and parole expenditures, we spend nearly $50 billion annually on corrections.

We know that these corrections dollars have, for the most part, not funded more programs, but have funded, instead, prison staff, construction, and rising prison health care costs. Medical budgets comprise, on average, 10 percent to 15 percent of state corrections' operating budgets, and that percentage is increasing each year. Prison treatment programs, however, comprise 1 percent to 5 percent of state prison budgets, and that percentage is decreasing each year.

Public Sentiment and Punitive Incarceration. But it is not only that resources are scarce. Public sentiment and political rhetoric have also forced the reduction of many prison programs. A number of new "no-frills" statutes have been passed, eliminating smoking, weightlifting equipment, hot meals, personal clothing, telephone calls, family days, and so forth. Proponents argue that reducing such privileges is deserved—after all, incarceration should be punitive. Former Massachusetts Governor William F. Weld said that prisons should be a "tour through the circles of hell," where inmates should learn only "the joys of busting rocks."

The "Principle of Least Eligibility." Treatment and work programs have also been affected by society's expectation that prisoners should not receive free any services for which law-abiding citizens must pay. Taken to its extreme, this "principle of least eligibility" prohibits many benefits for prisoners, such as education and work programs. In 1994, Congress eliminated Pell grants for prisoners, which paid their tuition for college courses taken while in prison. Scholarships to prisoners were seen as unfair to hardworking citizens who could not afford to pay for college. In fact, fewer than 1 percent of all Pell grant funds went to prisoners. Nonetheless, the Pell program died, and prison college programs are now virtually extinct in most states.

The Pell controversy was but a small part of a huge and largely undocumented trend to drastically scale back all prison vocational and education programs. At least 25 states report having made cuts in vocational and technical training, the areas most likely to provide inmates with an alternative career when they leave prison.

More Idle Inmates Equals More Violence. More punitive attitudes, combined with diminishing rehabilitation programs, mean that more inmates spend their prison time being idle. In California, for example, with about 160,000 inmates, nearly 20 percent of all inmates have no assignment to a correctional program during their entire prison stay. Yet, research shows that California inmates who spend more time in programs are less likely to return to prison and less likely to participate in prison violence. Although some of this relationship reflects differences in the ways in which prisons select inmates for programs (in other words, the most motivated are given priority), the relationship between participating in prison programs and reduced recidivism has been documented repeatedly.

Idle hands are indeed the devils workshop—as any prison warden knows. Gangs and racial tensions increase, and gang wars started (or continued) in prison get settled after release. As an article in the *Atlantic Monthly* put it: "There is an awful lot of potential rage coming out of prison to haunt our future."

"Maxing Out" with No Supervision

In 1977, just 4 percent of all prisoners released "maxed out," that is, served the maximum amount of time allowed by law for their criminal convictions. But in 2002, 18 percent, or nearly one in five, of all exiting prisoners maxed out, having no obligation to report to a parole officer or abide by any other conditions of release. That is about 150,000 prisoners a year (or about the same number of total parole releasees in 1980).

An ironic situation has resulted from the public's desire for harsher, longer sentences and its dislike of parole. In sixteen states, governors elected on tough-on-crime platforms abolished discretionary parole. But even in the other states, the rate of release for inmates appearing before parole boards has been cut dramatically. In Massachusetts, for example, a state that still retains discretionary parole, 70 percent of state prisoners appearing before the parole board in 1990 were granted conditional supervised release, but by 1999, just 38 percent were paroled. Yet, these inmates were not kept in prison forever—they eventually maxed out and returned to the community without supervision. During these same nine years, Massachusetts reported that the number of prison releasees increased nearly 20 percent.

Unsupervised High-risk Releasees Jeopardize Public Safety. Inmates, anticipating that they will be denied parole, simply waive their right to a release hearing and max out instead. This is particularly true for high-risk inmates who presume they will not be judged eligible, and herein lies the irony. Massachusetts is seeing an increase in the number of high-risk inmates released directly from high-security prisons without the benefit of parole supervision. As a report by Community Resources for Justice wrote: "The joke is on us. . . . The very thing the public wants—community safety—is jeopardized when inmates are released without the supervision and support of parole."

This is happening in state after state: those who are released on parole supervision may be those who need it *least*, and those who are released unconditionally—*without* parole supervision—may need it *most*. Today, 60 percent of all inmates coming out of prison have not appeared before a parole board to have their readiness for release considered but have, instead, been released automatically at the end of a set prison term.

Some worry that prisoner reentry equates with prisoner recidivism and increases crime rates. As *Time* magazine reported in a cover story on prisoner reentry: "The looming fear is that their return—just at the time the country is fighting a recession and a war—will boost crime again, just as their incarceration helped bring it down." FBI statistics show that violent crime was up about 2 percent for the first six months of 2002, after having declined for the previous several years.

Already, crime increases in Boston, Chicago, and Los Angeles are being blamed on prisoner returns. When former Los Angeles Police Chief Bernard Parks was asked to explain the nearly 25 percent increase in Los Angeles' murder rates in 2002, he said: "Surely it is attributable to the fact that a wave of convicted offenders has recently hit the streets." Los Angeles receives 3,000 new parolees a month, nearly one-third of all those released in California.

What Does Parole Supervision Mean?

Prisoners who do not max out are released to parole supervision. But what does that mean for most inmates? Most of them will be given a bus ticket and told to report to the parole office in their home community on the next business day. If they live in a state that provides funds upon release (one-third of states do not), they will be given $25 to $200 in gate money.

Parolee Almost Solely Responsible for Transition Plan. Some states provide a new set of clothing at release, but these "extras" have declined over time. Sometimes a list of rental apartments or shelters is provided, but the arrangements are generally left up to the offender to determine where to reside and how to pay for basic essentials such as food, housing, and clothing during the first months—although a housing voucher for a few weeks at a local hotel or shelter may be provided. Employment is also mostly left up to the offender. Few prisons have transitional case managers to assist offenders, and the current process places the offender almost solely in charge of, and accountable for, his or her own transition plan.

Parolees Last in Line. Parole services have been hit as hard financially as prisons have—and perhaps even harder. Community treatment centers and social service agencies, which provide the majority of services, have been badly affected by the recession, and parolees find themselves at the end of long waiting lists. Parolees are also among the least desirable clients to treat from a social service agency perspective. They present higher risks to other clients, high dropout rates, complicated payment and eligibility arrangements, low motivation, and so forth.

High Abscond Rate. National statistics show that 10 percent of all state parolees who are required to report to parole offices after release fail to do so. They abscond supervision and their whereabouts remain unknown. In California, which supervises one out of five parolees nationwide, the abscond rate is a staggering 22 percent. Warrants are routinely issued for parole absconders, but scarce police and parole resources may mean that such warrants are given low priority.

Nearly 200,000 Unsupervised Releasees Each Year. So, if we add the number of absconders (about 44,000) to the number of releasees who were not required to report to parole in the first place (150,000), we have nearly 200,000 inmates coming out of prison each year who remain unsupervised or whose whereabouts are unknown on a daily basis—fully one-third of all exiting prisoners. Clearly, this should be a cause for public concern, particularly for the inner-city communities to which most ex-convicts return.

Reducing Services, Increasing Barriers

In addition to what is happening within the criminal justice system, a number of social policies have been enacted in recent years that, although not intended specifically to affect prisoners coming home, have had dramatic impacts on them. It is the intersection between these more broadly based social policies and prisoners coming home that makes prisoner reentry a more difficult issue today than in the past.

While corrections was reducing services to inmates behind bars and after release, Congress and many state legislatures were independently passing a number of laws and regulations that would *increase* the barriers to employment, welfare, and housing that inmates face after release. These new laws have remained largely unnoticed and undebated, but their effects are profound. The United States has passed dozens of laws since 1980 restricting the types of jobs for which ex-prisoners can be hired, easing the requirements for the termination of their parental rights, limiting their right to vote, and maybe most important, restricting their access to public welfare and housing subsidies. In the author's book *When Prisoners Come Home*, she has a chapter entitled "How We Help" followed by one on "How We Hinder" prisoner reintegration. It is safe to say that the "How We Hinder" chapter is much longer than the review of how we help.

Job Restrictions. Since 1985, the number of occupations from which ex-prisoners are barred has increased dramatically. The most commonly barred jobs are in the fields of childcare, education, security, nursing, and home heath care—exactly the jobs that labor economists say are growing the fastest. Moreover, more jobs are unionized, and some unions flatly exclude ex-convicts. Further obstacles are presented by the licensing requirements applied to many jobs. Nearly 6,000 occupations are licensed in the United States—including cutting hair and collecting garbage.

In-prison Training for Jobs Denied Offenders. It is also important to remember all of these barriers when we question the relationship between in-prison work programs and post-prison employment. Many prison job-training programs are training prisoners for jobs on the outside for which they are ineligible. And even if they can *legally* qualify for some jobs, a recent employer survey in five major U.S. cities for unskilled jobs found that roughly 65 percent of all employers would not knowingly hire an ex-offender (regardless of the offense), and between 30 percent and 40 percent actually checked the criminal history records of their most recently hired employees. So, the number of jobs for ex-convicts has declined.

Exclusion from Public Assistance and Housing Vouchers. Congress has also excluded certain offenders from receiving public assistance and housing vouchers. This is critically important. The 1994 Welfare Reform Act eliminated tens of thousands of former offenders from welfare eligibility. One provision of the law requires that states *permanently* bar individuals with drug-related felony convictions from receiving funded public assistance and food stamps during their lifetime. This applies to all individuals convicted of a drug felony after August 22, 1996. The effect of this law on women and their children is particularly severe, because women constitute the most rapidly growing segment of the U.S. prison population (the majority are serving a sentence for a drug crime), and 65 percent of them have children.

Loss of Voting Rights. There has been a great deal of publicity about the fact that once convicted of a felony, convicts in most states are barred from voting. Only Maine and Vermont impose no restrictions, and ten states permanently deny convicted felons the right to vote after a single felony conviction. Disfranchising felons for life is a custom unheard of in other democratic countries. Recent analysis suggests that if just 15 percent of the nearly 900,000 disfranchised felons in Florida—those unable to vote as a result of a felony conviction—had participated in the last presidential election, Albert Gore would have prevailed in Florida and President Bush would not have been elected.

Expanded Public Access to Criminal Records

The expansion of legal barriers has been accompanied by an increase in the ease of checking criminal records by means of new technologies and expanded public access to criminal records through the Internet.

Historically, criminal records were restricted to law enforcement and those with a "need to know." Today, those restrictions have been lifted and, for all practical purposes, one's criminal past is public. In twenty-nine states, anyone can obtain at least some type of criminal record information on anyone he or she wishes. In twenty-five states, that information can be publicly accessed through the Internet.

Fifty-nine Million Americans with Criminal Arrest Records Affected. Expanded restrictions now apply to a greater percentage of the U.S. population simply because the number of people convicted and imprisoned over the past decade has exploded. The Department of Justice reports that more than 59 million Americans have a criminal arrest record on file with state repositories—that is, 29 percent of the nation's *entire* adult population—and that the number of records has more than doubled during the last decade.

Thirteen Million Ex-felons. Further, researchers estimate that more than 13 million Americans are ex-felons, that is, they had been convicted of a felony and served or are currently serving a felony probation, parole, prison, or jail sentence. This equals 6 percent of the entire adult population, 11 percent of the adult male population, and an astounding 37 percent of the adult black male population.

Weighing the Benefits and Costs. Of course, it is undeniable that greater public access to criminal records enhances public safety and feelings of safety, and that protecting our children and vulnerable adults from ex-convicts who might work with them, and ultimately exploit them, makes perfect sense. But we have to weigh those benefits against the number of lives disrupted and the families and communities—especially minority communities—that are affected.

Target Policies to Offenders Representing Serious Threats

Ideally we should target these policies specifically to those offenders who represent serious threats. The neighbor who wants to know if a sex offender lives nearby, the school district that does not want to hire a convicted felon, the gun dealer who wants to avoid selling guns to a felon, and so forth. There are many violent and chronic inmates coming out of prison today, and we need to use all available means to monitor them at release. But today, these policies are applied equally to offenders representing very different risks.

Many First-time Offenders Labeled for Life. As we have expanded the numbers of people and types of crimes for which individuals are sentenced to prison, more first-time drug offenders have these restrictions applied to them—often for life. These people, who would not have gone to prison just twenty years ago, and who would not go to prison in other countries, are now forever labeled as ex-convicts. Once someone's record gets on the Internet, there is no pulling it back.

We are sending people to prison in greater numbers, and we now have the technology to assure that the ex-con label follows them for life. Once that label is applied, the chances of getting a job, securing housing, or developing solid social relationships—the very things we know help offenders succeed—is severely limited. Our policies may well threaten the very society their imprisonment was meant to protect.

Index of States' Felon Exclusion Policies. In *When Prisoners Come Home*, the author created an index that ranks each state on its felon exclusion policies, taking into account its laws regarding the sharing of criminal records, felon voter disfranchisement, and convict eligibility for welfare, food stamps, and public housing. States differ significantly in these policies. Felons face the most exclusionary policies in the South and in Texas, although Arizona, Kansas, and Nebraska also scored in the highest categories. States that were more inclusive, in that they continued to provide welfare and housing subsidies to convicted felons and did not post criminal records on the Internet, were in the northeast section of the nation, but Indiana, Ohio, Oregon, and Utah were also included in this category. California lies near the national average.

More Inclusive States Appear to Have Higher Levels of Civic Engagement and Social Trust. It is not clear what causes states to have such different policies, but social historians have found higher levels of civic engagement and social trust in these more inclusive states as well. What is more important for our interest in prisoner reentry is: what difference do these polices make, and how do they enhance or impede an inmate's chances of remaining crime-free? That is a critical but unanswered question.

Rising Rates of Recidivism

It is not surprising that most prisoners do not succeed. In June 2002, the Bureau of Justice released the most comprehensive study ever conducted of prisoner recidivism. The study tracked 300,000 prisoners released in 1994 in fifteen states. They found that 30 percent, or nearly one in three, released prisoners are rearrested in the first six months, 44 percent within the first year, and 67 percent within three years of release from prison.

Comparing these recidivism rates with a nearly identical study conducted in 1983 reveals some disturbing trends:

Overall, rearrest rates increased slightly (about 5 percent).
The time to first rearrest was shorter.
The overall percentage of serious crime arrests attributable to ex-prisoners had increased.

Ex-convicts appear to be doing less well than their counterparts released a decade ago. No one working in the system believes that the current prison and parole system is working. Of course, it is much easier to document that a problem exists than to figure out what should be done to fix it.

Addressing the Problem

Prisoner reentry is a complex and multifaceted problem. It involves tackling some of the central issues in crime policy—sentencing, prisons, and parole practices. It also requires us to revisit the effectiveness of treatment programs and the government's responsibility in helping convicts and ex-convicts acquire new living and work skills.

Who Should Operate Assistance Programs? If we decide to assist the six to seven million convicts coming home over the next decade, we must also rethink which agencies should be involved. Some question whether parole officers, given their current law enforcement stance, can operate "helping" programs. Perhaps other social service agencies, or even the courts, should be more involved in delivering and monitoring rehabilitation.

At an even broader level, some ask whether state-initiated crime policies—or any of their programs—can remedy what is criminogenic in urban communities. Perhaps nonprofit organizations, inmate self-help groups, and faith-based programs hold the key to successful reentry? These are all good questions, and we need to debate them.

Recent Funding for Reentry Programs. Of course, there has been a flurry of interest in prisoner reentry since the Department of Justice gave $100 million in 2000—$2 million to each state—for reentry programs. The Department of Justice is also supporting the Reentry Partnership Initiative and the Reentry Courts Initiative. Maryland, Ohio, Pennsylvania, and Washington have revised their approaches to offender reentry. All have developed new risk assessment instruments that tie prison programs with postrelease risks and needs

Everyone Wants Successful, Safe Reentry. The newfound focus on prisoner reentry is encouraging, and it may be just what the nation needs to bring balance back to a corrections system that has become too punitive. Reentry could serve as an "elevating goal" for corrections, because regardless of one's political preferences about who should go to prison or how long they should serve, they all return home. There is therefore a zone of consensus around the reentry issue that may provide unique opportunities.

Remember the Intensive Supervision Probation Programs. At the same time, however, caution should be exercised and the lessons of the past remembered. One should remember the "intermediate sanctions movement" of the 1980s and 1990s. The federal government provided financial incentives to develop intensive supervision probation (ISP) programs, and within a few years, hundreds of local programs emerged across the nation. Despite good intentions to deliver more effective programs, the dollars were insufficient to fund social services and were used instead to fund more surveillance, such as drug testing and electronic monitoring. In the end, the intensive supervision probation programs, which were supposed to reduce recidivism through more effective rehabilitation, simply identified the failures more quickly and revoked greater numbers of them to custody.

We have a history of implementing programs that are initially designed to help offenders but, instead, result in harsher treatment. A similar scenario could befall prison reentry initiatives. Yet, this author believes that we are wiser today and more skeptical of quick fixes, and that there is much promise in the reentry initiatives she is seeing.

What To Do? Reforming Prisoner and Reentry Practices

In *When Prisoners Come Home*, the author made twelve major policy recommendations. Four of them are here.

Reinvest in Prison Work, Education, and Substance Abuse Programs. First, we must reinvest in prison work, education, and substance abuse programs. We simply cannot reduce recidivism without funding programs that open up more substance abuse treatment and work programs for ex-convicts. We can all agree that treatment programs can reduce crime—not in every case, not for every person, and not for every program, but we can no longer say, "nothing works." Today, there is ample evidence that treatment programs can reduce recidivism if the programs are well designed, well implemented, and targeted appropriately.

In this case, the devil is not in the principle, but in the details. Ironically, just as research evidence was building that certain rehabilitation programs do reduce recidivism, state-strapped corrections departments had to dismantle those very programs in response to budget constraints. Effective programs include:

> Therapeutic communities for drug addicts
> Substance abuse programs with aftercare for alcoholics and drug addicts
> Cognitive-behavioral programs for sex offenders
> Adult vocational education and prison industries for the general prison population

Each of these programs has been shown to reduce the recidivism rates of program participants by 8 percent to 15 percent. Even with these relatively modest reductions in subsequent recidivism, these programs pay for themselves in terms of reducing future justice expenditures. For example, prisoners who participate in vocational education programs have about a 13 percent lower likelihood of recidivism, and the programs cost about $2,000 per participant per year. Analysts have estimated that such programs result in an average $12,000 savings per participant in future-saved criminal justice expenditures. Similar cost savings accrue for the other proven correctional programs. It is thus highly likely that investing in selected rehabilitation programs generates several dollars' worth of benefits for every dollar spent. In addition, the more important social benefits of reduced recidivism cannot be measured in economic terms. There is no longer any reasonable justification for not funding proven rehabilitation programs.

Reinstate Discretionary Parole in States that Have Abolished It. Second, we should reinstate discretionary parole in the sixteen states that have abolished it and reverse the trend toward automatic mandatory release in the states that are moving in that direction. Abolishing parole was a politically expedient way to appease the public, which wrongly equated parole with letting inmates out early. But the public was misinformed when it judged parole to be lenient. On the contrary, recent research shows that inmates who are released through discretionary parole actually serve *longer* prison terms, on average, than those released mandatorily, and the difference is most pronounced for violent offenders. Prisoners released by a discretionary parole board also have higher success rates. Both of these results hold true even after statistically controlling for crime type, prior criminal history, and other demographics.

These data suggest that having to earn and demonstrate readiness for release, and being supervised postprison, may have some deterrent or rehabilitative benefits—particularly for the most dangerous offenders. Discretionary parole systems also provide a means by which inmates who represent continuing public safety risks can be kept in prison. And discretionary parole serves to refocus prison staff and corrections budgets on planning for release—not just opening the door at release.

No one would argue for returning to the unfettered discretion that resulted in unwarranted sentence disparities among offenders, but we have "thrown the baby out with the bath water." We should be using inmate risk assessments and parole guidelines to structure and control discretion, not eliminate it.

In the long run, no one is more dangerous than a criminal who has no incentive to straighten himself out while in prison, and who returns to society without a structured and supervised release plan. As ironic as it may seem, it is in the interests of public safety that discretionary parole systems should be reinstituted. We must get that message to the public.

Front-load Postprison Services during the First Six Months after Release. Third, we must front-load postprison services during the first six months after release. Recidivism data show that return to crime happens very quickly—30 percent of all released prisoners are rearrested for a serious crime within the first six months. By contrast, recidivism declines dramatically after three years, and after five years of arrest-free behavior, recidivism is extremely low. These data suggest that the first three to six months after release are critical to success, and we should concentrate our limited resources on that time period. At the same time, parole terms of longer than five years, for all but the most serious offenders, should be eliminated for parolees who have remained arrest free during that time. As logical as this sounds, parole services are not currently organized this way in most states. Parole terms commonly last three to five years—and even longer in some states. (However, life parole terms for predatory sex offenders may well be justified.)

Ideally, all inmates who have spent a considerable amount of time incarcerated (say, more than two years) would transition to a halfway house or day-reporting center. During the critical first six months, these agencies would work to coordinate surveillance, drug testing and treatment, job training and placement, health and mental health services, family services and transitional housing.

It makes no sense to spend $23,000 a year on an inmate—even three times that amount if he or she was in maximum security—and then on the day of release, spend from zero dollars (for unconditional releases) to about $2,500 a year—most of which is used to pay parole staff. Little of it pays for direct services such as housing, medical attention, and drug treatment, although ex-convicts often consume significant public dollars when they show up at homeless shelters, get rearrested, or access benefits and social services.

What if we were to spend the same amount of money per month during the first three months after release as we do for the three months prior to release? This would cost about $7,000 for every prisoner returning home, roughly the same as we spend for the entire period of parole supervision. But let's front-load this expenditure to the first three months back in the community. This money would support transitional housing, if needed, employment if no other job could be found, drug treatment, medical attention, family counseling—in short, whatever was required to increase the odds of successful transition.

In *When Prisoners Come Home*, the author also recommend a "goal parole" system, in which work, education, and treatment incentives are built into the system and parolees can earn time off their parole term by succeeding in prosocial activities. Again, there is little public risk, and much to gain, from the *informal* social controls—those interpersonal bonds that link ex-inmates to churches, law-abiding neighbors, families, and communities. These informal social bonds are the strongest predictors of ultimate desistance from crime.

Establish a U.S. "Rehabilitation of Offenders Act." Fourth, we must establish procedures by which some offenders can put their criminal offending entirely in the past. The United States has the highest incarceration rate of industrial democracies, and yet unlike all other democracies, we have virtually no practical means of sealing or expunging adult criminal records. A criminal conviction—no matter how trivial or how long ago it occurred—scars one for life. In terms of this issue, we have the worst of both worlds: higher conviction and imprisonment rates, combined with no legal way to move beyond their stigmatizing effects.

The author recommends we consider adopting something similar to England's "Rehabilitation of Offenders Act," which allows some criminal convictions to become "spent" or ignored after a period of time has elapsed from the date of conviction, if no felony convictions occur during this time. The rehabilitation period varies depending on the sentence imposed, and convictions receiving a prison sentence of more than two and a half years can never become spent.

For example, a first-time burglary conviction, which might result in a one-year prison sentence, would qualify. If an adult were given that one-year prison sentence and then remained conviction free for ten years, the original conviction would be considered "spent" or legally ignored in future matters, such as employment. Those former offenders who meet this criterion are allowed by law to answer "no" when asked: "Have you ever been convicted of a crime?" England's act is actually more stringent than those of most other countries, where all criminal offenses become spent after specified time periods.

To be sure, there are valid reasons for wanting to know the criminal backgrounds of persons with whom we come in contact; a prior criminal record is a strong predictor of future criminality. But there are ways to protect the public from those criminals who wish to continue committing crime, while not allowing those same procedures to prevent criminals who wish to go straight, from doing so. Establishing procedures to seal some adult criminal convictions seems especially urgent now, as public access to criminals' records is becoming more widespread via the Internet. Current legal barriers and prohibitions are simply overly broad.

Again, there are few public safety risks in such a scheme, given that so few prisoners return to crime after seven to ten years of crime-free living. Yet, the benefits may be quite large, as a greater number of ex-convicts are able to find stable housing, meaningful employment, and support their children. Those persons who establish a stake in the welfare of their community are also less likely to engage in illegal activities that will bring harm to others.

Both *for* Prison and *for* Alternatives

The author does not consider herself a liberal on crime policy, but rather a moderate. She believes that many of those in prison should remain there—we need to remember that half of those now in prison have been convicted of violent crime, and these people need to be removed from society. We often become polarized in our policy discussions by having to choose sides—either *for* prison or *for* alternatives. She is *for* both, depending on the seriousness of the offense and the risks the offender represents.

Those who say that *most* prisoners are nonserious, nonviolent "light-weights" and should be released are just as wrong as those who say that all prisoners are vicious predators. There are significant numbers of prisoners in each of those categories, and recognizing that and finely tailoring sentencing and corrections programs to those subpopulations is critical to effective sentencing and reentry policy. This more honest message is also more likely to garner public and political support.

The author believes the reforms she suggests will help get us to a more finely tailored system—in which those who are dangerous will remain in prison—through discretionary decision making—and those who are not, will self-select themselves out of surveillance and services through programs in prison and activities on the outside. Our policies should not continue to impede—*for a lifetime*—the efforts of those who wish to go straight but are often prevented from doing so because we put up barriers that none of us would be able to overcome.

We face enormous challenges in managing the reintegration of increasing numbers of prisoners, but we have to focus our attention on prisoners coming home, not because it will be good for them, which it will be, but because it will ultimately be good for their children, their neighbors, and the community at large.

Revisiting Responsivity: Organizational Change to Embrace Evidence-Based Principles and Practices

7

Frank J. Porporino, Ph.D.
T3 Associates, Inc.
Ottawa, Ontario, Canada

Introduction

Trends in criminal justice and corrections should not follow prevailing social-political rhetoric. The field is inevitably more pulled than driven when this is the case, prone to endorsing correctional "quackery" more than working towards true professionalism (Latessa, Cullen, and Gendreau, 2002). Corrections clearly should not be comfortable in behaving "iatrogenically," a medical term referring to the kind of disease created in the process of treating the disease. Pursuing evidence-based practice in working with offenders (Chapman and Hough, 1998), what has come to be termed doing "what works," should be the singular preoccupation of our field, not the luxury or good fortune of a few who have the resources or the expertise to embrace it. Instead, it should be the defining feature of every correctional agency. In probation and parole, what works should matter even more critically, since what is or *is not* done with offenders in the community context can put public safety at risk quite immediately and very tragically (Rhine, 2001).

Doing what works, and not tolerating what doesn't work, should be the defining feature of our field. But despite a compelling, supporting base of theory and an impressive range of evidence that has been integrated and documented repeatedly (Andrews and Bonta, 1998; Blackburn, 1993; Hollin, 2001; McGuire, 1995; Sherman et al., 1997), few would suggest that what works has become the defining quality of the field, or even that it is the quality to which the field generally and decidedly aspires.

Most correctional agencies in the past decade have struggled in implementing and sustaining any notable and broad-based change towards what works. Immersion in evidence-based practice still remains something that we know more about in the abstract than in the concrete.[1] And what works is stalled in some other important respects, even in those jurisdictions that are attempting to pursue it with vigor.

Widespread implementation of evidence-based programs increasingly seems to end with "impotency" of impact, a not so impressive demonstrable reduction in the likelihood of reoffending. The *Times* newspaper in England and Wales recently reported the findings of a large-scale Home Office research study with the humorous headline "I Think . . . Therefore I'm Still a Criminal" intended to poke fun at the fact that what was supposed to be the programmatic approach of choice in working with offenders, teaching offenders new "thinking skills." This approach conceived originally in Canada, but now used internationally in many countries, an approach with an impeccable pedigree within the social learning and cognitive-behavioral movements in psychology (Porporino and Fabiano, 1999), was evaluated with very large samples in United Kingdom prisons over the last several years and found to make absolutely "no difference" on reoffending rates (Falshaw et al., 2003).

There have been similar disappointing findings from other studies. For example, in a study out of the University of Cincinnati, a statewide implementation of cognitive-skills programming within the Georgia Board of Pardons and Parole was found to have very little impact on rates of reoffending, and especially striking, no impact for an African-American population, which happened to constitute about 70 percent of their caseload (Van Voorhis et al., 2003).

It has been suggested that in contrast to smaller-scale implementations that can be well controlled and defined, larger-scale, system-level implementation initiatives risk diluting program integrity (in other words, programs are not delivered as they were intended). The inevitable consequence will be less impact (Lipsey et al., 2001; Wilson et al., 2000). This may be the case to some degree, and it is certainly possible that attention to detail and quality dissipates as one moves from the enthusiasm of introducing something new to the effort of sustaining and maintaining it. Possible yes, but should this really happen with a good idea? Shouldn't evidence-based practice be self-reinforcing? If it works, and we can see that it works, shouldn't we want to keep doing it, and keep doing it better?

If a what-works approach only can demonstrate results on the small scale, can it truly become the "defining quality" of the field? Obviously, we need documented evidence that it can work systemically, not just in pockets. The motive for pursuing what works should not be simply altruistic in nature, because it is the right moral thing to do. A business case needs to be mounted for why what works should be the standard mode of operation in our business. In the end, nothing short of showing clear impact on offending behavior will count (Paparozzi, 2003).

It is striking that after more than two decades of determined accumulation of an empirical "bibliotherapy for cynics" (Gendreau and Ross, 1980), what works continues to be ideologically challenged.

Changing offenders through "intervention" is still strongly rejected within the ideology of the right, since, of course, despite indisputable evidence to the contrary, there is a commonsense belief (Gendreau et al., 2002) that reductions in reoffending are best assured through other means. The correctional mandate, it is argued, should be limited to (Logan, 1993):

> Keeping prisoners . . . to keep them in, keep them safe, keep
> them in line, keep them healthy, and keep them busy—and to
> do it with fairness, without undue suffering, and as efficiently
> as possible.

Indeed, the right would crystallize their wisdom about what is wrong with our business by suggesting that we should simply learn to "Condemn a little more and understand a little less" (Michael Howard; John Majors' Conservative Government Home Secretary, England and Wales).

We have had to become accustomed to managing this kind of tenacious philosophy of correctional purpose.

And as what works has become more legitimate, officially endorsed, and formalized by correctional agencies in one country after another, the ideology of the left has interestingly aligned with that of the right in also rejecting the aims of intervention with offenders . . . for different underlying reasoning, of course, but strong rejection nonetheless.

Here are a few of the key points from the critical voice of the intelligent left:

1. What works has too readily promoted overgeneralization from mostly white, male-based models and evidence as if these had any valid implications whatsoever across, for example, gender and/or culture and race.

2. As we have refined our technologies for assessing offender needs, have we not also transformed the notion of need into the "label" of risk?

3. In the delivery of cognitive interventions to severely marginalized groups, are we in the end doing anything more than aiming to pacify, simply trying to teach these individuals to learn "to rationally cope with their own oppression"?

4. And does not delivery of programs in effect "responsibilize" offenders, a notion out of feminist criminology (Carlen, 2002) to refer to how corrections does their little part by delivering the "program," and if the offender does not respond, then we can feel justified in holding the offender even more responsible . . . we "responsibilize" them.

There is some validity in each of these criticisms, and especially (as we will elaborate later), when doing what works deteriorates into something considerably less than what it was supposed to be.

We can conclude that what works has not gained any significant degree of support from the pragmatic "right" who are looking for simple evidence of an investment payback. At the same time, it seems to have managed to create a serious dissonance with the morally and ethically sensitive left, who see correctional efforts to change offenders as misplaced. Despite an incredibly rich knowledge base as grounding, the what works movement has neither translated well into systemic practice, shown clear and replicable impact on a large scale, nor has it been able to win many allies from the ideological spectrums of the right or the left.

This paper tries to come to grips with the apparent implementation "glass-ceiling" to what works, a prevailing phenomenon where key elements of the approach are introduced by an agency or jurisdiction, but the full potential in terms of broad-based systemic change and impact is never realized.

This paper elaborates on the notion that the key struggle in the implementation of what works may be rooted in the failure of correctional agencies, and the managers in those agencies, to come to grips with the fundamental issue of "responsivity"—how to introduce, and incrementally develop, the methods and processes that constitute what works in a manner that engages and mobilizes staff to deliver the services correctly, and motivates offenders to benefit from them optimally.

Implementation failure, it will be argued, is occurring primarily because of a basic misconceptualization of what is implied in pursuing evidence-based practice. The paper tries to hone in on what the idea of doing what works was "supposed to mean" and how, unfortunately and increasingly, it seems to have "come to mean" something else. A reframing of what works along an overriding "responsivity" perspective is presented wherein it is suggested that "responsivity," as usually understood, has been defined too narrowly as part of the tradition of looking at what works as a set of techniques and methods to apply in "fixing" offenders. But what works has to begin to be seen as much more than a set of useful techniques or a menu of programs. It needs to be more clearly articulated and refined as an integrated process for developing both organizational and offender "responsivity."

Accounting for Implementation Failure

Implementation of what works has not been studied methodically as a process of change in organizational direction and arrangements, practitioner culture, and service delivery systems to offenders. It certainly has not been studied in terms of how all of these can interact toward success or failure. There is a lacuna of documented evidence about what can go wrong, how, why, and when in attempting to unfold what works, either in a small agency or a whole jurisdiction. Some thoughtful historical accounting of the origins of a what works focus in a particular jurisdiction has been provided (Vanstone, 2000), and there are some interesting anecdotal descriptions of what can spur an agency toward the approach and the early pitfalls that can be encountered (Knott, 1995). But the stages or phases of implementing a what works agenda clearly deserve more systematic analysis so that we can understand both implementation obstacles and strategies for overcoming them.

Discussion of implementation is beginning to receive the attention it deserves, however, and at least at a very basic level, there seems to be agreement on a few points (Gendreau, Goggin, and Smith, 1999, 2001; Harris and Smith, 1996; Leschied, Bernfeld, and Farrington, 2001).

> Enthusiasm is not enough. It will not last. There is an overarching need for a master plan to reorient the workings of the agency and the "professionalism" of staff with an enduring sense of purpose.
>
> There are no magic bullet programs that work effortlessly. Good programs and good services for offenders require effort to get right.
>
> The "Maytag" philosophy does not apply. You cannot implement any facet of what works and then leave it alone to fend for itself.
>
> What works is not doable in piecemeal, grab-bag or fast and easy fashion.

At the core, there is a need to ask whether implementation of what works is being underpinned by the pursuit of "quality." Or, is it being undermined from the start, jostled and challenged persistently by the imperatives of a more-for-less culture? Implementation compromises and shortcuts may seem to be driven by resource realities in the short-term. But, since implementation of what works is fragile, it can be derailed easily if we create:

1. Staff resistance in circumstances where they feel:
   unskilled (or de-skilled relative to what they were doing previously)
   unsupported in what they are doing
   unrewarded for how well they are doing it

2. Sloppiness in program delivery rooted in:
   time pressures and conflicting demands
   lack of adequate training and/or supervision
   ignoring the professional inclination toward tampering ("adjusting" and "adapting")

The end result of this strategy of good initial intentions but with limited follow-through is the following:

inconsistent application of program models
a burst of activity followed by inertia and lessened momentum
high program-attrition rates leading to labeling of the program as "too long," "too difficult," or "too structured and inflexible" (by staff and/or inmates)

The ultimate cost to the organization is the following:

wasted training dollars
lack of penetration of any programming model
staff turnover and/or disengagement and loss of trust in the organization that may be doubly difficult to rekindle in the future

What Works: Two Interpretations

What works, at the end of the day, is about insisting on following all of the evidence or, at least, following as much of the best evidence that we may have at hand. Agencies that only test the waters with what works methods will not sustain them. Introducing a risk/needs instrument and purchasing a program or two will not plateau them into evidence-based practice. In many instances, when implementation failure has to be contended with, it can lead to a discouraging backlash, even among those staff who initially may have subscribed to the philosophy (Palmer, 1992).

What works was supposed to be about what we know regarding the onset, persistence, and desistance of criminal conduct: how it starts, why it continues, and what makes it stop (Clarke and Cornish, 1985; Farrington, 1995, 1997; Sampson and Laub, 1993; Zamble and Quinsey, 1997). This evidence we speak about tries to clarify how some individuals, with a particular mix of dispositional traits, exposed to a complex interplay of circumstances and experiences, can be propelled toward rejecting conventional norms and developing antisocial sentiments that underpin antisocial lifestyles.

The basis of what works is what we know regarding how individuals "change" in this fashion toward adopting criminal and antisocial orientations to living. Translated into practice, it is about how we can take this knowledge and learn to ask what we could we do to be more successful in influencing change in these individuals in the other direction.

And this type of change does occur. Here is some "consumer feedback" from an offender who participated in one of our short reentry programs in the United Kingdom, suggesting rather poignantly that some change has occurred: "I've known for a long time that my life was shit . . . but until I took this program, I always thought it was all just because of bad luck."

It is this type of fundamental shift in "thinking" that what works should aspire to help engender. It is what sociologically oriented ethnographic criminologists like Maruna (2000) in his Liverpool Desistance Study have termed "narratives of desistance," or helping offenders arrive at different accounts or understandings of their situation and the possible responses, options, and strategies to alter it.

What works was supposed to be about how we could bring our knowledge of crime and criminality to bear in developing an effective "process" of service delivery for offenders that could help activate, accelerate, and solidify this sort of change. The operative notion being "process," implying some type of interaction with individuals over the course of time, with multiple components, that work together to influence change.

It is not the one thing that we can do to offenders that will change them, nor the one program or intervention we can deliver. It is how offenders end up reacting, and the resources and capabilities they believe they might have acquired, after they experience all of the things we do to them that might help them change.

But what works seems, unfortunately, to have been simplified and distorted into something else, an easy formula for correcting the "thinking and behaving" of offenders, or what we can refer to as a "Fix the Offender" misconceptualization, seeing what works as simply the application of a set of methods or techniques to fix offenders.

This kind of "fix them" orientation to what works, which creeps into practice relatively easily, is more about efficient processing of offenders while imposing or mandating change to happen. It seems to degenerate too commonly into:

> risk/needs assessment that gets overly preoccupied with identifying and targeting offender "deficits" and/or problem areas and ignores strengths and/or protective factors
>
> treatment planning that, in theory, should revolve around streaming offenders into "services" that address their dynamic needs but that, in reality, allocates them into those programs that are available to do it
>
> program design that tries to develop the "right stuff" (cognitive-behavioral) to fix offenders efficiently, preferably in ways that

are flexible enough to accommodate agency constraints (for example, continuous entry, ease of delivery, shorter, not too onerous training requirements)

program delivery that becomes frustrated with offender "non-compliance" and "uncooperativeness" and turns its focus to the amenable few, while demanding/waiting for some evidence of motivation from the typical many

We could be generous in calling this a "process" for influencing change, but from the offender's point of view, it is typically seen as our way of managing them with determined effort to slot them as square pegs through our round program holes.

This author knows of one jurisdiction that has quickly evolved their new intake risk/needs assessment process into a computerized program scheduling or "booking" routine. Offenders are booked (in other words, a space is reserved) to participate in a specified program, in a particular setting during a given quarter of their sentence. It is unclear how appropriate sequencing of programming is arrived at, but undoubtedly it has more to do with availability of program space than any thoughtful treatment planning. And whatever circumstances, crises, or issues the offenders may be contending with when their "program reservation" comes due is really irrelevant, since their time has come.

In theory, dynamic risk factors have been conceptualized as interrelated and interactive—impinging on each other. But, in practice, we segment them into broad areas or "domains," and some sort of intervention is seen as necessary to tackle or eliminate each, one by one. We know that the more of these dynamic factors that are present, the greater the risk of offending, but does this mean that each dynamic factor has to be "programmed out" of the offenders and that we should sequence or "stack" program upon program without consideration of the offenders' sense of continuity, integration, or consolidation of their personal change experience?

It is relatively easy to take impulsive, angry, substance-abusing offenders who have had several DUIs (Driving Under the Influence) and some history of perpetrating domestic violence and suggest they take cognitive skills plus anger management, a substance abuse program, a drunk driving program, and a domestic violence program for good measure. In jurisdictions that are fortunate enough to be program rich, this is what actually can occur. In a large-scale evaluation of cognitive-behavioral treatment for substance abusers within the Correctional Service of Canada, average offenders completed 6.4 institutional or community programs during their sentence (Porporino et al., 2002). More likely in most jurisdictions, though, regardless of how many dynamic risk domains are identified, one intervention or two might be delivered. The key question is whether it will be the intervention that the offender could benefit from most or only *the* intervention that is available.

The effect of stacking or sequencing program interventions is relatively unexplored and needs to be taken much more seriously. In the substance abuse study referred to above, it was found that when a prison-based cognitive-behavioral intervention was followed through with a community "booster" type intervention, there was a statistically significant "additive" effect. But the additive effect occurred as well, and was actually even more pronounced, when offenders followed through on their prison-based cognitive-behavioral intervention with self-help AA/NA type support in the community.

What works has to progress to understanding how some interventions might serve as the "fulcrum" for change for some offenders where, together with some effective case managing of the offender and other supportive influences, continuity, integration and consolidation of change occurs and dynamic risk factors are impinged upon meaningfully. In particular, the potential for effective case managing to become the central active ingredient in the process will be addressed later in the paper.

The "Fix Them: What Works" type of program, of course, is an illusion, and when queried to reflect on how much programs can achieve in changing offenders, line staff clearly recognize what sort of tall order this entails. Here is some revealing data from Canada on staff attitudes about the effectiveness of programs. A quite comprehensive correctional strategy has been in place in Federal Corrections in Canada for over a decade, and there is no delusion that programs are a quick fix. Staff members at every rank across the prison service were asked the following question as part of a comprehensive all-staff survey: "Do you think the goal of reducing criminal behavior or recidivism with our correctional programming strategy can be achieved?" The findings were as follows:

1. Yes, generally quite possible   10 percent
2. Yes, but very hard in some cases   37 percent
3. Maybe, but very hard in most cases 35 percent
4. No, can't be achieved   15 percent
5. No opinion   3 percent

Some of the explanations were interesting to note. For example, 80 percent of staff thought that many offenders participated in programs only to manipulate the system rather than to improve themselves;

60 percent thought that waiting lists for programs were too long and this de-motivated them.

The important lesson to be drawn is that these are probably realistic attitudes that we are capturing. Line staff who work daily with offenders do not have a blanket rose-colored endorsement of what works as a fix-them strategy (Robinson et al., 1997). When implementation of any what works paradigm shows no real appreciation of this, when staff are led to believe (or we try to convince them) that programs can fix offenders, when they begin to judge that an agency is not acknowledging the difficulties that they encounter, when they see no truly coordinated or integrated strategy to help influence change in offenders in different encounters and interactions that they have with the agency, and when staff end up judging that an agency is only pretending to do what works, then implementation will unravel and fail.

The "Fix Them What Works" misconceptualization, in many ways, has seriously hampered the unfolding of true evidence-based practice in our field. This can be seen most obviously in the fact that there is still:

> only surface understanding of what really works and how or why
>
> a pervasive misconstruing and misplaced emphasis on good program delivery as dynamic delivery of content—as if this were all that was needed to assure program effectiveness
>
> an unrealized potential for examining different ways of targeting dynamic risk factors (other than through structured programs) and for highlighting the effective "case managing" of offenders as central to the process of influencing change

Each of these aspects of the problem will be taken up in turn in what follows. Underscoring the discussion is the point that the pitfalls of a fix them model only can be avoided if what works practice is embedded (anchored), generally and seamlessly, within motivational theory of change that acknowledges that offenders cannot be fixed that easily.

What Really Works and Why

At the crux of all the efforts that are made in corrections to influence offenders is the issue of "responsivity" (in other words, the lack of response to the services and/or programs that we deliver). Antisocial thinking maintains antisocial attitudes, and holding on to antisocial attitudes makes it easier, and considerably more likely, for individuals to continue to behave antisocially (Andrews and Bonta, 1998). Practitioners can relate to this conceptualization of the antisocial attitudes-antisocial behavior link very quickly. They experience it in their interactions with offenders every day, and in many ways. They are exposed persistently to the reality of the link and have to bear the brunt of dealing with the resistant, hard-to-budge, difficult-to-supervise, manipulative and/or disingenuous offender who continues to think antisocially, and eventually, despite our best correctional efforts, relapses or fails.

It is questionable whether the scope of service delivery that offenders can access, in and of itself, is at all consequential for them. What criminal justice practitioners have to learn to accept is that:

1. Effort toward change for offenders, as for people generally, does not occur without a self-perceived need for change.
2. Most offenders have not developed any well conceptualized (or very insightful) "case" for change.
3. Any approach that relies on persuading, convincing, shaming, confronting, or coercing will not work (even when it deceptively seems to be working in the short-term).

Motivational theory would argue, fundamentally, that meaningful take-up of services that can have some enduring impact on reoffending is unlikely unless, in all aspects of practice in how offenders are dealt with, there is an appreciation of how best to manage offenders' resistance and ambivalence concerning change (Fabiano and Porporino, 2003; McMurran, 2002).

Curiously, though it is acknowledged that change is difficult for most people in most situations, when applied to offenders, we seem to see it as something rather different—in many ways, as something that should be rather easy for offenders to do. Routinely, practitioners will express some degree of frustration (or puzzlement, confusion, or exasperation) at having to deal with so many offenders who "don't want to change" or "don't want to do anything to help themselves." It is as if there is an obvious reality that all offenders should be aware of—that change is something they must do and obviously need to do. It is naive to expect most offenders to see change as we do—as necessary and in their best interest.

For many criminal justice practitioners, motivation is another problem in the offender that they try to fix or do something about (and the quicker the better). Unfortunately, without any real awareness that it is occurring, this orientation towards motivation as something that must be "fixed" or "set right" can engender behaviors and approaches that are actually "antithetical" to what might be effective.

This "righting" reflex, as it has been referred to (Miller and Rollnick, 1992; 2002) puts in motion a series of responses from staff that are either subtly or quite blatantly directed toward "imposing" change on offenders. In turn, this only leads to increased resistance and the consequent labeling of individuals as either "in denial," "resistant," or "recalcitrant."

Those who have tried to master downhill skiing know that there is a quite natural reflex to lean backwards as we sense we may be loosing our balance. This, of course, only ensures that we fall. To learn not to fall means learning the not-so-natural reflex of leaning further forward.

This righting or "fix them" reflex seems to be the more natural reflex in working with offenders (possibly because there seem to be so many apparent aspects that need to be righted). But it leads to responses and all types of interactions that are actually counter to building any momentum toward change—interactions that are neither defusing nor reinforcing.

To be effective in influencing offenders to change their "thinking and behaving" means learning to react in ways that may not always "feel" or seem right to do in the moment—and that is what makes it so difficult.

Without an overarching motivational framework that strives to consistently manage offenders' resistance and ambivalence concerning change (not merely classifying it, assessing it, or labelling it), the interventions we deliver may go mostly for naught. All correctional staff—whether working individually in probation or parole or supervising offenders in prison living units—need to adopt an attitude, and a posture, a style of interaction, and a specific set of skills that can guide them consistently in dealing with offenders in a "motivationally focused manner." Importantly, they also need to be able to reconcile easily how working "motivationally" with offenders is neither inconsistent nor incompatible with the ultimate aims of using risk management and contributing to public safety.

Embedding what works in motivational theory is essentially about finding ways for developing a process (or processes) of effective service delivery for offenders, engaging them to take up our services because they think they need them and want them (because we have made them appealing). It is about inculcating the "motivating reflex" in every facet of work that the agency delivers in its contact with offenders.

Embedding what works in motivational theory implies that agencies should abandon the inclination to simply imitate or join the latest program bandwagon. The challenge of implementing what works means making steady effort toward true, thoughtful, integrated, and specific application.

What works methods can be easily borrowed or bought, but in developing a "process" for influencing change in offenders, there has to be a disciplined emphasis on continuity and consistency of service provision by the agency as a whole. What works should act as a guiding framework for assessing all of the component parts of this service delivery so that they mesh toward one fundamental aim—moving the offender gradually and methodically toward embracing change.

Agencies need to thoroughly examine and reexamine if, when, and how what they do with offenders is at all prone to the "fix them" reflex. Every process or method that is being misconstrued by offenders, and every intervention that is being misapplied or mistimed in a way that engenders resistance, needs to be corrected for what works to take shape.

We know from the addictions field, for example, that how useful or helpful offenders judge services to be is predictive of how much service they access, how often, and for how long they remain (Fiorentino et al., 1999). It is irrelevant how good we think our services are if offenders remain unconvinced. We all prefer choice, but with offenders, we seem to work to constrain it; yet, we nonetheless want their cooperation.

Now, of course, looking for ways to motivate offenders—to want to take programs or benefit from the services we can provide, participate in them fully, complete them, and follow-through on them with some further work—is not new. And motivational theory is certainly not new. But motivational concepts and approaches cannot be simply "tacked on" to what works practice; they have to be truly interwoven with it, and this is considerably more challenging. In particular, the implications of motivational theory have to be understood for:

1. how we can go about achieving greater levels of "responsivity" with structured interventions that are delivered to offenders
2. how "case managing" of offenders can become motivationally attuned to initiating, focussing, and maintaining change

What Is Effective Program Delivery?

What does it mean to say that program delivery, within a "fix them" perspective, is stuck on better ways of delivering content—rather than truly focusing on influencing change? Teaching "content" is all about how we think offenders *should* change and the skills we think they *should* learn. Following "process" is about helping offenders make the choice to change, providing them opportunity to gain insight, learn relevant new "thinking and behaving" skills, then begin to apply them successfully in their lives.

It should be recognized as axiomatic that structured, group-based, curriculum-guided programs will not stick, or help change anyone, unless there is mindful, motivationally attuned respect of individuals within the group process. Unfortunately, the factors that can contribute to "responsivity," the genuine engagement of offenders during program delivery, seems to have once again become too narrowly defined within a "fix them" conceptualization of what works.

The first facet of "responsivity" is the need to match the learning styles and personality of offenders to the intervention. This is primarily about program design and delivery methods and, narrowly defined, it has led to an obsession with making programs involving and entertaining for offenders, especially within the cognitive-behavioral framework, where every possible attempt is made to create stimulating, participatory exercises to teach various concepts and skills. In the extreme, this has led to, as examples:

> packing sessions as much as possible with activities from ice breaking to closing
>
> overloading with simplified explanations of too many concepts (with overuse of acronyms)
>
> setting the agenda (often with poor sequencing) and assuming that offenders are willing to move on to new concepts or learn new skills at our pace
>
> constantly questioning offenders, supposedly "Socratically" as a technique to engage, but oftentimes without any rhyme or reason at all (and in such a repetitive, staccato fashion that would undoubtedly enrage most of us)
>
> packaging "motivational enhancement" front pieces to programs to adequately "motivate" before programs are actually delivered
>
> perhaps most importantly, giving little if any time for offenders to reflect, for themselves, on the meaning and significance of what is being said

The second facet of "responsivity" calls for matching the qualities of the "intervenor" to the characteristics of offenders. There is no evidence-based matrix that has been derived in this respect and, other than the fact that individuals "intervening" with offenders should obviously have some capacity for social-perspective taking and clearly demonstrate as prosocial models (Andrews and Bonta, 1998; Paparozzi, 1994; Trotter, 2000), it is not at all clear what types of offenders respond best to what types of personal qualities in staff. Again, however, a rather narrow interpretation of "responsivity" in this respect seems to have led to the practice of selecting staff as program facilitators, often primarily on the basis that they are "dynamic and energetic" (regardless of whether they also might be overwhelming and anxiety-provoking for some offenders).[2]

The third aspect of "responsivity" relates to the matching of the skills of the "intervenor" to the type of program being delivered. Again in the extreme, and especially with structured programs requiring a facility for organized preparation and lesson planning, facilitators who may be less able to do this well in the beginning (for example, because of lack of certain types of educational experience) may never be given an opportunity (or the time) to ever learn to do it well (regardless of their other qualities or abilities in relating to offenders). Without support and supervision, discouragement sets in, and these facilitators drop out of the game.

If we put all of this together, a mistakenly narrow interpretation of "responsivity" leads to the conclusion that if programs are appropriately participatory, delivered with the right pace and energy, and with all of the content covered thoroughly, then offenders should be willing to receive what we have to give. We know otherwise, of course, and we know that despite all of these elementary "responsivity" issues that are attended to in some fashion, most facilitators delivering most programs continue to struggle and "wrestle" with offenders, instead of finding a way to "dance" with them smoothly and effortlessly.

Perhaps one of the most consistent findings in the what works literature is that program dropouts reoffend at a much higher rate than program "completers"—and even at a much higher rate than various matched comparison groups (Dowden and Serin, 2001; Porporino et al., 2002; Robinson, 1995; Van Voorhis, et al., 2003). The problem is so serious that it severely hampers any attempt at evaluating programs to find a true "treatment" effect (Gaes et al., 1999). Programs seem to do a very good job of streaming out the offenders who are not going to do so well. Even with relatively decent implementation of program models and fair attention to issues of program integrity, dropout rates of 30 to 50 percent have been reported in community-based programming initiatives (VanVoorhis et al., 2003; Roberts, 2003). Detailed analysis of the characteristics of these "dropouts" (and their justifications for dropping out, perceptions and/or reactions about the programs) is not at all common, but we know these offenders are typically the higher-risk, younger offenders (Robinson, 1995; Van Voorhis, 2003). Not surprisingly, they seem to be less motivated before the start of programming (Stewart and Millson, 1994). One somewhat more detailed study of this phenomenon of program dropouts in a probation service in the United Kingdom (Roberts, 2003) showed that these individuals were those with more practical obstacles in their lives, more entrenched criminal lifestyles, younger, more likely to have been breached or served custody in the past, had more criminal associates and fewer supportive influences, and were the most inadequate in problem-solving and communication skills. In other words, the offenders who dropped out of the programs seemed to be those who needed them the most.

Delivery of structured programs clearly should be geared to "engaging" the most likely to fail, finding ways to keep them at least modestly interested in the beginning, and more and more interested as the program unfolds so that whatever value the program might have for them has some opportunity to take root. It seems silly to allow our programs to be delivered in such a way that only the "good risks" survive.

What seems to lead to both less program attrition and better impact on reoffending outcomes is a facilitator's demeanor that shows sensitivity and understanding of the offender's perspective (without collusion), encourages active participation and rehearsal of previously learned skills and concepts, and keeps control (but not rigid authoritarian control) over the group process so that relevant material is covered (Van Voorhis, 2003). This is essentially good group work skills coupled with an awareness of how offenders will tend to react to and reject what is proposed to them in the program material (Porporino and Fabiano, 1999). It is not rocket science, but neither is it very common in correctional realities where facilitators become "program delivery machines."

Avoiding program drift and preserving treatment integrity is something the what works literature has attempted to hammer home repeatedly (Hollin, 1995; Palmer, 1992; Van Voorhis et al., 1995). Obviously, if the essence of what a program is trying do is not being done in delivery, if content is presented in a muddled and confusing way, if free-wheeling discussion is allowed, if facilitators substitute willy-nilly their own preferred material, exercises, and sequencing of content, and so forth, then the integrity of the program is clearly violated.

But, on the other hand, curriculum-based programs cannot be delivered to offenders in rigid, lock-step fashion. A "balance" of interpersonal interaction skills and content knowledge is required in delivering cognitive-behavioral interventions to offenders, where the program material always serves as the only the platform for engaging offenders to examine their "thinking and behaving." The content is not the message; making the content come alive in delivery is the message (Porporino and Fabiano, 1999; Tamans and Jurich, 2000).

We have incorporated motivational concepts in much of our recent training for group-work delivery and have found that practitioners repeatedly ask (and are desperate for answers) to these sorts of questions:

How do you avoid being "an expert" when teaching a session?

How do you balance getting all the content in a session covered while attending to the motivation of each participant?

Which should I do first—skill build or motivate?

How do I distinguish bored from unmotivated?

Why does motivation appear to change between sessions?

When this happens, what do I do? Am I starting all over again?

How can I tell whether the group members are really motivated or if they just want me to think they are?

How can I be motivational with someone who is using racist, sexist, or other discriminatory language or expressing strong antisocial sentiments? Isn't a prosocial modeling approach required?

How do I deal with other members of staff "crushing" any motivation I have created?

What does it look like when you have a successfully motivated group?

What does a "motivational" facilitator look like?

Andrews (2001) has recently differentiated a deeper level of responsivity that he refers to as specific: the delivery of a program taking into account the personality, motivational state, strengths, and various impinging personal characteristics of the offender (in other words, gender, age, ethnicity/race, language, and so forth that might function as barriers to successful completion).

There are some general responsivity features that apply to the delivery of programs to most offenders because of their particular learning styles. For many offenders:

experience makes it "meaningful" and "memorable"

>precise makes it clear
>concrete makes it easier
>elicited makes it personal
>relevance makes it possible—doable
>linked makes it purposeful—usable

But what needs to be added to this is the following:

>an alert and "mindful" tuning in to individuals within
>the group—guiding "in-the-moment" interactions with those
>individuals
>sensitivity to the "ebb and flow" of motivation and skill in how
>to respond
>steady out-of-the group monitoring and reinforcement to keep
>offenders on track

Resistance ignored during program delivery with offenders becomes apathy, disruption, and/or sabotage. Resistance attended to appropriately with some simple and well-timed motivational techniques can be turned into motivated engagement, for example, adopting a posture of "curious inquiry"; knowing when and how to raise doubt; recognizing when uncooperativeness is coming from low self-efficacy (lack of confidence in the ability to change some behavior) versus low motivation (attaching little importance and questioning the need to change) (Fabiano and Porporino, 1999).

An explicit (in other words, coherent, clear, and convincing) model of change that has been articulated by program designers should guide every intervention framework that is implemented as part of what works. The components of effective delivery are shown schematically in Figure 1 on the next page. This should allow for:

>staff to develop a depth of understanding of how to work with
>program material for successful intervention
>self-correcting in motivationally attuned delivery to happen
>over time
>supervision to be supportive (and effective in figuring out with
>what aspects staff may need assistance or help in fine tuning)

Ineffectiveness can creep into each component:

>in the initial design (by not properly elaborating and/or linking
>program content within a coherent model of change)

Figure 1

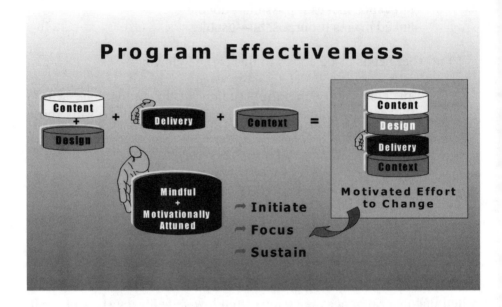

in delivery (by not learning to balance adherence to the program with a mindful, motivationally attuned style of interaction)

in context (by not creating conditions that can recognize, support, build upon, sustain, and reward program gains)

This last point is critical. We certainly should deliver programs in ways that are motivating, relevant, and absorbable by offenders, teaching skills systematically and methodically that are applicable and usable in changing behavior in their real lives.

But that still is not enough if we want to be truly serious about what works as a "process" for effective service delivery for offenders. Now, the only possible way to "pull together" our efforts for influencing change in offenders that might be enduring is through effective case managing of offenders that is motivationally astute, alert, and skilled.

Case Managing Offenders Toward Change

Within a what works paradigm, the case managing of offenders should be about something methodical and focused that is pursued to move the case toward "change"—change that results in a reduced risk of reoffending. Arguably, however, case managing of offenders is the Achilles' heel of the what works framework. It continues to be seen as something that needs to be and should be done well, but it is generally left unspecified as to what exactly this means in practice. Despite the considerable efforts that have been directed toward developing effective programs, no overarching framework has been provided for community workers to adopt in supporting, reinforcing, and building on the "change" process that these programs might initiate.

It needs to be acknowledged that many offenders do respond genuinely and positively to the assistance they might receive with community supervision. In motivational terms, though, it could be suggested that this is not necessarily because of the way they are case managed, but because they are already "in readiness" for change. Effective case management should be a much more powerful force. It should do more than simply pick up on preexisting readiness to change. It should awaken it, strengthen it, and support it, as necessary.

Too often, case management falls into the trap of "telling" offenders what they should be doing—even going so far as telling them how they should be doing it. For example, offenders should be looking for employment, should be getting assistance from a local employment agency, should stop giving excuses about lack of transportation (they can work on this later), and should settle for whatever job they can get, at least in the beginning. If an offender has participated in some cognitive-behavioral intervention, then they might be told as well that they should be "problem-solving" rather than rationalizing or justifying. Offenders who seem to be unwilling to take concrete action in dealing with risk factors and reentry issues, despite the fact that they may have participated in some intervention where they should have learned something, are seen as needing more intervention. Depending on the preferred natural style of the case manager, messages would be communicated to the offender in either a matter-of-fact (you should take responsibility) fashion, in a somewhat confronting (and possibly threatening) manner or, quite often, in a rather persuasive to and fro way where arguments are presented to the offenders for what they should do, and counter arguments are then judiciously introduced to keep convincing the offenders that their perspective is mistaken.

Examined from a motivational framework, this approach of "pushing" offenders toward action that is good for them—be it by encouraging taking responsibility for their future, benevolently confronting, or by cajoling, persuading and convincing—typically has but one outcome. It engenders "resistance" that leads to a tug of war with the offender that the case manager inevitably loses in the short term (but where the offender loses much more considerably in the longer term). Some offenders will boldly defy the case manager, others will keep them at bay with excuses for their limited efforts, while still others will seem to be doing what they can but knowing all along that it is only limited effort being expended simply because it is preferable to the alternative (in other words, a possible noncompliance of a probation order or other condition). What is missing in all of this is finding ways to arouse and channel the offender's own commitment to change.

Case managing offenders in a motivationally attuned manner implies, first and foremost, that we listen to their perspective, and not try to impose our own from the outset. We listen to this perspective—not to accept it or to "empathize" with it—but to understand it so that we can reflect it back, if and as necessary. We listen first to assess where the offenders are positioned and how much acknowledgment of problems they have developed. We listen as well for types of concern and sources of ambivalence. When motivational practitioners refer to "rolling with" the individual or "rolling with resistance," they are not suggesting that they are giving the individuals the latitude to go wherever they may wish to go. Rolling with the offender, in a case-management context, allows us to take the lead rather than to forego it. It helps us gather the information we need to determine the offenders' presenting stage of readiness, regarding whichever issue we may be exploring with them, and it sets the stage for us to help offenders move forward—if we know how to continue interacting motivationally, and what techniques or strategies to apply.

At a stage where some comfortable compliance seems to be occurring, maintaining a "motivational approach" would allow case managers to pursue the critical ongoing work of reinforcing/supporting action. Offenders will need to get themselves over and past the tough spots and the ups and downs that normally accompany change. Case managers would respond appropriately because they would know, for example, when the issue required:

> resolving some hesitation (resolving of ambivalence) where it could be a matter of simply reminding the offenders why (reasons) they started all of this and showing them the gains made so far

removing an emerging obstacle for the offender where there may be need for an adjustment or modification in the "plan for change"

contending with a slip or relapse where there may be a need to revisit concerns and highlight benefits for change, build greater self-efficacy, learn to anticipate and avoid high-risk situations, monitor and challenge negative self-talk, and build a strong network of supports and positive influences

For offenders who begin to "change," this requires learning and applying new thinking skills, developing and becoming comfortable with a new behavioral and interpersonal repertoire, and challenging the entrenched attitudes and beliefs that they can easily slip back into. This is a persistent and relatively long-term challenge. When we ask them to focus on changing antisocial lifestyles, we are asking them to accept quite fundamental "change." Indeed, for offenders, it typically implies dramatic lifestyle-altering change. The task of case managing them is fundamentally about helping them "negotiate" this process. This process includes:

building momentum toward change (but not by pushing)
helping create direction (but not by directing)
detecting inertia in effort (but not just when it is obvious)
working with resistance (but as a signal to attend to, not a label to describe with)
linking them to the right resources and services, but only when the time is right—too early and resistance resurfaces—too late and an opportunity may be lost
responding to lapses, setbacks, discouragement and/or dismissal as it relates to a particular issue of change
engendering "active" participation—not just compliance

This kind of motivational case managing has to be seen as distinct from the notion of "boosting" of programming gains. Case managing offenders motivationally should not be directed to just recharging or amplifying their motivation by:

reminding them of what they have learned (or should have learned in some program in which they participated)
rehearsing it over again
teaching them (or monitoring them) in how they should apply it in real life

This is essentially antimotivational and, again mistakenly, preoccupied with the "content" of interventions rather than the process of change. Regardless of how much effort is made to introduce and deliver effective programs, results will be limited when offenders are not case managed in ways that help them see the benefits of taking programs and staying on track as determination wanes.

Getting the case management process "right" has now been positioned at the forefront of an impressive what works agenda in England and Wales, where implementation in the last several years has been unprecedented in its scale and breadth (some of the elements of this are detailed in a short case study at the end of this paper).

A new National Probation Service (recently joined with the HM Prison Service into a new Offender Management Service) has introduced an impressive menu of "accredited" evidence-based interventions that are being buttressed by wide-ranging, specialized training of staff, extensive recruitment of young probation service officers to deliver them, new management structures, and all of the essential offender risk/needs assessment protocols and targeting criteria, program management frameworks, quality control mechanisms, performance measurement checks, and independent auditing of implementation. In the attention paid to refinement of the basic elements of what works, little more could be asked of any agency over such a short period of time.

But after several years of this very methodical elaboration, attention is now turning to an understanding of some key blockages—and "program attrition" is among the most significant. Recent data show that about 40 percent of offenders referred to programs never start, and of those who do, only an average of 51 percent complete them.

A recent analysis of forty-two audit "indicators" of performance across thirty-six different probation areas showed how different aspects of how what works were being managed in those areas were correlated with success in getting program completions (in other words, what differentiated those areas that seemed to be able to get the most program completions). The strongest correlation (+.39) was with the item "effective liaison between case managers and program staff."

How to effectively case-manage offenders is possibly one of the least well-articulated aspects of the what works paradigm; yet, it is one of the most powerful to properly deploy. It is in how offenders are case managed that we can try to help create awareness of problems when such understanding is not there, resolve hesitancy about efforts needed to change whenever it surfaces, and help focus attention on maintenance and avoiding relapse when this becomes important. Case management of offenders needs an articulated model or framework that becomes the profession's standard and its identity and basis for training. Procedural case management guidelines will not suffice, no matter how detailed.

We also need to explore how to incorporate specific motivational case management frameworks as follow-through to the delivery of interventions. When this is done, there is evidence that the effects can be pronounced.

We have worked with the United Kingdom Probation and Prison Services for the last several years to explore a realistic approach for increasing the odds that revolving-door, short-term offenders would take up services after release. This is important, especially in view of the high proportion of persistent offenders in this group who have personal and social difficulties and a high reconviction rate. Helping these short-term prisoners with reentry issues in the United Kingdom, as in many countries, is almost the exclusive responsibility of voluntary aftercare agencies—well-meaning agencies which take this work seriously and strive diligently to "offer" advice, support, advocacy, and referral services to offenders—housing, assistance in finding employment, addictions treatment, and so forth. All of these are social factors that we know can contribute to reoffending. The crux, of course, is that only very few offenders decide to take advantage of these services (less than 20 percent in the United Kingdom). Most of the rest undoubtedly believe it would make no meaningful difference to their lives.

So, we helped design a very short intervention, to be delivered by probation staff prerelease, the same staff who then would carry on with a motivational case management approach after release. The intervention was not designed to teach offenders life-skills (or to correct their thinking in any structured way) but only to suggest that they may want to look "at their life story," assess their lives to that point, ask what might have held them back in the past, and if they chose to do so, guide them toward developing their own SMART Action Plans for Release with specific, meaningful, accessible, realistic and timely goals for change. As part of the intervention, a Community Resource Marketplace would be organized as the closing session, where community agencies would gather in one place and offenders could "shop" for the services they believed they needed, making their contacts in advance and reassuring themselves that there is actually a real person and a real "service" with which they could connect. Motivational case management then would be used as a flexible but focused approach for community follow-through with these offenders to keep them working on the right issues (Fabiano and Porporino, 2003).

A recent evaluation of three probation areas adopting the approach showed a doubling in the likelihood of postrelease continuity of contact, compared with the more traditional voluntary advocacy/aftercare model. Moreover, clear evidence of sustained change in offenders was noted, with significant lowering of crime-prone attitudes, fewer self-reported problems, and lower reconviction rates (Raynor, 2004).

Organizational Responsivity to Support What Works

The discussion thus far has suggested that for what works to survive and thrive, it needs to be reframed. It needs to be organized, implemented, and refined, not as a fix-the-offender model, but as an integrated process for influencing change towards desistance of antisocial behaviors and lifestyles. Motivational theory and practice has made a "paradigm shifting" contribution in the last number of years in psychology, health, education, and a host of other fields (for example, Skinner, 2002). It can do the same within the field of corrections by bringing an overarching framework and workable set of strategies of interaction to the difficult task of intervening with offenders.

But to return to the opening question in the paper, can what works as this kind of motivationally anchored, evidence-based practice become the defining quality of the field on the large scale? Is it possible for an entire agency to become immersed in the model and show results? The short answer is yes, it should be possible, but only as long as we stop pretending that it should be easy. What works methods cannot help create offender "responsivity" unless we also can create what we can refer to as organizational "responsivity" (Ingstrup and Crookall, 1998).

In social and organizational terms, correctional agencies, whether big or small, are essentially "street-level" bureaucracies. Within street-level bureaucracies, resources will never match the level of client needs. There always will be more work, less time to do that work, more complex work to attend to, more difficult clients to work with, and more unrealistic expectations about what that work can possibly achieve. Line staff "know" this and they remain vigilant in developing their own compelling arguments for why "nothing new" that is proposed can possibly make things easier or better for them or their clients. Supervisors and managers are also aware of this hard reality and though they may publicly endorse the need for change, as their role requires, they privately can harbor considerable hesitancy about the promised benefits of change.

Organizational change efforts within "street-level" bureaucracies, as a consequence, often do not translate into any real and lasting improvement in the quality or quantity of services delivered to clients. Protection from change permeates organizations, and this is particularly true at the middle management and line levels where countervailing strategies hold back, slow down, or even more actively and directly, sabotage change.

The end result is that organizational-change efforts sputter along in achieving varied and mixed results. They even may claim some short-lived victories. But in time, the determination and stamina to sustain change in a particular direction begins to fade and, after some period of transition, another organizational change effort is initiated.

Reorganizing structures, policies, mechanisms, or procedures certainly can appear to be changing the organization at the "behavioral" level. Some organizational theorists would argue that behavior in this sense is the key; simply build in processes to hold staff accountable for new behaviors and in time those new behaviors will lead to improved results. At the other extreme is the view that one need only inform staff of the results that are expected and in time those results will be forthcoming, as staff feel empowered to implement their own methods and procedures to achieve them.

But the psychology of change would argue, once again, that neither approach will be very successful unless there is a prevailing and necessary precondition—a widespread "preparedness" for change at the line staff and individual level.

A fundamental problem with many management approaches to organizational change is the focus on "behavioral change" (in other words, how to do things differently) rather than a focus on the more enduring aspects of psychological or "cognitive change" (in other words, how to think differently about what we do). Staff will not change "practice" simply because they are encouraged to do so, regardless of whether that encouragement is subtle, forceful, or even enthusiastic, and visionary. On the other hand, staff will willingly change practice if what they begin doing differently actually begins "working" differently (and more successfully) in managing their clients.

An emerging perspective in the theory on organizational change suggests that how the members of an organization (a body of persons organized for some end or work) acquire knowledge of, organize, and make sense of changes in the organizational environment is key to understanding the success or failure of change initiatives (Armenakis and Bedeian, 1999; Bartunek, Lacey, and Wood, 1992). This "cognitive" orientation in organizational theory argues that staff members are constantly active in "sensemaking"—a process of examining their various core beliefs and assumptions to make sense of organizational change, and resolve any ambiguity, anxiety, and conflict inherent in accepting this change.

"Sensemaking" is seen as an ongoing process of adjustment of views about change that are both cognitive (in other words, attitudinal) and emotional in origin (Huy, 1999) and where the nature of the cognitive "schemas" about change that staff may develop, they will vary dramatically, leading in the end to acceptance or rejection of change for very personalized sets of reasons.

Particular features of this "sensemaking" process have been strongly related to organizational commitment to change (Lau and Woodman, 1995). Obviously, when the reasons for change are not fully appreciated or accepted, when there is little significance attached to the change (in other words, within the grand scheme of things), or when members of the organization make predictions of future personal outcomes that are negative, then commitment to change will wane.

To carry the parallel with the psychology of personal change a little further, members of the organization will remain stuck in a precontemplative or contemplative state and will not move forward toward any real committed action unless there is a tipping of the balance that resolves their ambivalence (Egan, 1998; Miller and Rollnick, 1992; Prochaska and DiClemente, 1994).

Implementing what works in corrections is a challenge at many levels. But attempting to implement any thoughtful and integrated what works agenda may be futile if the sensemaking of staff is not acknowledged and dealt with along the way.

What works was originally practitioner led and dynamic. As it has had to become organizationally led, especially in an environment that is obsessed with accountability and performance measurement, it also has become more mechanistic, prescriptive, and demanding. But what works can only thrive in a culture where there is a blossoming of practitioner curiosity and a commitment to self-correcting ways of working.

Staff attitudes and desire to implement what works will tend to be shaped by what they see as realistic and achievable, not by what we tell them should be realistic and achievable. Staff will work with us if they believe that we are genuinely interested in enhancing their talents, and if they see that the time and resources invested in this are adequate. They will be more genuinely exuberant if they do not feel boxed in, if they believe they have meaningful choices in altering their roles, if they can see their work as having some rhythm and matching what they desire and feel able to do, and if they see themselves and others being rewarded consistently for:

> trouble-shooting—anticipating problems and addressing them before they escalate
> creating flexibility—elbow room in meeting the needs of individual clients
> speeding up the system—always reminding components of the system to keep moving, keep connecting

Success in implementing what works hinges on getting broader organizational "responsivity." It deserves a fine-tuned and orchestrated managerial response, but not one that dismisses practitioner wisdom and that befuddles and disengages them. From agencies this requires:

> committed leadership—vision, gumption, stamina, strategy, and a genuine belief in quality
> implementation planning—strategic and operational, slow but methodical persistence in a building-blocks approach with a dogged stubbornness balanced with a respect for others' views
> adequate knowledge to discern—to be able to tell the good from the merely acceptable and to be able to clearly identify the bad
> risk analysis and profiling of obstacles and vulnerabilities—at all levels of the organization; among key stakeholders, the public, and at political and legislative blockages
> planned action for dealing with implementation failures and an ability to create an understandable, nonthreatening mode of new "thinking and behaving" for the organization

Conclusion: "What Works" on the Grand Scale

The following very brief case study shows, under each of these headings of organizational "responsivity," how what works can be leveraged into reality. It is an outline of one jurisdiction's approach to developing and implementing a culture of evidence-based practice that seems to be sustaining and able to show results. It is the National Probation Service of England and Wales. Here are a few of the elements that are giving it shape:

Committed Leadership

Following a long reign of social and economic conservatism, there was an opportunity to "re-invent" probation (after it had nearly been dismantled). Strong labor government support was obtained by linking this, in a policy context, to a much broader "social-inclusion" initiative (Halliday, 2001). The challenge was taken up speedily, with massive organizational change to support it, and a series of very thoughtful practice/policy "think pieces" to ground it (Underdown, 1998; Chapman and Hough, 1998).

Consistent, attention-grabbing, sensible and convincing "language" was developed to introduce new initiatives—a mode of communicating that government officials and the public could accept. Here is an example. Eithne Wallis, the head of the New National Probation Service, talking about one aspect of her New Choreography, a new community supervision approach for high-risk young offenders to divert them from custody (Wallis, 2003):

> "Programme X is first and foremost about placing restrictions on young adults that limit opportunities to offend and stop them from causing grief and disorder in their communities. Then, to do work which stands the best chance of achieving genuine rehabilitation. High levels of control are not sustainable—these have to be replaced by change from within the offender. It has to be a 'control and change' programme"

— Eithne Wallis

Implementation Planning

Broad-based developmental work was pursued quickly. For example,

> Their own tailored risk/needs assessment and case planning process—OASys (Offender Assessment System)—was used.
> Some best practice program models were imported, and where holes existed, new programs were commissioned (for example, to address ethnic diversity and gender issues).
> Across-the-board training of staff in motivational principles and practice was employed.
> Initial testing and refinement of intervention models was done through probation area "pathfinders," what we call pilots.

Information and performance management systems were developed to monitor key indicators; evaluation frameworks were put in place for all major program initiatives.

Evidence-base was brought to bear not just in introducing programs but in significantly altering other service delivery "systems" (for example, a new model for community service orders aiming to use the community work experience as "treatment"; development of specific risk management "regimes" for their hostels [in other words, our community correctional centers]).

Adequate Knowledge to Discern

A formal process is necessary for external, expert scrutiny of programs before national rollout, where programs have to pass the litmus test of detailed evidence-based criteria before they are implemented.

Accreditation is used as a process for raising the bar for theoretical depth and coherence of interventions. Programs that wish to be accredited have to articulate, with an accompanying theory manual and literature review, how and why the "model of the change process" that the program is pursuing might impinge on reoffending:

> Which combination of dynamic risk factors is it targeting?
> Why in that combination?
> With what intensity and what order/what sequence and why?
> For which offenders?

Risk Analysis and Profiling of Obstacles and Vulnerabilities

Many examples could be given of this, but here is one very significant and bold move that was taken. It was refreshing the workforce with a new category of probation officer, several thousand probation service officers—junior but young and energetic and not stunted from moving forward by old-style social work and welfare notions of probation.

But, at the same time, every effort was made not to alienate probation officers. They remain the senior case managers and supervisors whose central role is emphasized in a continuing series of training seminars and practitioner what-works events and conferences.

Planned Action (for dealing with implementation failure)

A formal change-control strategy was introduced to prevent local program drift. It welcomes comments/observations from practitioners, but manages the process of introducing broadly agreed to and necessary adaptations to program curricula and procedures. Practitioners are involved, but they do not institute changes on their own. They are asked to respect cumulative experience.

For programs to be accredited in the United Kingdom, they have to be sound conceptually, deliverable, and properly targeted. But they also have to specify:

> What preprogram work might need to be completed?
> How will program through-care happen in terms of post-program continuity of services and case management?
> How will the program be checked in action and monitored for impact and for ongoing quality of delivery? (All programs are delivered within a tripartite arrangement of a "team of tutors" supervised by a program manager and treatment manager)
> What provisions are being made to ensure response from an ethnically diverse offender population? All programs have to pass a separate "diversity review" examining possible discriminatory content and methods.
> Who is accountable for delivery management? All programs require a management manual detailing staff selection, training, and supervision requirements, minimum operating conditions, roles of program mangers, and treatment managers.

We could go on with much further detail, but this should paint a broad-brush picture of how what works can take hold of an agency and become its defining feature. This author personally remains hopeful that what is transpiring in England and Wales will not be just a grand experiment, cataloged historically but not sustained. Resource constraints are now on the horizon, and the clamoring for results has begun. The rationale of "we've only just begun" no longer holds weight, and the next several years will be key to showing whether an entire probation service can prove to government officials that they have become both evidence-based and more effective.

Recently, another bold move was announced, the joining up of the Prison and Probation Services into one National Offender Management Service with the singular aim of managing offenders as seamlessly as possible throughout their sentences (Carter, 2003). The entire system, the argument goes, should work together to use resources as effectively as possible in doing one thing: reducing crime. What a simple and refreshing thought!

Conclusion

"What works?" will always remain a question at some level. It has a future in becoming the defining quality of correctional practice, but only if we become courageous enough to accept that it is not easy and never will be.

This paper argues that we can certainly reach a further plateau by intertwining motivational principles into the fabric of everything we do with offenders. Staff who facilitate programs and case manage offenders have to be given the time, training, supervision, and support they need to learn to do this "skillfully."

In the end, we have no choice but to acknowledge that everything we do in corrections will influence offenders regardless of our systems, procedures, methods, and all of our interactions with them. We can choose to do it to make a difference—with every bit of evidence we can find about what truly works and why. Or, we can go about doing it like we always have or as best we can. The choice is ours!

References

Andrews, D. A. 2001. Principles of Effective Correctional Programs. In L. L. Motiuk and R. C. Serin, eds. *Compendium 2000 on Effective Correctional Programming*. Ottawa, Ontario: Correctional Service Canada.

Andrews, D. A. and J. Bonta. 1998. *The Psychology of Criminal Conduct*. 2nd ed. Cincinnati, Ohio: Anderson Publishing Co.

Armenakis, A. A. and A. G. Bedeian. 1999. Organizational Change: A Review of Theory and Research in the 1990's. *Journal of Management*. 25(3): 293-302.

Bartunek, J. M., C. A. Lacey, and D. R. Wood. 1992. Social Cognition in Organizational Change: An Insider-Outsider Approach. *Journal of Applied Behavioral Science*. 28: 204-223.

Blackburn, R. 1993. *The Psychology of Criminal Conduct*. New York: John Wiley and Sons, Inc.

Carlen, P. 2002. New Discourses of Justification and Reform for Women's Imprisonment in England. In P. Carlen, ed. *Women and Punishment.*: Cullompton, Devon, United Kingdom: Willan Publishing.

Carter, P. 2003. Managing Offenders, Reducing Crime. Correctional Services Review submitted to the Prime Minister, Home Secretary and Chief Secretary of the Treasury. London: Home Office Publications

Chapman T. and M. Hough. 1998. *Evidence Based Practice: A Guide to Effective Practice*. London: Home Office Publications Unit.

Clarke, R. V. and D. B. Cornish. 1985. Modelling Offenders' Decisions: A Framework for Research and Policy. In M. Tonry and N. Morris, eds. *Crime and Justice: An Annual Review of Research*, Vol. VI. London: University of Chicago Press.

Devereaux-Ferguson, S. 1994. *Mastering the Public Opinion Challenge*. New York: Irwin Professional Publishing.

Dowden, C. and R. Serin. 2001. *Anger Management Programming for Offenders: The Impact of Program Performance Measures*. Ottawa, Ontario: Research Branch, Correctional Service of Canada.

Edna McConnell Clark Foundation. 1997. *Seeking Justice: Crime and Punishment in America*. New York: Office of Communications.

Egan, Gerrard. 1998. *The Skilled Helper! A Problem Management Approach to Helping*. 6th ed. Albany, New York: Brooks/Cole Publishing Company.

Fabiano, E. and F. Porporino. 1999. *Manual for Cognitive-Motivational Tools for Negotiating Behavior Change*. Ottawa, Ontario: T3 Associates.

———. 2003. *For A Change Part 2: Community Case Management Guidelines*. Ottawa, Ontario: T3 Associates Inc.

Falshaw, L., C. Friendship, R. Travers, and F. Nugent. 2003. Searching for "What Works": An Evaluation of Cognitive Skills Programmes. Home Office Research Findings No. 206. London: Home Office.

Farrington, D. P. 1995. The Development of Offending and Antisocial Behaviour from Childhood: Key Findings from the Cambridge Study in Delinquent Development. *Journal of Child Psychology and Psychiatry*. 36: 929-964.

———. 1997. Human Development and Criminal Careers. In M. Maguire, R. Morgan, and R. Reiner, eds. *Oxford Handbook of Criminology*. 2nd ed. Oxford: Clarendon Press.

Fiorentiono, R., J. Nakashima, and M. D. Anglin. 1999. Client Engagement in Drug Treatment. *Journal of Substance Abuse Treatment*. 17: 199-206.

Gaes, G., G. Flanagan, T. J. Motiuk, and L. Stewart. 1999. Adult Correctional Treatment. In M. Tonry and J. Petersilia, eds. *Prisons*. Chicago: The University of Chicago Press.

Gendreau, P., C. Goggin, and P. Smith. 1999. The Forgotten Issue in Effective Correctional Treatment: Program Implementation. *International Journal of Offender Therapy and Comparative Criminology*. 43: 180-187.

———. 2001. Implementation Guidelines for Correctional Programs in the "Real World." In G. A. Bernfeld, D. P. Farrington, and A.W. Leschied, eds. *Offender Rehabilitation in Practice: Implementing and Evaluating Effective Programs*. Chichester: John Wiley and Sons.

Gendreau, P., C. Goggin, F. T. Cullen, and M. Paparozzi. 2002. The Common-Sense Revolution and Correctional Policy. In J. McGuire, ed. *Offender Rehabilitation and Treatment: Effective Programmes and Policies to Reduce Reoffending*. Chichester: John Wiley and Sons.

Gendreau, P. and R. R. Ross. 1980. Effective Correctional Treatment: Bibliotherapy for Cynics. In R. R. Ross and P. Gendreau, eds. *Effective Correctional Treatment*. Toronto, Ontario: Butterworths.

Halliday, J. 2001. *Making Punishments Work: Report of a Review of the Sentencing Framework for England and Wales*. London: Home Office.

Harris, P. and S. Smith. 1996. Developing Community Corrections: An Implementation Perspective. In A. T. Harland, ed. *Choosing Correctional Options that Work: Defining the Demand and Evaluating the Supply*. Thousand Oaks, California: Sage Publications.

Hollin, C. R. 1995. The Meaning and Implication of "Program Integrity." In J. McGuire, ed. *What Works: Reducing Reoffending, Guidelines from Research and Practice*. Wiley Series in Offender Rehabilitation. Chichester, United Kingdom: Wiley and Sons.

———. 2001. *Handbook of Offender Assessment and Treatment*. Wiley Series in Offender Rehabilitation. Chichester, United Kingdom: Wiley and Sons.

Huy, Q. N. 1999. Emotional Capability, Emotional Intelligence, and Radical Change. *Academy of Management Review*. 24(2): 325-345.

Ingstrup, O. and P. Crookall. 1998. *The Three Pillars of Public Sector Management: Secrets of Sustained Success*. Montreal and Kingston: McGill-Queen's University Press.

Isabella, L. A. 1990. Evolving Interpretations as Change Unfolds: How Managers Construe Key Organizational Events. *Academy of Management Journal*. 33(1): 7- 41.

Kennedy, S. M. 2000. Treatment Responsivity: Reducing Recidivism by Enhancing Treatment Effectiveness. *Forum on Corrections Research*. 12(2): 19-23.

Knott, C. 1995. The STOP Programme: Reasoning and Rehabilitation in a British Setting. In J. McGuire, ed. *What Works: Reducing Reoffending, Guidelines from Research and Practice*. Wiley Series in Offender Rehabilitation. Chichester, United Kingdom: Wiley and Sons.

Latessa, E. J., F. T. Cullen, and P. Gendreau. 2002. Beyond Correctional Quackery: Professionalism and the Possibility of Effective Treatment. *Federal Probation*. 66(2): 43-49.

Lau, C. and R. Woodman. 1995. Understanding Organizational Change: A Schematic Perspective. *Academy of Management Journal*. 38: 537-554.

Leschied, A. W., G. Bernfeld, and D. P. Farrington. 2001. Implementation Issues. In G. A. Bernfeld, D. P. Farrington and A. W. Leschied, eds. *Offender Rehabilitation in Practice: Implementing and Evaluating Effective Programs*. Chichester: John Wiley and Sons.

Lipsey, M., G. Chapman, and N. Landenberger. 2001. Cognitive Behavioral Programs for Offenders. *The Annals of the American Academy of Political and Social Science*. 57(8): 144-157.

Logan, C. H. 1993. *Criminal Justice Performance Measures for Prisons*. Washington, D.C.: U.S. Department of Justice, Bureau of Justice Statistics.

Maruna, S. 2000. *Making Good*. Washington, D.C.: American Psychological Association.

McGuire, J., ed. 1995. *What Works: Reducing Reoffending, Guidelines from Research and Practice*. New York: Wiley and Sons.

McGuire, J. and P. Priestley. 1985. *Offending Behavior: Skills and Stratagems for Going Straight*. London: Batsford.

McMurran, M., ed. 2002. *Motivating Offenders to Change: A Guide to Enhancing Engagement in Therapy*. Chichester: John Wiley and Sons.

Miller, W. R. and S. Rollnick. 1992. *Motivational Interviewing: Preparing People to Change Addictive Behavior*. New York: The Guilford Press

——. 2002. *Motivational Interviewing: Preparing People to Change Addictive Behaviors*. 2nd ed. New York: The Guilford Press.

Millson, W. A., D. Robinson, and A. P. Stringer. 1999. 1999 *Survey of Non-National Substance Abuse Programs*. Submitted to Correctional Service Canada, Ottawa, Ontario.

Palmer, T. 1992. *The Re-Emergence of Correctional Intervention*. Newbury Park, California: Sage Publications.

———. 2002. *Individualized Intervention with Young Multiple Offenders*. New York: Routledge.

Paparozzi, M. A. 1994. *A Comparison of the Effectiveness of an Intensive Parole Supervision Programme with Traditional Parole Supervision*. Unpublished doctoral dissertation, Rutgers University, New Brunswick, New Jersey.

———. 2003. Probation, Parole and Public Safety: The Need for Principled Practices Versus Faddism and Circular Policy Development. *Corrections Today*. 65(5): 46-52.

Porporino, F. J. 1995. Intervention in Corrections: Is "Cognitive" Programming an Answer or Just a Passing Fashion? *The 1994 State of Corrections: Proceedings of the American Correctional Association Annual Conferences*. Lanham, Maryland: American Correctional Association

———. 1999. What Works from a Canadian Perspective. Invited address to conference on Producing the Evidence: Effective Work with Offenders in the Prison and Probation Services. London, Home Office.

Porporino, F. J. and E. Baylis. 1993. Designing a Progressive Penology: The Evolution of Canadian Federal Corrections. *Criminal Behavior and Mental Health*. 3: 268-289.

Porporino, F. J. and E. Fabiano. 1999. Program Overview of Reasoning and Rehabilitation Revised. *Theory and Application Manual*. Ottawa, Ontario: T3 Associates.

Porporino, F. J., D. Robinson, B. Millson, and J. Weekes. 2002. An Outcome Evaluation of Prison-based Treatment Programming for Substance Abusers. Substance Use and Misuse. *An International Interdisciplinary Forum*. 37: 1047-1077.

Prochaska, J. O. and C. C. DiClementi. 1994. *The Transtheoretical Approach: Crossing Traditional Boundaries of Therapy*. Malabar, Florida: Krieger Publishing Company.

Raynor, P. 2004. Opportunity, Motivation and Change: Some Findings from Research on Resettlement. In R. Burnett and C. Roberts, eds. *Evidence-Based Practice in Probation and Youth Justice*. London: Willan Publishing.

Rhine, E. 2001. Why What Works Matters Under the "Broken Windows" Model of Supervision. *Federal Probation.* 66(2): 39-42.

Roberts, C. 2003. The Way Ahead: A Systems Approach Using Research Evidence. Paper presented to the What Works Conference: Promoting Practitioner's Experience, Manchester, England.

Robinson, D. 1995. The *Impact of Cognitive Skills Training on Post-Release Recidivism among Canadian Federal Offenders.* Ottawa, Ontario: Research Branch: Correctional Service of Canada.

Robinson, D., P. Lefaive, and M. Muirhead. 1997. *Synopsis of Results of the 1996 CSC Staff Survey.* Ottawa, Ontario: Research Branch, Correctional Service of Canada.

Sampson, R. J. and J. H. Laub. 1993. *Crime in the Making: Pathways and Turning Points Through Life.* Cambridge, Massachusetts: Harvard University Press.

Sherman, L. W., D. Gottfredson, D. Mackenzie, J. Eck, P. Reuter, and S. Bushway. 1997. *Preventing Crime: What Works, What Doesn't, What's Promising.* Washington, D.C.: Office of Justice Programs.

Skinner, H. 2002. *Promoting Health through Organizational Change.* San Francisco: Benjamin and Cummings Publisher.

Stewart, L. and W. A. Millson. 1994. Offender Motivation for Treatment as a Responsivity Factor. *Forum on Corrections Research.* 7: 5-7.

Tamans, J. and S. Jurich. 2000. Overview of Cognitive-Behavioral Programs and Their Applications to Correctional Settings. *Perspectives.* 24(4): 48-53.

Trotter, C. 2000. Social Work Education, Pro-Social Orientation and Effective Probation Practice. *Probation Journal.* 47: 256-261.

Underdown, A. 1998. *Strategies for Effective Supervision: Report of the HMIP What Works Project.* London: Her Majesty's Inspectorate of Probation.

Vanstone, M. 2000. Cognitive-Behavioral Work with Offenders in the United Kingdom: A History of Influential Endeavour. *Howard Journal.* 39: 171-183.

VanVoorhis, P., F. Cullen, and B. Applegate. 1995. Evaluating Interventions with Violent Offenders: A Guide for Practitioners and Policy Makers. *Federal Probation.* 59: 17-28.

Van Voorhis, P., L. M. Spruance, P. N. Ritchie, S. Johnston-Listwan, R. Seabrook, and J. Pealer. 2003. *The Georgia Cognitive Skills Experiment: Outcome Evaluation Phase II.* Cincinnati, Ohio: School of Criminal Justice, University of Cincinnati.

Wallis, E. 2003. *Intensive Change and Control Programme: A Briefing for Ministers.* London: Home Office.

Weber, P. S. and M. R. Manning. 1998. A Comparative Framework for Large Group Organizational Change Interventions. In R. W. Woodman and W. A. Pasmore, eds. *Research in Organizational Change and Development.* 11: 225-252.

Weick, K. E. and R. E. Quinn. 1999. Organizational Change and Development. *Annual Review of Psychology.* 50: 361-386.

Wilson, D., L. Allen, and D. MacKenzie. 2000. *Quantitative Review of Cognitive Behavioral Programs.* College Park, Maryland: University of Maryland.

Zamble, E. and F. J. Porporino. 1988. *Coping Behavior and Adaptation in Prison Inmates.* Syracuse New Jersey: Springer-Verlag.

Zamble E. and V. L. Quinsey. 1997. *The Criminal Recidivism Process.* Cambridge: Cambridge University Press.

Endnotes

[1] There are more encouraging exceptions if we gaze beyond America and look at the picture internationally. For at least the last decade, the federal correctional system in Canada has sustained a program-oriented correctional strategy (Porporino and Baylis, 1993) despite the repeated attacks it has had to face from a conservative media, victim interest groups, and get-tough-on-crime government officials. A more recent example is the new National Probation Service in England and Wales that has been organized around an expressed, systemwide what works agenda that is being implemented at breakneck speed. The Scandinavian countries, the Netherlands, a number of state systems within Australia, and especially the correctional system in New Zealand have all attempted to realign in the last number of years toward implementation of evidence-based principles and practices.

[2] It is interesting to note that in a study that looked at the personality characteristics of offenders as these related to outcomes of cognitive-skills programming (Van Voorhis et al., 2003), neurotic offenders as assessed by the Jessness Inventory were more likely to drop out of the program, and those who remained reoffended at a higher rate than neurotic offenders in the comparison group. In other words, the delivery of the program seemed detrimental for these offenders.

About the Authors

Linda Baker, Ph.D., C. Psych.

Linda Baker is presently the executive director of the Centre for Children and Families in the Justice System of the London Family Court Clinic. She is an adjunct professor in both the Department of Psychology and the Faculty of Education at the University of Western Ontario. She is a clinical psychologist whose areas of expertise have been children and youth experiencing mental illness, children and adolescents affected by violence, and youth in conflict with the law. Currently, Dr. Baker is on the regional advisory board for the Child and Parent Resource Institute and on the board of directors for the Sexual Assault Centre of London. She is also on the editorial board for *Youth Violence and Juvenile Justice: An Interdisciplinary Journal.* Recent research and publications include *Waiting for Mommy: Giving a Voice to the Hidden Victims of Imprisonment; Youth Exposed to Domestic Violence: A Handbook for the Juvenile Justice System to Enhance Assessment and Intervention Strategies for Youth from Violent Homes;* and *Protecting Children from Domestic Violence: Strategies for Community Intervention.* She is invited to speak and facilitate workshops in her areas of expertise throughout Canada and the United States.

Brad Bogue

Brad Bogue is a partner in Justice System Assessment and Training (J-SAT) in Boulder, Colorado, a justice system consulting firm specializing in evaluation, assessment tools, and training public and private sector systems to build capacity in systems and individuals. In addition, he is the director for a licensed juvenile and a licensed adult treatment agency. Prior to establishing J-SAT, Mr. Bogue worked as the project director for the Standardized Offender Assessment Project with the Colorado State

Court Administrator's Office. This project entailed the design, development, and implementation of statewide, multisector assessment protocols for all adult and juvenile offenders in the state and won the American Probation and Parole Association's President Award for 1997. He has worked in a variety of public and private sector corrections and treatment agencies. He has been the primary investigator in more than fifty different corrections and treatment agency evaluations. Mr. Bogue has delivered more than 200 training seminars to state and local agencies throughout the country. He co-authored the book *The Probation & Parole Treatment Planner*, which provides detailed information about effective case interventions based on cognitive-behavioral principles.

Nancy M. Campbell

Nancy M. Campbell helps organizations and individuals develop the management and leadership skills needed in today's dynamic and challenging work environment. She combines more than twenty years of leadership experience in the public and nonprofit sectors with superb communication skills and practical problem-solving techniques to bring clients new perspectives and insights when faced with complex problems. A charismatic speaker, who combines practical experience with theoretical knowledge, her training is both useful and engaging. As a an Affiliate Associate Professor for the Evans School of Public Affairs at the University of Washington, she provides training in leadership for mid-career professionals. Ms. Campbell served as the director of community corrections for both the Colorado and Washington State Departments of corrections. She also served as the director of the King County Department of Youth Services and the Community Responsibility Center, a nonprofit residential community corrections program. A graduate of the School of Criminal Justice, State University of New York at Albany, Ms. Campbell is a well-known speaker and lecturer in the field of criminal justice.

Mark Carey

Mark Carey served as the deputy commissioner of community and juvenile services in the Minnesota Department of Corrections from 1999 to 2003. He was the director of Dakota County Community Corrections and, prior to that, the director of Dodge-Fillmore-Olmsted County Community Corrections. He is currently the warden at the only state women's prison in Minnesota, MCF-Shakopee. He has more than twenty years of experience in the correctional field serving as a counselor, probation/parole officer, planner, administrator, and consultant. He taught juvenile justice at the Community College in Rochester, Minnesota and has published two books and more than a dozen articles. Mr. Carey has served as president and chair for a number of associations and task forces and frequently is requested as a speaker and trainer. He has been on the American Probation and Parole Association (APPA) board of directors since 1997 and is currently the president-elect. In 1996, he received APPA's Sam Houston University Award. In 1993, he was selected as the Corrections Person of the Year by the Minnesota Corrections Association.

Elyse Clawson

Elyse Clawson is the executive director of the Crime and Justice Institute, an organization committed to creative collaborative approaches to complex social issues. She has twenty-nine years of experience and a substantial background in education, substance abuse treatment, mental health, and criminal justice. Ms. Clawson began her career as a teacher for emotionally disturbed children. Among other positions, she has been an educational director for a program serving delinquent youths, the primary therapist for the Salt Lake City Mental Health System, and a co-director for a nonprofit organization providing mental health and substance abuse services to the criminal justice system. She served as the director of community corrections for the Oregon Department of Corrections and as the director of the Department of Community Justice for Multnomah County, Oregon. Under Ms. Clawson's direction, the Crime and Justice Institute has a cooperative agreement with the National Institute of Corrections for the implementation of effective management of offenders in the community using evidence-based practices in Illinois and Maine. They are also working with a number of other states assisting them in their implementation of evidence-based practices, development of reentry systems, and other organizational change efforts.

Anne L. Cummings, Ph.D.

Anne L. Cummings is a professor of counseling psychology at the Faculty of Education at the University of Western Ontario. Her research interests include women's issues in counseling, aggression in adolescent girls, and the counseling process.

Kate Florio

Kate Florio has been with the Crime and Justice Institute (CJI) since June, 2000. As an assistant project manager, she helps to coordinate the National Institute of Corrections/CJI initiative entitled Implementing Effective Correctional Management of Offenders in the Community. She also coordinates CJI-sponsored public forums and expert panel discussions. She worked extensively on the Safety First Initiative in Lynn, Massachusetts, a collaborative effort between law enforcement agencies and community-based treatment organizations designed to tackle the issue of heroin overdoses. Providing research and data analysis, Kate worked with the drug task force to understand trends, identify "hot spots" in the city, and track any significant changes that could inform the strategic attack on this social problem. Ms. Florio received a bachelor of science in sociology from Bridgewater State College in 2000, where her focus of study was criminology.

Lore Joplin

Lore Joplin currently works with the Crime and Justice Institute in Boston, Massachusetts. In that capacity, she manages a cooperative agreement with the National Institute of Corrections, Community Corrections Division entitled *Implementing Effective Correctional Management of Offenders in the Community*. The project's integrated model is designed to guide implementation of evidence-based principles in community corrections with an equal focus on organizational development and collaboration. Previously, Ms. Joplin worked as a senior policy and budget analyst for the Department of Community Justice in Multnomah County, Oregon, where she helped to coordinate major system reform efforts in juvenile justice and adult community corrections. Her work included policy and budget analysis regarding adult and juvenile programs, detention reform, and system enhancement efforts. Prior to her work in Multnomah County, Ms. Joplin worked as a trial court program analyst with the Office of the State Court Administrator in Oregon.

Alan W. Leschied, Ph.D.

Alan Leschied is a psychologist and professor in the Faculty of Education at the University of Western Ontario. He began working in children's mental health in 1977 at the London Family Court Clinic. Since then, he has worked at the Clinic with the exception of from 1980 – 1982, when he worked at the Children's Hospital of Western Ontario. He joined the faculty at Western in 1998. Currently, his research interests have included the completion of the clinical trial with Multisystemic Therapy, funded by the National Crime Prevention Centre and the examination of factors related to increases in the demand for child welfare services in London and Middlesex. Dr. Leschied chairs the graduate program in counseling psychology at Western's Faculty of Education. He is a Fellow of the Canadian Psychology Association, and a recipient in 2003 of both the Edward G. Pleva Award for Excellence in Teaching and the Judge Wendy Robson Award for outstanding service to children in Ontario.

Peggy McGarry

Peggy McGarry has been with the Center for Effective Public Policy since 1983. She served as a principal with the Center for most of those years. She is the director of the Community Justice in Rural Communities and Tribal Courts project, the Community Prosecution Regional Trainings project, and the Police-Prosecutors Partnership project, all three for the Bureau of Justice Assistance, Office of Justice Programs (OJP). She has directed many projects for the Center for more than twenty years, most recently "Improving Community Responses to Women Offenders" for the National Institute of Corrections (NIC) and "An Agenda for the Nation on Violence Against Women" for both the Department of Justice and the Department of Health and Human Services. Ms. McGarry has worked on a variety of Center projects in recent years. She directed ten years of the Center's work on intermediate sanctions, working with more than fifty policy teams in twenty-one states and the District of Columbia. Ms. McGarry has served as staff on many other Center projects, including the Criminal Justice Systems Project for NIC and the Center for Sex Offender Management for the Office of Justice Programs. Ms. McGarry is the author of *The Handbook for New Parole Board Members;* co-author of *Community Justice in Rural America: Four Examples and Four Futures*, and co-editor of *The Intermediate Sanctions Handbook*, a comprehensive guide to the development of policy to guide the use of intermediate sanctions. For many years, she was the lead trainer for the National Institute of Corrections in its annual training program for new parole board members. She has been involved in Center work providing training and technical assistance to paroling authorities, courts, probation agencies, state and local corrections departments, sentencing commissions, and a variety of other criminal justice and local government agencies. Previously, Ms. McGarry founded and directed Women Against Abuse in Philadelphia, a shelter and legal services program for victims of domestic violence, and served as the first president of the Pennsylvania Coalition Against Domestic Violence.

James McGuire, Ph.D.

James McGuire is professor of forensic clinical psychology at the University of Liverpool, UK. He is the director of studies for the doctorate in clinical psychology program and also holds an honorary post of consultant clinical psychologist in Mersey Care NHS Trust. He is a chartered clinical and forensic psychologist and carries out psycho-legal work involving assessment of offenders. He has conducted research in prisons, probation services, and other settings on aspects of the effectiveness of treatment with offenders and related topics and has written or edited twelve books and approximately a hundred other publications on this and related areas. In addition, he has been involved in a range of consultative work with criminal justice agencies in the United Kingdom, Sweden, Canada, Australia, and Hong Kong.

Joan Petersilia, Ph.D.

Joan Petersilia is a professor of criminology, law and society in the School of Social Ecology, University of California, Irvine. Prior to joining UCI, she was the director of the Criminal Justice Program at RAND. She has directed major studies in sentencing, probation and parole, juvenile justice, intermediate sanctions, and racial discrimination. She has served as president of both the American Society of Criminology and the Association of Criminal Justice Research. She is an elected fellow of the American Society of Criminology and received its Vollmer Award for her overall contributions to public policy. She has also received awards from the International Community Corrections Association, the American Probation and Parole Association, and the California Probation, Parole, and Corrections Association for her dedication to community corrections. Her most recent book is *When Prisoners Come Home: Parole and Prisoner Reentry* (2003). Other recent books include *Crime: Public Policies for Crime Control* with James Q. Wilson (2002), *Reforming Probation and Parole* (2002), *Crime Victims with Developmental Disabilities* (2001), *Prisons*, edited with Michael Tonry (1999), *Criminal Justice Policy* (1998), *Community Corrections* (1998), and *Crime*, edited with James Q. Wilson (1995). Dr. Petersilia has a bachelor of arts (1972) in sociology from Loyola University of Los Angeles, a master's degree (1974) in sociology from Ohio State University, and a Ph.D. (1990) in criminology, law, and society from the University of California, Irvine.

Frank Porporino

Frank Porporino has a Ph.D. in clinical psychology from Queen's University and has specialized for the last thirty years in the application of sound research knowledge to correctional and criminal justice practice. His public sector career began in 1974 as a psychologist in Canada's oldest maximum-security prison, Kingston Penitentiary. He spent twenty-two years with the Correctional Service of Canada (CSC), eventually serving as director of strategic planning and director general of research and development. In 1993, he cofounded T3 Associates Training and Consulting, Inc. in order to disseminate the cognitive model and provide other research-based training and technical assistance in effective practice to correctional jurisdictions internationally. Dr. Porporino has provided general research and evaluation consultancy and delivered numerous workshops, seminars, and staff training sessions to all levels of management and line staff for both government and private agencies. He has worked for numerous agencies throughout Canada and the United States, and internationally. He was adjunct professor of psychology at Carleton University in Ottawa from 1987-1994. He is on the editorial board of the *Journal of Substance Use and Misuse* and was the founding editor of *Forum on Corrections Research*, a quarterly journal dedicated to promoting effective, accountable, and knowledge-based corrections. He has authored numerous monographs and journal articles on the assessment and treatment of offenders, has developed a number of well-respected cognitive-behavioral programs for both juvenile and adult offenders, and has also co-authored the book *Coping, Behavior, and Adaptation in Prison Inmates* (with Edward Zamble, Springer-Verlag, 1988).

Billy F. Wasson

Billy F. Wasson has more than thirty-five years of experience in the criminal justice system, working a variety of positions from headquarters to the field. He served as the founding director of the Marion County (Oregon) Department of Corrections from 1979 to 1999, when her retired. His agency operated a full continuum of sanctions and services, including the jail and all alternatives to incarceration in the county. Mr. Wasson has also served as a consultant and trainer for the National Institute of Corrections, and in this regard, has been to more than fifty jurisdictions throughout the United States assisting with issues in all aspects of the criminal justice system. Mr. Wasson holds a master's degree in correctional administration from Western Oregon University.

William Woodward

William Woodward is a faculty member at the University of Colorado at Boulder's Center for the Study and Prevention of Violence. Prior to this he was a Senior Project Manager at the Center for Effective Public Policy. At CEPP, he managed the National Resource Center for Collaboration in the Criminal Justice System and the resource sites for the Center for Sex Offender Management. From 1984 to 1999, he served as the director of the Colorado Division of Criminal Justice, managing a budget of more than $46 million. Mr. Woodward was the President of the National Criminal Justice Association for two years, 1996 and 1997. From 1982 to 1984, he was appointed executive director of the Colorado's Prison Overcrowding Project. In 1980, he was appointed deputy director of the Division of Criminal Justice. In this position, he oversaw projects ranging from prison population projections to statewide jail standards. Mr. Woodward worked in law enforcement for twelve years in positions ranging from officer to police captain. He served with the 140th tactical Fighter Squadron in 1968 and 1969 in Kwang Ju, Korea. He has authored and co-authored several publications and holds both a bachelor's degree in psychology and a master's degree in public administration with a specialization in organizational development and criminal justice from the University of Colorado at Boulder.

INDEX

242

245

A Blueprint For An Offender Job Retention Program

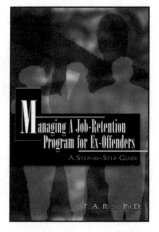

Managing a Job-Retention Program for Ex-Offenders: A Step-By-Step Guide

T. A. Ryan, Ph.D.

One of the primary reasons for recidivism is the inability of offenders to find and maintain work upon their release. **Managing a Job-Retention Program** has four sections that provide practitioners with a blueprint for creating programs which will help offenders retain employment. The first section documents the need for programs to decrease ex-offender crime, which can occur through increased job retention. The second part presents a generalized model that sets forth directions and guidelines for developing delivery system models to achieve ex-offender job retention. It includes an example of an organization that utilized this program. Part Three presents guidelines for implementing the delivery systems. The final portion of the book provides conclusions and a discussion. The programs within this resource are time- and cost-effective. (2005, approx. 100 pages, 1-56991-217-3)

"No one will question that employment may well be the most important factor in post-release success. Dr. Ryan has collected and organized the data to support that fact. More importantly she provides a road map to ex-offender employment retention. Rather than a cookie cutter approach to retention, she presents a model for planning and implementing programs for job retention for ex-offenders."

Howard Skolnik, Assistant Director
Nevada Department of Prisons

Call 1-800-222-5646, ext. 1860 to order!
American Correctional Association
4380 Forbes Boulevard
Lanham, MD 20706-4322
Order online at www.aca.org

ACA
FOUNDED 1870

Cutting Edge Community Corrections Resources

Heading Home:
Offender Reintegration Into the Family
Vivian L. Gadsden, Editor

Many people assume that when offenders return from prison, their life picks up as before their incarceration. This is far from the truth. The incarceration process affects offenders and their families. How can you prepare offenders and their families for this reunion? *Heading Home* has the answers. Chapters include: "Parent Education for Incarcerated Parents: Understanding What Works"; "Families, Prisoners and Community Reentry"; "Children of Prisoners"; "What Works in the Treatment of Family Violence in Correctional Populations"; and "What Works in Faith-Based Programs." (2003, 307 pages, index, 1-56991-165-7)

Risk Reduction:
Interventions for Special Needs Offenders
Harry E. Allen, Editor

Risk Reduction illustrates what leading thinkers in corrections are doing to identify risk and lower recidivism. Published in cooperation with the International Community Corrections Association, this book examines programs, which can lower recidivism and prepare individuals for everyday life. Programs discussed include: Reaffirming Rehabilitation: Public Support for Correctional Treatment; What Works: Effective DWI Intervention; The Spousal Assault Risk Assessment Guide (SARA): Reliability and Validity in Adult Male Offenders; Effective Intervention with Sex Offenders; Assessing Psychopathy in Juveniles; and Effective Family-based Treatment for Juvenile Offenders: Multisystemic Therapy and Functional Family Therapy. (2002, 271 pages, index, 1-56991-148-7)

ACA/ICCA Partnership

The American Correctional Association and the International Community Corrections Association have now co-published seven books. To view a complete listing of these titles, visit www.aca.org and click on the ICCA search category!

Call 1-800-222-5646, ext. 1860 to order!
American Correctional Association
4380 Forbes Blvd.
Lanham, MD 20706-4322
Shop online at www.aca.org